# PRACTICS

## Handgun Defense System

## Albert H. League III

# Practics - Handgun Defense System

Copyright 2018 - Albert H. League III

Formatting by Rik - Wild Seas Formatting (www.WildSeasFormatting.com)

Manuscript editing by Jeanette Cameron (Risen Editing)

*For the good guys.*

# Acknowledgments

Knowledge is not invention; it's collection. This book would not have been possible but for the hard work, experience, and generosity of more people than I can recall, and I apologize for any omission in my acknowledgment of that debt. My earnest thanks to The Cigar Fellowship; Officers Gregory Hibbard and Martin Hogan; Deputies Stacy Barker and Robert Riley; New York City Police Department for their intelligent and relentless effort toward improved officer safety; Philadelphia Transit Officer Ken Ganiszewski; Patrolman Bruce Perry, who pounded the boardwalk; Corporal Blessing and the boys at Camp Pendleton; Officer Adam Millard; Senior Deputy Vernon Huggins; Sergeant Rod Trumpf; Captains Winfrey, Fried, and Morelock; Sheriff Rod Mitchell; my patient and meticulous editor, Jeanette Cameron of Risen Editing; Thomas J. Aveni, Executive Director of the Police Policy Studies Council, whose work, *Officer-Involved Shootings: What We Didn't Know Has Hurt Us,* may be the most usable piece of research concerning police shootings currently available; California Commission on Peace Officer Standards and Training; and all the nuts, scoundrels, hoodlums, and suspects who schooled me in the tangible benefits of prudence. Finally, I would like to thank that olive-drab seafaring organization whose tender encouragement of my budding shooting skills began affectionately with, "Tell me something, League. How can somebody so (expletive) they can't even walk, shoot like that?"

Sir, the private still doesn't know, sir.

# Introduction to Practics

*Change is the end result of all true learning.*

Leo Buscaglia

The Whitechapel Killer, or "Jack the Ripper," was world news near the close of the nineteenth century. It was the beginning of media-named serial murderers and the recognized birth of the modern spree killer. Newspapers from around the world followed the story. A New York Times correspondent wrote that the murders demonstrated a "ghoul-like brutality." Today, as I write this introduction, I find nothing in the Times about serial killers, though several are currently at-large within the United States. The fact is there have been so many serial killers in the past 120 years that, for the most part, the media doesn't even bother giving them names anymore. In terms of profligacy, Saucy Jack isn't even in the top 100. God forgive us that demonic violence has become passé.

Now teenage degenerates prey on their classmates with firearms before passively surrendering or committing suicide. As late as the 1980s American high school students were encouraged to take rifles to school for hunting clubs and gun-safety classes. Guns did not change, but the juvenile population surely did. On the other hand, violent crime is generally dropping in the U.S. Much of that has to do with changes in policing and incarceration, but not exclusively. We live in a social paradox where conformity and passivity live next door to unrestrained violence and boiling hatreds. Criminal violence for the sake of personal gain is dramatically fading, whereas emotionally driven violence is steadily increasing. Today you are much less likely to be robbed solely for the contents of your wallet or purse but much more likely to be beaten to death for the enjoyment of your attackers. The world is not necessarily more violent by the numbers, but rather it is a different kind of violent.

Personal protection was once a debatable choice for the general population. Conscientious people could reasonably choose to lose property rather than risk increased violence. *Things* can always be replaced. That point-of-view is increasingly difficult to maintain with any intellectual honesty. Submission to predators is now, by and large, an invitation to greater injury or death. However, the moral and legal use of firearms for personal protection cannot honestly be expected to turn back the tide of mad, ravenous violence. That war is being lost in the souls of men. No, the reason for a personal defense is only to allow freedom of movement, property ownership, and public participation without fear of serious injury or death. That's the limited ambition of Practics and the practical intent of this book.

One-handed, formal marksmanship shooting was once the standard in law enforcement training. During the first half of the last century American and British firearm trainers recognized that traditional handgun training was failing to provide sufficient field skills. Traditional handgun training, which lasted at least into the 1970s in some locales, was based largely on seventeenth-century dueling postures. The British colonial experience and America's urban crime boom gave somber and substantial proof that close-range, moving targets required more than single-handed bullseye training could provide.

Practics (practical tactics) is a personal defense system based on the moral, legal, and effective use of firearms. This book addresses that portion of the Practics system that focuses on defensive use of the pistol and revolver.

Practics has seven unique characteristics:

1. **Firearm Based**—Practics is not an unarmed martial art adapted to firearm use. European swordsmanship, for example, was built upon the advantages and limitations of swords. Traditional sword techniques included full use of the sword, from tip to pommel, whereas hand-to-hand range techniques for the firearm-equipped defender have tended *not* to include the use of the gun. Today most progressive police training regimens include some form of defensive ground fighting. However, the techniques taught to law enforcement officers are almost exclusively for *unarmed* defenders, despite a reasonable expectation for the legal use of deadly force. Practics is a defense system designed specifically for firearms.

2. **Holistic**—Practics is a complete handgun defense system. It is not my intention to suggest that popular and established

techniques and training have no current value. Certainly, some have been less effective over the years than was hoped by their innovators, but modern training has unquestionably elevated the general skill of the shooting population. The problem is continuity; the draw does not always match the requirement of point shooting, and popular point-shooting methods don't marry well with aimed-fire techniques. Practics is a system of interrelated techniques and skills based on the entirety of an armed defender's needs rather than simply a collection of standalone techniques.

3. **En Motion Fire**—Practics emphasizes shooting as movement, not just position. Starting with the good work of William E. Fairbairn and Rex Applegate in the first half of the twentieth century, there has been a march toward practical defense techniques. These efforts have focused on transitioning shooting from traditional slow-fire marksmanship to close-range, point-shooting techniques. Today the practical crowd has all but won the argument. Police agencies have largely abandoned formal marksmanship instruction. Everybody now knows how to crouch and jerk shots; "missing the mark" has sadly become American police orthodoxy. Having said that, the desire to advance defensive-shooting effectiveness is a worthy one. Unfortunately, after six or seven decades, all we've accomplished is another form of target shooting. Those who disparaged traditional marksmanship replaced it with "crouch, grimace, and jerk" (a faster way to miss). Both disciplines have value, but both are static, positional firing—two sides of the same coin. To better understand this problem, consider how close-range firing techniques are taught to police and private defenders. Shooters stand on the firing line; on command draw the handgun to the hip, waist, or chest level; cease motion; and fire. Now consider the way knives, clubs, and fists are used in fighting—always within motion. Those weapons were intended to transfer force *during* motion. In medieval Europe and Asia, swordsmen, not archers, were used for close-range fighting. The blade is used fluidly, slashing within an arc of movement. The handgun is typically fired after a movement—bringing the handgun onto target—which is significantly different than a sword pierce at

the end of a thrust because a strike with the sword point always occurs within the thrusting movement. Knife or sword operation includes using the blade during the arcing movement or thrust. Likewise, the handgun user must also be capable of accurately discharging the handgun without pausing or stopping handgun motion. Pause-and-fire techniques are appropriate for most applications but are insufficient for some fast-moving, close-range encounters. If the handgun is to fully replace the bladed weapon for close range, it must also be used *en motion.*

4. **Practical, Non-sporting Origins**—Sports kill. That is, sports can kill practical effectiveness when conforming good defensive practices to fit within the confines of an organized game. Practical shooting sports have tremendous defensive training value but by necessity compromise best defense practices. Firing ranges have directional limitations, organized events require shooters to keep firearms unloaded off the firing line, shooters may be required to run when they should stay, and subjective legal requirements of deadly force can never be objectively scored. Shooting sports do have value for all shooters seeking to improve their technical skills but not without some cost to practicality. Practics has no sporting roots and is not intended to be an organized game. As an answer to a legitimate defense need, Practics is simply practical tactics.

5. **Adaptable**—Practics can be modified to include and exclude techniques based on the practitioner's fitness and health. The handgun portion of Practics includes techniques that some readers will find physically impossible. Each general type of threat, however, has one low-movement Practics response. Practics is a defensive plan as well as a collection of techniques. Those defenders requiring wheelchair use, for instance, will find the offered strategies relevant and some of the techniques sufficiently flexible.

6. **Inclusive**—Practics does not replace other defense systems but rather enhances them. Pugilists, wrestlers, and traditional martial artists will find Practics an excellent supplemental system for defensive firearm use. Nothing in Practics discourages practitioners from pursuing non-deadly-force

defensive training. In fact, Practics recommends further training.

7. **Evolutionary**—Practics will continually be improved by its varied practitioners based on their own expertise, experience, and needs. Practical tactics are only practical as long as they serve their purpose. It is impossible to be dogmatic and practical at the same time. Constant improvement of the system is necessary for Practics to sustain a competitive effectiveness.

The Practics handgun defense system is not more reinvention of existing techniques. In fact, it is intended to be a whole lot less: the most direct, concise answer for the defensive handgunner. We must be able to apply marksmanship and point-shooting techniques beyond currently accepted limits. Even so, open-distance shooting is not enough. Handgun training must include defensive solutions previously provided by hand and knife techniques. Sub-contact shooting—that is, shooting into compressed flesh—is the logical extension of the handgun as a tool, a true magnifier of the hand, not just a better bow and arrow. Some of what you're about to read is generations old, forgotten and ill-advisedly replaced. The starting point for Practics Handgun was a melding of old-pattern Marine Corps training with successful rural law enforcement practices. Development of the system was oriented toward effectiveness and achievability for a sole defender. In other words, no regard was given to physical grace, competition, or tradition. Practics can have no loyalty to form, system ideology, nor—if I'm to be intellectually honest—myself. Either it works or it is abandoned. Practics is simple, legal, brutally effective, and morally justifiable.

The design goals for Practics were also simple:

- **Firearms must be effectively used to leverage superiority in all likely deadly force encounters**, even to their mechanical and ballistic limits. Guns can do magic things. They can shoot around corners, find targets in the dark, and control remarkable amounts of space—provided the operator has the knowledge and skill.
- **Techniques must be successful against larger, stronger, better-trained, and more-violent attackers.** I don't blame you for doubting this one. Every martial-arts huckster from the beginning of time until now has made this claim. Practics uses

Brazilian Jujitsu for an *attacker benchmark*, as opposed to the old self-defense standard of a hapless idiot who always seems to grab the defender in just the right place. In formalizing Practics, techniques were tested with an average-size woman defending against a heavyweight, male Brazilian Jujitsu practitioner. Let's be clear: She didn't beat him in a grappling match or a fistfight, but she was able to use her gun. *Practics works only within its intended scope of purpose.* Nobody will ever get beat up in a bar by a Practics practitioner, thank God. What Practics can do is help you to succeed in encounters that merit your use of deadly force. In the dark, on the ground, or from a few hundred yards away, Practics is for those poor souls on the wrong end of trouble and the right side of the law.

- **Tactics must be usable for the lone defender.** Practics is not a modification of military or SWAT team tactics but is specifically designed for the lone defender. Most tactical training currently available comes from special operations, conventional military forces, or SWAT, all of which are team efforts. It is insufficient to cut these tactics down and repackage them for personal defense. For example, all team tactics include a rearward-looking member. The need to know what is behind you does not disappear when you are on your own. Dynamic (fast) entries make much more sense when half a dozen trained members move quickly into a room. Each team member has a responsibility for a limited and specific portion of the room. Obviously, a lone defender forced to enter the same room has greater burdens for information gathering and personal protection from all corners of the unsecured space. Lone-defender tactics need to originate from good single-operator practices. Much of the interior-tactical-movement portion of Practics comes from remote, rural America, where peace officers have been working alone for well over 100 years.

- **Techniques must be executable for a wide range of defenders.** Having arthritis or getting on in years doesn't lend itself to boxing lessons or wrestling matches. Most people can use Practics. Some of it does involve getting on the ground, and some of it involves a little pushing or pulling, but not much. If you can handle your own groceries, are steady on your feet, can get up and down, and operate your handgun well, you're a good candidate for some usable level of Practics. Choose those techniques that are within your ability and train to master them.

- **The totality of techniques must cover the broad range of typical threats.** Practics is designed to give the defender a sufficient skill platform for use in a variety of spaces and conditions. The experience of law enforcement was used to determine the most likely threats. As an example, being attacked at close range by two or more criminals is common enough to require defensive preparation. On the other hand, the likelihood of six armed, bad men attacking you from 15 yards is extremely remote. So Practics tends toward close encounters and includes long-range, single-attacker defense but avoids the common type of practical pistol training that is often geared toward very improbable scenarios. Close indoor encounters often involve physical contact. Outdoor encounters may involve ranges substantially beyond your quick-fire abilities. Practics is a three-sixty response to common threats faced by armed defenders.

- **Defensive system must be logically organized.** Defensive shooting techniques without proper strategy behind them or failure tactics to support them are not sufficient for the home defender. You must already know your tactical objectives when your window is forced open at three in the morning. Practics starts with understanding the use of force, includes techniques and tactics necessary to execute defense, and is fully based on the *individual's predetermined defensive goals and strategies*.

- **Safety must be balanced against risk.** Practics includes techniques that involve risk. Previously, a desire for institutionally approved defense techniques prevented exploration of sub-contact shooting techniques. Nobody wants to get sued, including me. I do not advocate recklessness, and following proper use-of-force guidelines is mandatory. Safety is the cornerstone of pistolcraft. However, when we're discussing worst cases and final options, *safety must share a proportional risk*. Being choked unconscious and then being killed with your own gun is not better than suffering serious facial injury from flying bone fragment as you shoot your attacker. Modern law enforcement trainers misrepresented the goal of safety when we switched our focus from tactical objectives to civil liability. Defensive techniques now need to develop outside of law enforcement and military circles, wherein risk-management efforts are running amok to the detriment of human life. A practical firearm defense must balance safety and risk.

- **Use of force must be understood in terms of logical principles.** All defense strategies and supporting tactics must begin with an understanding of the legal use of force. Lawyers and academics have written a sea of excellent books on this subject. Despite plenty of good information in the public sphere, most defenders do not have sufficient grasp of the principles that govern deadly force laws and, therefore, are never quite certain of the rights and responsibilities of the self-defender. Those underlying principles are the simple building blocks used to educate American peace officers in the use of force. Six months of police academy training cannot possibly include years of legal study, but the elemental principles behind the use of force are readily understandable. Learn the *why* and you'll know the *when*.

If you discover something in Practics that doesn't work for you, abandon it, and use what works. Please try all the recommended techniques before seeking alternatives. Practics is a platform of replaceable elements. If you can't use my movement techniques, use ones that better suit you. However, it is the practitioner's responsibility to ensure that the goals of specific techniques and the system's continuity are met and maintained when replacing elements. Practics serves you, not the other way around. Some techniques in this book are not offered in *all* usable versions nor are they always the only reasonable choices. For instance, we currently train in only one method of dealing with pistol malfunctions. The reason is simplicity and recall. If you have one solid technique for each attacker problem, you are more likely to be victorious. Students who have more information than they can make instinctual are likely to stumble without ongoing training. Bear in mind that tired, pot-bellied, middle-aged cops get some pretty stout boys into the backs of America's patrol cars. In part that is because the hood is swinging, kicking, pushing, and screaming, while the officer is only trying to get *one* arm behind the back and execute *one* wristlock. Then it's handcuffs and off to jail. You can add to and modify Practics, but always keep it simple.

When I was a new deputy, I was taught to imagine my own emergency reactions to possible threats as I drove around my beat. For example, I would imagine my reaction to someone running up and yanking my door open at a stop sign or my immediate reaction if a bigger man was throwing haymakers at me in a confined space. It really worked, not because of some psycho-babble-power-of-positive-thinking nonsense, but because in stressful situations we go back to what we know. We know whatever we've been trained to do, and we *can* train ourselves. Much technique training requires physical commitment, but tactics and strategy rely mostly on forethought. Practics is, in part, a strategy—an organization of thought—designed to address the *why*, *when*, and *how* of armed defense. When a defender understands the problems, he can react with pre-determined solutions.

## Practics' Six Truths:

1. Firearms are the best magnifier of human self-defense capabilities.
2. Complicated problems require simple solutions.
3. Safety must stay proportionate to risk.
4. Attacks are likely to initially succeed; defenses are likely to initially fail.
5. Weapons will malfunction.
6. Deadly force is morally justified when no reasonable alternative exists.

"What-ifs" plague firearm training; second-guessing can run to the absurd. Practics is not the perfect answer to any situation, because no such thing is achievable. Defense is not like anything else, including sports. In sports, there is always that unknown element that can make an underdog a champion. The best teams don't always win the Super Bowl, and the best boxers don't always win the fight. Nonetheless, games have rules, which limit action. No football player can hop in a car and drive to the end zone to score a touchdown, which would be the most sensible use of his time. In defensive situations there are no time limits, no teams, and no rules. Everything in Practics has a thousand possible "what-ifs." Probability, more than possibility, informs the material included in this book. Not everything will work for everyone in every situation. The reader who expects otherwise will be severely disappointed. Practics includes knowing how to use deflected fire (ricochets) and, in some cases, deliberately putting yourself on the ground. I am well aware that many of the techniques in Practics will be met with skepticism. Fair enough. I ask that the reader consider that Practics is intended for the last-minute, final-inch, and no-alternative moment when traditional point-fire techniques have little hope of succeeding. Practics assumes that everything will go wrong, and, based on my experience and that of law enforcement officers whose counsel was instrumental in the formation of this material, failure is the natural environment in which defenders must expect to act.

Mercifully, I am not the last word on the use of firearms or self-defense. Others have taught me over the years, and I hope I may continue to learn. There can be reasonable disagreement on defensive tactics. The information in this book is intended to be part of a broader knowledge that each reader will use in the continual development of personal skill. Test everything, including the material you're about to read. Regardless of the advocate, information has to make sense to be of value. No instructor has sufficient expertise to rewrite the laws of common sense and good judgment. *You are the final arbiter of your shooting education.* Test and evaluate everything before you accept or reject it. Make certain that you haven't gathered bad practices or useless habits. Honest self-evaluation is the responsibility of everyone who picks up a weapon. Be your own worst critic. The well-being of those around you may depend on it.

Be safe.

*A.H. League III*

# Getting the Most from This Book

The material in this book equates to a lesson plan for a three-week training course; therefore, the material is interrelated and presented in a particular order. To enjoy the greatest benefit from this book, the student must read it cover to cover. Practics is not a loose collection of skills, and each section of the book depends on the student having understood previously read material. As each new skill is introduced, its purpose is explained so that the student may understand the *why* before trying the *what*. After explanation of the skill or topic, specific training designed to assist the student in acquiring that particular skill or topic knowledge is presented. The reader will find that approaching the text as a single continuous lesson will be much more beneficial than flipping back and forth through the book.

Many shooting books tend to be very heavy on pictures and light on text. In fact, many of them would be too small for publishing if it weren't for a generous inclusion of full-page photos and very liberal formatting. This book has more text because the goal is for the reader to understand concepts rather than merely imitate actions. The *why* is the basis for the *how*. There is a commercial problem in all this: Shooting books are expected to be light, easy reading for people who would rather shoot than read. Self-defense is not a light and easy topic, however. Imitation is insufficient for mastery because once circumstances change, duplication may not be possible. Memorizing a shooting stance has no value once the defender is pushed against a wall or knocked off his feet, but the principles of successful shooting can be applied in all circumstances. In other words, armed self-defense requires legitimate study and perhaps a sliver of academic rigor. I didn't want to divide the material into separate volumes, which could leave the reader with less than a complete system, and I couldn't omit much more material in good faith. Consequently, space did not allow for continually repeated information. The reader must be responsible to carry knowledge forward throughout the study.

Practics Handgun Defense System contains a good amount of "lecture" but also an enormous amount of training. The drills and exercises are necessary to acquire experiential knowledge. The text is divided into four major sections, and each section is divided into topic chapters, which contain training and knowledge or preparation requirements. Skills training have both installation and maintenance requirements. Ongoing training requirements are heavy. I was torn concerning training requirements and opted to list what I believe to be necessary baseline requirements with the understanding that some students will not be able to execute all the training. Impaired students or those shooters who do not have access to outdoor ranges will be precluded from some training. The reader should train as instructed to the extent that training can be done safely. A training partner is required to properly and safely execute the training portions of this book. Use the text as a field workbook to guide you through skill-installation requirements.

Here's the best way to organize your Practics maintenance training:

- Read the entire book at least twice.
- On the second or third reading, annotate 12 months' worth of training-maintenance requirements on a large wall or desk calendar. Schedule only those exercises that you are able to conduct safely and properly.
- Use the book as a training guide, consulting it before and during scheduled events.
- Near the end of the year, repeat the process with a fresh calendar.

The above calendar method ensures the student stays on track with relatively little effort. Make certain each year that you consider adding or dropping events based on any changes to your firing range, physical abilities, or alterations in equipment. Do all that you can—don't cheat yourself.

The overwhelming majority of required skills training include duplication for ambidextrous training. From years of training shooters I have learned that ambidextrous training is slightly more popular than measles. However, the inability to effectively use the weak hand may mean one broken finger will prevent your defense. You must train both hands.

A final word about training: When learning a Practics technique, begin by executing the entire technique slowly. Never break the technique into smaller parts. Doing so will prevent fluid movement, frustrating competence. Fluid movement is the basis for speed. We regulate speed to learn new techniques but never break the movement.

In addition to normal range safety gear, a water pistol or toy pistol will be needed. Other needed items are listed throughout the text but tend to be fairly common, easy to make, or at least readily accessible. Admittedly, some of my training-aid recommendations are primitive in a world of electronics and lasers, but having been a trainer for a dirt-poor sheriff's office, I learned how to stretch a training dollar. The absence of expensive, commercially produced equipment must never prevent a student from benefiting from essential skills training.

Regarding language, gun enthusiasts, particularly law enforcement shooters, are vulnerable to a bit of cult speak. For instance, we used to refer to the preferred shooting hand as "strong" and the other hand as "weak." About 30 years ago, it became fashionable to switch to "shooting" and "support." The reason for the switch was supposedly to prevent shooters from becoming convinced that accurate fire with the *weak hand* was unobtainable. It was well intended though probably not worth the effort. I would have preferred to use *primary hand* and *secondary hand* in this text, but we need more terms like we need more reality shows. Practics uses the standard terms *shooting hand* and *support hand* when discussing in-progress firing, such as "Use the support hand to retrieve a magazine." We'll use the traditional *strong hand* and *weak hand* when making a distinction between a shooter's hands, such as "Learn to shoot with your weak hand as well as your strong hand." Otherwise we're all apt to get confused when we begin switching hands and supporting hands become shooting hands and vice-versa. Also, I will use the term *trigger press* to mean a shooter engaging the trigger and *trigger pull* to mean either the force needed to move the trigger rearward or the mechanical quality of the trigger, such as "The trigger pull is four pounds and has a rough, uneven quality." The expression *low ready* means the handgun is held in front of the tactically alert shooter at about the beltline, properly indexed and pointed downrange, while *high ready* means the gun is held at about chest level. Hopefully, writer and reader will speak the same language over the next several chapters.

Let's get to it.

# PRACTICS 101:
# Baseline Knowledge and Core Skills

# Chapter One: Safety Reminder

*Experience keeps a dear school, but fools will learn in no other.*

Benjamin Franklin

*Fear is the foundation of safety.*

Tertullian

In *The Perfect Pistol Shot*, I included a more in-depth safety *refresher*, assuming the reader had already obtained formal safety training with his or her handgun. Since we are discussing tactics and well beyond entry-level shooting, I assume no one will attempt the exercises and practices in this book without having received formal handgun-operations training with subsequent safety refreshers.

Accidents happen. We won't beat a dead horse here, but we ought to revisit our first priority. You may never experience a criminal assault, but if you spend a lot of time around shooters, you will certainly witness firearm accidents. Most accidents don't result in injury. Some do. Time spent in safe handling is never wasted.

Let's take another look at the Four Rules of Firearm Safety.

1. **All guns are always loaded.** Unload it or treat it as if it's locked and cocked. If you don't *need* to touch it, leave it alone.
2. **Never point your gun at anything you're not willing to destroy.** If your handgun never points at anyone or anything that can cause death through a high-energy ricochet, you will never be found guilty of manslaughter as a result of an accidental shooting.
3. **Keep your finger off the trigger until ready to shoot.** Your trigger finger must remain extended and pressed against the frame of your weapon (indexing) until you are ready to address the trigger. Lifting the finger off the trigger will NOT prevent

a sympathetic muscle reaction. Index, index, index.

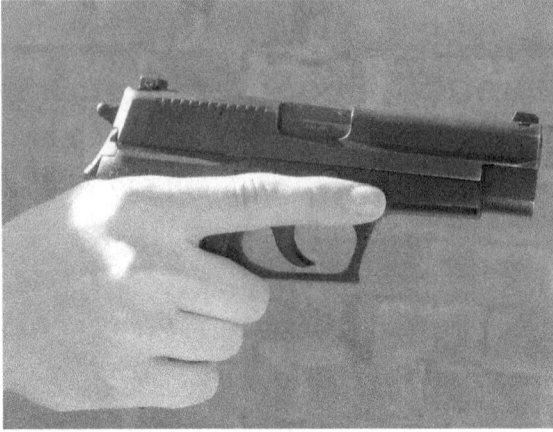

Index means a firm press into the frame. This is a bedrock skill.

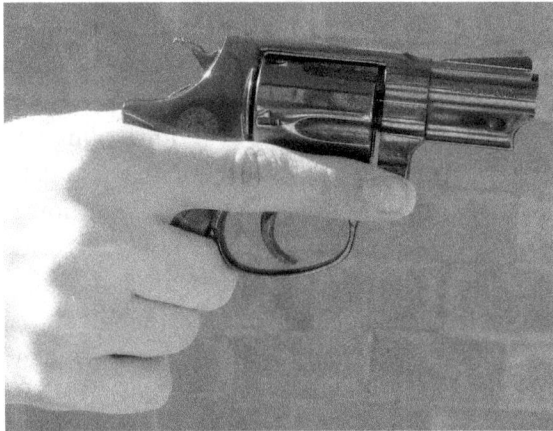

Indexing with a revolver means pressing the frame not the cylinder.

4. **Be aware of your backstop.** Your rounds will travel somewhere. They will stop in the dirt, or they will stop somewhere else, but bullets will never evaporate. When the round is in the pistol, you are legally responsible for everything within your control. When the bullet leaves the weapon, you are an ineffectual bystander who is now *legally responsible for things beyond human control.* Know where your bullets are headed and how they are going to be stopped.

Safety is tactically sound. It prevents premature firings, misses, injuries to allies, legal penalties, and assists in maintaining noise discipline and situational awareness. If you have not had formal, competent safety training, get it now. Untrained owners of firearms are far more likely to injure themselves than are trained owners. Safe gun handling is much more than common sense. Accomplish competent training and practice the Four Rules of Safety every time you encounter a firearm.

Normal discussions of safety involve absolutes. Practics embraces absolute safety to the extent that the absolute practice of safety doesn't get you or yours hurt or killed. For instance, being fired at through a wall, floor, or closed door may require you to return fire without being able to see your target or know your backstop. In such a case the burden is on the defender to weigh circumstances and determine whether the greater hazard to life lies in action or inaction. We'll discuss the moral and legal principles behind the use of force later on. For now let's agree that the proper application of safety requires an informed and somber thoughtfulness.

The use of force, deadly or otherwise, is a serious moral and legal matter. This book attempts to assist the reader in better understanding the responsibilities inherent in the right to self-defense. It is incumbent upon the reader to be informed about current applicable law and to seek competent legal advice. Safety prevents lawsuits, injuries, and death. Unfortunately, good reason is no longer sufficient to successfully navigate those waters. Your legal responsibilities exist, whether you choose to accept them or not.

This book is about nothing other than safety; the entire subject matter is instruction in personal safety. There is no interest on the part of the author to profit from someone else's misfortune. Self-defense is a serious matter. Although I have taken a certain license in creating a brand with memorable keywords and training techniques, I have not forgotten this is a gritty business involving human life with too many dangerous variables for me to dare claim the final word on armed self-defense. While I sincerely believe in the material offered, I am aware that not every Practics technique will work for every defender or every situation. I urge the reader to earnestly and diligently test the material offered and then keep the better ones while discarding anything that cannot be personally executed in a safe and effective manner. Safety requires forethought and reason. The personal safety system offered in this book is called "Practics," not "Dogmatics." The material is intended to serve the practitioner, not the other way around.

## Safety Skills Training

Most of the following exercises must be conducted in an area safe for firearm manipulation with either a training pistol or a *modified* storage-safe weapon. "Storage-safe" means the slide is home on an empty chamber, empty magazine is inserted, hammer is at rest, and safeties are engaged, as required. Our training modification will be the omission of the magazine whenever possible. No ammunition may be present during non-firing training. Like other Practics training, safety skills require a training partner to ensure the participant is executing the drills properly. Very often a shooter thinks he is indexing or controlling the muzzle when that is not the case. Students need an extra set of eyes to guarantee that "feel" matches reality.

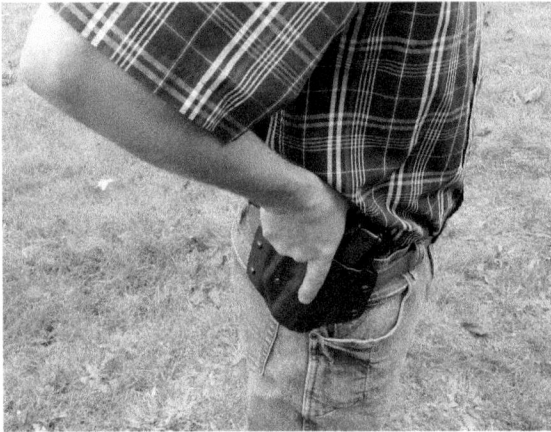

Indexing is part of a good draw. Safety begins in the holster.

**Practics Preferred Pistol Reload Technique**

In order for the reader to properly complete all of the following drills, we will have to jump ahead and discuss the Practics method for slide operation. The Practics preferred load/reload technique (Modified-Slingshot) requires the shooter to grasp the rear of the slide between the thumb and middle knuckle of the bent support-hand index finger (the other fingers provide increased pressure). Think of this position as a full-hand pinch. As the shooter sharply pulls the slide to the rear, the pistol is rotated toward the support side to no less than 90°. A slight push forward with the shooting arm, as the supporting arm pulls rearward, greatly eases this movement. The release of the slide is done as the support hand continues rearward with a clean release—letting go of the pinch. The reason this method is used will be explained later in the text, along with an alternative method for shooters whose hands or weapons will not support this method.

A slingshot cycling of the slide.

1. **Memorize the Four Rules of Safety**. You can't *do* what you don't *know*. The titles for the four rules are self-explanatory. Memorize the titles and you'll remember the rules.

2. **Index Drill**—This drill will assist you in executing proper indexing of the trigger finger from the holster. Draw your holstered handgun onto a target while keeping your trigger finger along the frame of the handgun throughout the entire

movement. Disengage the safety *during* the draw. Your trigger finger must move onto the handgun as it is being lifted from the holster. After acquiring perfect sighting, press the trigger for one dry fire. Engage the safety and re-holster while indexing. Indexing will assist re-holstering by letting you feel the retention strap. Do not stop the motion during practice but perform the first two sets of 10 draws very slowly. The remaining eight sets should begin slowly and increase in speed until the shooter is drawing onto the target at the maximum possible speed at which the drill can be done properly. When an error is made, the set must be repeated. Errors include failure to index, failure to engage/disengage the safety, and looking at the handgun during draws or re-holstering. Keep any break between sets limited to two minutes.

Skill-Installation Requirement: 10 repetitions · 10 consecutive sets

Maintenance Requirement: 10 reps · five consecutive sets weekly (first month), 10 reps · three consecutive sets (monthly for the first year), no fewer than 10 consecutive reps per month thereafter

Place a small waist-high table in front of you with the pistol resting on top and the muzzle pointed away from you. Using the table as your offside holster, repeat the above training with your weak hand.

3. **Index Slide Drill**—You must be able to cycle the slide of your pistol while properly indexing. This drill will help you develop that skill. Remove the magazine from your storage-safe pistol. Hold the handgun directly out in front of you with the muzzle pointed straight downrange. Place a penny under the tip of your trigger finger, against the frame of the pistol. Use the pressure of trigger-finger indexing to hold the penny in place. Grasp the end of your slide between the thumb and the middle knuckle of your support-hand index finger (as previously explained in the "Practics Preferred Pistol Reload Technique" inset box). Forcefully pull the slide to the rear as you rotate the pistol 90° to the support side. At the end of the pull, cleanly release the slide and allow it to travel forward. During the entire exercise you must index the penny against the frame, keeping the muzzle downrange. The training partner will ensure that the muzzle stays pointed straight downrange. The

student will be mindful of whether the penny drops. In the event of a wandering muzzle or dropped penny, the entire installation requirement must be repeated.

The Penny Drill

Learn to keep the trigger finger pressed into the weapon.

Skill-Installation Requirement: 12 repetitions · eight consecutive sets (slide cycles)

Maintenance Requirement: 10 repetitions · four consecutive sets (twice weekly for the first two months), 12 repetitions · five consecutive sets quarterly thereafter

The above requirements must also be executed with the weak

hand.

**4. Muzzle-Control Drill**—Successful gun handling is muzzle control. Whether we're concerned about accuracy or avoiding tragedy, muzzle control is the key. This drill will help you attain muzzle awareness while drawing/loading.

The first variation of this drill is for reloading with the firearm close to the beltline. The second variation is for reloading while keeping the arm extended toward the target. I've taken some liberty in naming them "Unsighted" and "Sighted." Neither name is an accurate description of intended use, but the names will give the reader an understanding of the proximity of the handgun to the body. Both variations must be done without the shooter looking at the hands. The training partner will look for extraneous and inaccurate movements and ensure that the shooter is not drifting focus onto the handgun. We will begin slowly and increase speed but always stay within the limits of what we can do perfectly. In other words, don't overrun your ability and, by virtue of moving too fast, actually delay the load or reload. This drill involves inserting an empty magazine and is best reserved for live-fire ranges.

Begin by placing two poles upright and 8" apart. (We use a lot of poles on the range and during dry-fire exercises. Poles can be wood stakes knocked into the ground, beams with bases attached, or just pitchforks and spades shoved into the earth.)

*Unsighted*: Stand an elbow-to-fingertip length from the poles on the "up-range" side. Center your body directly facing the poles and facing downrange. Slowly draw your storage-safe firearm and place the muzzle between the two poles but without striking either. Insert an empty magazine; sharply pull your slide to the rear and release. The goal is to load/reload while keeping your handgun between, but never touching, the poles. Increase speed throughout the set to achieve a brisk pace. If you touch a pole, repeat that set with a reduced speed. Speed in reloading comes with repeated and proper execution. During this exercise you will not see the handgun, but you will see the top half of the poles. The visible portions of the poles combined with the shooter's sense of handgun location are what actually instruct the shooter. At the completion of each training session it is important to conduct the drill with the training partner but without the poles. If the pole drill is properly executed, you will have acquired an awareness of muzzle location during loading or reloading.

*Sighted*: Stand a shoulder-to-fingertip length from the poles and repeat the drill as described above.

Muzzle Control Drill

Touching the poles with hand or handgun is a training failure.

The hand must not ride the slide forward causing a malfunction. Clean release.

The below requirements are necessary for both unsighted and sighted training.

Skill-Installation Requirement: eight consecutive reps · five sets for each of the two variations

Maintenance Requirement: five consecutive reps · five sets for each of the two variations (monthly for the first year), quarterly thereafter

The drill is not finished until weak-hand training has been successfully completed. You can easily lose the use of your strong hand. Ambidexterity is not optional in Practics.

5. **Safe-Movement Drill**—Place five standing poles in line and spaced at the following distances:

Poles #1 to #2 at 5'
Poles #2 to #3 at 4'
Poles #4 to #5 at 2'

Approximately 10' beyond pole #5, place a standing target at eye-level with an aiming point that appears no larger during sighting than your front sight tip. The student's beginning position is at pole #1, with the line of poles leading toward the target. Your objective is to move slalom-style through the poles, keeping good sighting on the target when your target view is unobstructed. However, you may not allow your muzzle to cross over a pole or to point at your feet. This will require you to lower the muzzle as you pass between poles and then immediately raise the muzzle the instant you have passed through the poles. The distances between the poles decrease as you approach the target. Initially you will be able to walk at an oblique angle between poles before the shorter distances require you to integrate your sidesteps with the location of your muzzle. At the end of the slalom, position yourself directly in front of the target with the last pole behind you. Then begin the slalom backwards, still keeping your sights on the target except when passing between poles. The training partner will watch for these violations: muzzle pointing at student's feet; muzzle crossing a pole; any part of the body or handgun touching a pole; sights not immediately on target when clear of poles; and student taking focus off the target, stumbling, or failing to index. Any violation requires the drill to be stopped and restarted at the beginning of the set.

Beginning position for the Safe Movement Drill.

11

Eyes downrange. You must be aware of your muzzle at all times.

Safe Movement Drill

Keep close to the polls; you're also learning how to move with cover and concealment.

Skill-Installation Requirement: 20 round trips through the poles

Maintenance Requirement: 10 round trips per month (first 3 months), 20 rounds trips per quarter for two years

Repeat the above requirements using the weak hand.

**6. Backstop Drill (Live Fire)**—This drill provides experience in selecting firing paths based on no-shoot obstacles beyond the target. You will need significant space behind the target to place your no-shoot obstacles (balloon clusters or full-size silhouettes). Typically, this can be done by placing the target closer to the shooter in the foreground of the range—provided such a thing is safe and permitted and leaves room to place the no-shoot obstacles in the background. Hammering a planter's stake into the ground and placing an old milk jug upside down over the end of the stake can install a good target. The stake should be about chest high for the shooter. A good starting distance is 10 yards.

Before the shooter approaches the firing line, the training partner will take four to eight similar stakes and place them randomly inside a 45° area behind the target. The shooter must not watch the positioning of the obstacle stakes. A good training partner will attempt to make the scenario as challenging as possible, tying clusters of inflated balloons or placing full-size silhouettes on the stakes or combining both for an improved no-shoot obstacle. Stake placement should be irregular, at varying distances, and changed between sets.

When the range is ready, the training partner will command the shooter to step forward onto the firing line. On the command to fire, the shooter will look downrange, ensure the range is safe, and fire on the target. Each shot must be fired from a different position along the firing line, and the pace should increase to brisk. The shooter may not hit any of the no-shoot obstacles. Instead the shooter will shuffle from side to side (no more than a few feet in either direction) in order to find a clear bullet path through the target and downrange. Kneeling poses a possible trajectory hazard and may render the obstacles useless and is therefore not permitted. The training partner will act as a safety officer and ensure the shooter does not fire at any angle that would result in a round exceeding the width of the range's bullet-stop.

Both types of obstacles are recommended. The balloon clusters require blowing up a few balloons and don't record shots as well, but they provide instant shooter feedback. The silhouettes will better record errant bullet paths but won't clearly react to hits. Silhouettes will additionally require some light framing to keep them from folding. Both types of targets are worthwhile. The obstacles should be slightly below the milk jug because the shooter will be firing at a slight downward angle. Find safe lines of fire by shuffling, not by firing above the obstacles. Treat the obstacles as innocent bystanders.

You must learn to be aware of downrange hazards beyond your target. Train for it.

14

It doesn't have to look nice. Use what you have.

<u>Skill-Installation Requirement</u>: 10- to 12-round course of fire
· four sets

<u>Maintenance Requirement</u>: four sets semi-annually

Of course, the weak hand requires the same training.

The Backstop Drill can be as difficult and varied as your abilities and firing range will permit. The goal is to develop an awareness of firing paths. Remember not every target stops every bullet and not every shot is a guaranteed hit. Increase your pace, change your course, use multiple targets at varying heights, employ bigger and more numerous obstacles, and you'll find this drill exceptionally useful and very enjoyable.

A final word about safety training and defensive handgun use in general: If you have two hands and can only effectively use one of them, you're only half prepared. Always train to use the weak hand.

# Chapter Two: Moral and Legal Use of Force

*Honesty is the first chapter in the book of wisdom.*

Thomas Jefferson

*The first thing we do, let's kill all the lawyers.*

William Shakespeare

A worthy goal is the defense of your life and the lives of those around you. Another good goal is staying out of prison and preventing your family's financial destruction. Objectives are targets of achievement based on goals. Strategy is planning based on objectives. Tactics are actions informed by strategy.

Knowing how to shoot without fully understanding the accompanying responsibilities of personal defense is a dangerous business. Your right to self-defense certainly exists but only within the parameters of local legal interpretation. In other words, you can be "right" and yet lose everything you have. Any discussion of defensive tactics needs to include the legal and moral reasoning that is the starting point for lawful self-defense. Prisons are full of those convicted of some form of unjustifiable homicide, many of which were committed without a pre-existing criminal motive. Self-defense depends on a moral and legal foundation.

Tactics are born in the mind, not the hand. In February 2012, in Sanford, Florida, George Zimmerman legally shot Trayvon Martin. Zimmerman had a God-given right, recognized by the U.S. Constitution, to defend himself— and he nearly went to prison for it. State laws vary, legal precedent keeps moving, and politics are increasingly intruding on jurisprudence. Defenders can win the battle but lose the war. In this chapter, we'll examine the strain of logic that provides the *honest* defender with a clear understanding of the lawful and moral use of deadly force.

## When Can I Shoot?

As punishment for becoming lawyers, assistant prosecutors are often expected to appear at public gatherings and answer questions concerning criminal law. I am always amazed at the ability of young attorneys to answer the same question a thousand times as if it had never been asked before. The favorite question asks something along the lines of "If a guy breaks into my house, can I shoot him?" The attorney's answer never satisfies the audience because *there is no magic shoot/don't shoot line*. Every deadly force encounter is made up of a thousand minute details that determine legality. Law concerning the use of deadly force is of necessity more spirit than letter.

Fortunately for us, a simple thread of reasoning runs through all self-defense and deadly force laws. The remainder of this chapter will walk you through that reasoning.

## Law

This union has 50 states. Each state has legislated laws regarding the use of force. It is your responsibility to know your state's applicable and changing laws. I am not a lawyer and not qualified to offer legal advice. What we're going to discuss in this chapter is how we can earnestly honor codified laws that don't always easily render themselves to clear, practical applications. This is the cop's-eye view. Don't be afraid to contact the office of your local prosecutor or state attorney general for legal clarification. Sadly, the best defense against a lawyer is a better lawyer. Think of it as a cockfight with silk ties.

Generally, there are two differing state standards for the use of deadly force. One burdens the defender with the responsibility to retreat when possible. The other grants the defender the same rights exercised by peace officers in deadly force encounters and is commonly referred to as "stand your ground." In some states a third standard exists for occupied dwellings. This is called the "castle doctrine" or "Make My Day" law. Castle doctrine recognizes the right of a legal resident to use deadly force without the requirement to retreat when confronted inside the home. *Each state is different and interprets these doctrines into markedly different laws.* The substance and particulars of the law in your state may not be what you think. Get a written copy of the law from your state and contact your state attorney general with any questions.

In general *stand your ground* is simply the right to not have to retreat when confronted with a threat that would justify the use of deadly force. It is the standard used by police. Cops don't have to back up before using deadly force if deadly force is otherwise justified. The Zimmerman case was not about *stand your ground* laws. That shooting occurred with Martin sitting on top of Zimmerman, punching downward and striking Zimmerman's head against the sidewalk—concrete can easily qualify as a lethal weapon. Zimmerman had no opportunity to retreat, and the normal threshold for the use of deadly force in self-defense applied. *Stand your ground* does not override the legal protections citizens enjoy against vigilantism, nor is it required for the legal use of deadly force outside the home. Learn the applicable laws for the jurisdictions you enter or dwell in.

If a state requires you to retreat, does that mean you have to climb out your bedroom window during a burglary? Probably not. Each case is based on the totality of circumstances. A man in an empty garage who is confronted by a drunk armed with a piece of firewood *may* do well to walk out the side door and go to a neighbor's home. On the other hand, a defender might not *reasonably* retreat down a home hallway, allowing a pursuing intruder access to occupied children's bedrooms. How can we recognize what is legally considered reasonable?

## Reasonably Prudent

First, we need to consider perspective. In other words, by whose standard must we be legally justified? That estimable fellow is called the *reasonably prudent person*. The RPP isn't a guy out to prove a point. He doesn't seek out trouble or lie in wait. He will defend himself when he must. Old RPP is the American middle class on a good day. He is also the court's standard for measuring your actions.

Here are some things a reasonably prudent person does:
- knows the general substance of applicable federal, state, and local laws relating to the firearms he uses
- measures responses to be proportionate to actual threats
- seeks to avoid confrontation
- exhausts all *reasonable* alternatives before using a firearm

- behaves in a logical manner, exhibiting behavior and experiencing emotions and thoughts common to the general population under similar circumstances
- exercises a degree of self-restraint commiserate with immediate circumstances
- calls for emergency services after a deadly force encounter
- tells the truth

Here are some things a reasonably prudent person does not do:

- remains ignorant of federal, state, and local laws relating to his firearms (*ex: cannot recall the legal limits of his concealed weapon permit*)
- exaggerates responses beyond actual threats (ex: in response to a vague verbal threat, drives around the neighborhood with a rifle on his lap)
- seeks confrontation (ex: What are you staring at, punk?)
- uses a firearm when more reasonable alternatives are available (ex: brandishes a gun at a verbally abusive man on his front porch rather than simply closing the door)
- behaves in an irrational manner, exhibiting behavior and experiencing emotions and thoughts outside of what is common to the general population (*ex: shows up at an ex-girlfriend's house, exhibiting anger and experiencing feelings of betrayal based on no further stimulus than his own imagination*)
- does not exercise a reasonable amount of self-restraint (ex: A kid scratches his car with a key, and he beats the vandal unconscious. Not an RPP.)
- cleans up crime scenes or alters appearance before calling emergency services (*ex: burns a bloody shirt before calling 911*)
- lies (ex: I did not raise my voice. All I said was "Please don't scratch my motorcycle with your key, sir.") The cops are going to read idiotic statements aloud in open court. Remember that.

*Reasonably prudent* evolves. In 1950 a reasonably prudent person could shoot a fleeing burglar. The thinking was that illegal entry with the intent to steal indicated a disregard for the personal safety of legal occupants. It makes sense in that light. If a crook were to break into a home and then flee, the homeowner would be justified in firing in order to capture the burglar or to prevent further crime. However, today, such action would likely land you in prison. It is not reasonably prudent to kill someone for stealing property. In fact, it's illegal. Though courts have *practically* overturned the fleeing-felon doctrine, some states still have fleeing-felon laws that allow police to shoot fleeing burglars. These are statutes that were never removed by legislation. However, no jurisdiction actually allows such force to be used by law enforcement. The same applies to the home defender. You can't shoot a man for stealing your television. An officer may shoot a fleeing murderer in extraordinary circumstances. For instance, if an officer were to witness a murder committed by an obviously unbalanced person and see that crazed killer fleeing with the weapon toward an occupied school and if the officer has no other reasonable alternative, deadly force may be used. But even that exception is not a slam dunk. The burden will be on the officer to articulate the immediate danger to others and the lack of reasonable alternatives. In short, "reasonably prudent" requires *extraordinary justification* when firing at a fleeing person in the twenty-first century. Make certain you are aware of current law and jurisdictional mores.

Above all, the reasonably prudent person behaves in an honest, sensible manner. Don't torture the RPP theory, trying to stretch it to fit your needs. Relax and be honest with yourself. If you're going to touch guns, you have a responsibility to be sufficiently self-aware to know your limitations. Measure yourself against the person you ought to be, morally and legally. Then behave accordingly.

Since we're both now reasonably prudent, let's consider when deadly force should be used.

## The Dilemma

Could you shoot a man charging you with a knife? Maybe. What if the man is 90 years old, charging you in his walker from half a mile away, and armed with a plastic knife? Of course not. You can see why the law cannot be universally specific. But what if the attacker is an amateur middleweight boxer armed with a hunting knife? He's certainly much more dangerous than the old man. But what if you're a professional heavyweight boxer, wearing pierce-resistant body armor, and armed with a high-velocity water cannon and two trained guard dogs? You get the idea. *Threat is always weighed in comparison to the potential victim and within the circumstances and environment in which it occurs.* No clear magic line.

## The Practics Gold Standard

The closest thing to a magic shoot/don't–shoot line, of which I am aware, is the following question:

> **Are you, a reasonably prudent person, in fear of imminent death, serious injury, or great bodily harm to yourself or others and have no reasonable alternative to the use of deadly force?**

That's the whole shebang, and the legal premise behind that question is why George Zimmerman is not in prison. Let's examine the Practics Gold Standard point by point.

**Reasonably Prudent Person**—a checkbook-balancing, two-beer limit, life-insurance buying, turn-signal using, employment-loving, directions-reading man or woman

**Fear**—After police shootings the involved officers' statements often include the phrase "in fear for my life." You're not allowed to shoot for anger, justice, vengeance, or moral outrage. You shoot only when you are afraid that not shooting will kill you or someone else. The phrase "in fear" is a legal requirement that must be met for the use of deadly force, but it is also a permissive caveat that allows a defender to act preemptively—you don't have to wait for death to occur. Otherwise, a potential hostage could *never* use deadly force to stay outside a kidnapper's van. In such a case, the victim is not responding to being shoved toward the van but responding to the *fear* of death, serious injury, or great bodily harm. Nothing in the above kidnapping example requires breaking the Gold Standard. This application will become clearer when we discuss the continuum of force (COF). Being "in fear" does not, of itself, justify the use of deadly force. That fear has to meet the reasonably prudent standard. The court will judge the validity of your claim to fear. It's simple: Fear is not the result of a long thought process; it's a visceral but reasonable reaction to immediate circumstances.

**Imminent**—Urgency is the key. Imminent tends to mean "immediate" in most circumstances but not necessarily in all situations. Think of imminent as *time combined with circumstance.* Generally, threats have to be in the now.

Let's say a sniper is hunting you through the deep woods. He has shot at you several times, nearly striking you. You run and he pursues until, finally, you gain some distance on him and hide, waiting three hours for him to pass close enough for you to split his head with a rock. That would *probably* pass legal muster, unless you had stopped and hidden across the road from where you had parked your car, choosing to lie in wait rather than simply drive away. Even then, it might fly, or it might not. The defender's honest reasoning is the key. There is no situation without an exception or possible challenge. *Imminent may allow for more time, but never wasted time.* In other words, there's no time limit, but *imminent* allows no break in the threat timeline.

I am aware of a singular case in which a man was sitting in a bar when a member of an outlaw biker gang threatened him with the death of his family. The man went home, got a gun, returned to the bar, and killed the biker. He was found not guilty because the threat from the biker was considered to be imminent, and the jury believed no reasonable alternative was available to the defendant. I only remember that decision because the jury's "not guilty" verdict was so far outside what we've come to expect in such cases.

More people go to prison monkeying around with *imminent* than with any other portion of the deadly force doctrine. Be honest with yourself. The key is not to try to hide behind a carved-in-stone point of law, but rather to live by a sincere, fair interpretation of the Gold Standard. The taking of life is a last resort for the reasonably prudent person. Did the urgency of the threat make deadly force the only reasonable action you could take? If so, you've behaved within the general understanding of the law.

**Death, Serious Injury, or Great Bodily Harm**—the imminent occurrence that you, as a reasonably prudent person, believe is likely to kill you, break bones, cause internal injuries, rape you, or torture you.

Fear of a black eye isn't a reason to use deadly force. However, fear of unconsciousness may qualify for the use of deadly force in two ways: believing more serious injury will occur when you are unable to resist or fear of a brain concussion, suffocation, or restriction of blood flow that would cause unconsciousness. On the other hand, if you willingly engage in a bare-knuckles contest and resort to using a firearm to prevent receiving a knockout punch, you're likely headed for prison. In other words, we can't contrive circumstances to endanger ourselves and then claim self-defense. Death, serious injury, or great bodily harm must be the feared result proposed by a legitimate external threat.

The defender has a burden to justify his action against the ability and means of the attacker. You can be in fear of being stabbed to death, but you can't be in fear of being stabbed to death by a quadriplegic with a knife sitting on his lap. The attacker's *means* (knife) is not sufficient to be a legitimate deadly threat without the *ability* to execute the act (stabbing with the knife).

**Yourself or Others**—Deadly force may be used to save your own life and person, as well as that of others. However, the same standard applies when defending others; they must meet the imminent, great-bodily-harm-or-death, and reasonable-alternative criteria. Think of it as acting as someone else's agent. Does the threat to that person fall within the Gold Standard? It is the same standard for yourself or others. Don't count on the court granting you any heroic license.

**Reasonable Alternative**—A gang of rioters spots you from across a large parking lot and runs in your direction. Instead of getting in your car and driving away, you draw your handgun and wait for them to arrive. In such a case you would have the legal challenge of explaining why you didn't take the reasonable and prudent action of leaving. Conversely, it may not be reasonable to try to get into your car when someone is pummeling you about the head. A stun gun may be a reasonable alternative when confronted with a fist but is insufficient when confronted with a firearm. *Having no reasonable alternative qualifies as exhausting all reasonable alternatives.* If you tried to wrestle with your attacker or hit him with pepper spray and your attempt(s) failed, you're not required to get beaten to death to show goodwill.

**Use of Deadly Force**—Deadly force is any force likely to cause death, serious injury, or great bodily harm. Legal force is not used to kill. It is used to stop the threat. *Death occurs incidentally in deadly force cases.* You are not Dirty Harry. You're permitted to address threats, not people. The legal defender does *not* shoot to wound but does not seek to kill either. Shots are aimed at where they will be most effective at stopping threats, which coincidentally tends to be where they also are most likely to cause death. Nonetheless, the defender's intent matters. Think, speak, and act only in terms of eliminating threats.

> **Reality Follows Theory**
> Nowhere does the tactical importance of guiding principles appear more clearly than in basic firing strategies. Planning to fire two rounds here and two rounds there may be technically solid, but it is a violation of the Practics Gold Standard. The amount of fire is always based on the imminent threat. Firing continues as long as the threat continues, no more and no less. Firing 2·2 or 4·2 may be too much, but it just as well may be too little. The Practics shooter does not plan to stop firing any more than a driver plans to stop his car on the freeway, but the shooter, like the driver, must be prepared to stop when the need arises. Technical skills must be based on foundational principles.

## Truth

If you want to avoid legal problems and prevent years of misery, behave within the spirit of the law. Interpret the Gold Standard honestly. You do have a right to defend your life or the lives of others. But if you know you don't have to shoot—don't. Any cop of some experience has had many opportunities to "legally" shoot and has chosen not to fire. Your own goodwill provides your best protection. Those who seek violence for violence's sake will wind up with costly court cases and a good chance of life in prison. Be honest with yourself. Don't ask "When can I shoot?" The question ought to be "When must I defend myself?" The answer is in the Gold Standard.

George Zimmerman's credibility suffered prior to his trial. His lawful act of self-defense was not aided by his purported attempt to deceive the judge who set his bail. Those involved in use-of-force cases are wise to be cautious in what they communicate. Discretion is not lying—deliberately misleading is lying. Not every convicted perjurer was an idiot. Don't assume that you're smart enough to outwit the system. Credibility, once gone, is hard to recover in a single court case.

## One Level Higher, More or Less

American law enforcement agencies all have (hopefully) a continuum-of-force policy. The COF tells officers where weapons and techniques fall within that jurisdiction's use-of-force doctrine. For instance, most COFs start off with officer presence as the lowest form of force, then verbal commands that are usually followed by pepper spray. Pepper spray is generally believed to cause no lasting or serious harm and is therefore often considered lower force than a shove on the shoulder. Tear gas (Mace) was ranked higher in the old days than pepper spray is ranked currently because some people had died from Mace. All COFs end with deadly force, which includes the use of firearms. Even deadly force varies by state. For instance, when adopting the carotid-artery restraint, California considered it to be deadly force. The "carotid" is a rear-neck compression that restricts blood flow to the head, quickly causing unconsciousness, with further application resulting in death. California law enforcement originally considered its use to be at the same level as a firearm. Other states disagreed.

The way officers are taught to select weapons is based on a rule of "one level higher." If a suspect has a fist, the officer may use a stick. If the suspect has a stick, the officer may use a gun. The same rule applies to private citizens. A firearm is not an acceptable choice when faced with a water balloon, but it may be acceptable when faced with a baseball bat. The underlying rule of COF is to *start at the lowest level reasonable and go no higher than necessary to prevent death or serious injury.* There are some instances in which the defender must go immediately to a firearm, even though it is more than one level above the threat. A much smaller defender may have no reasonable hope of defense with sprays, fists, kicks, and sticks. No magic line, just honest, realistic assessment.

Remember our kidnapping example? A victim who is overpowered by an attacker and is being pushed into a van can make some reasonable and prudent assumptions. There may be no time for even a shout. Being physically pushed beyond an ability to resist has already taken the defender beyond a bare-handed defense. She doesn't carry a baseball bat in her purse and is not required to get into that van. *Escalation occurring quickly is still escalation*, and, of course, it is the attacker who determines the defender's level of response. A charging attacker may take you from nothing to firearm within a second. In such a case, your escalation is an instantaneous decision based on urgency: no time to speak a command, no reasonable ability to punch, strike with an impact weapon, or run. If you have an attacker whom you have just witnessed beat someone into serious injury, great bodily harm, or death, and you don't think you can do any better than the victim just did, forget fist-fighting. If you're not specially trained to use an impact weapon or the killer is significantly larger than you (or both), drawing a firearm may be the proper escalation in the use-of-force continuum. Maybe the other guy is a known brawler and you've never been in a fight. The only person who will know which level is necessary is the reasonably prudent individual experiencing the incident. Good faith and knowledge are your best defense.

Be aware that regardless of the legitimate justification of your threat response, you must be able to articulate your reasoning. Think about the COF before you need it.

## Private Person's Continuum of Force

Private persons don't have a COF per se, but, nonetheless, they bear a responsibility for adhering to COF rules. For ease of understanding, let's look at what might be a private-person COF. Obviously, state law will play havoc with a universal rule, particularly as it relates to the ranking of sprays and stun guns. We'll keep it very general for our use here, but you can create your own according to your state's laws. A good pattern may be found in the policies of the law enforcement agencies within your jurisdiction. The value of a personal COF is not in showing it to anyone but in provoking forethought toward how you will escalate force. You want to *know* before you have to *do*.

- **Verbal Commands**—*"Stop!" "Leave me alone!" "I'll shoot if you come closer!"* Voice commands matter in court because they show an earnest intent to gain lawful compliance. That's why the presence or absence of verbal commands is so important to police in rape investigations, particularly when the parties are acquainted. In reality, voice commands very often work in low-level street encounters, such as in controlling drunks. Give clear commands whenever you reasonably can.
- **Hands**—When you have to put hands on someone, there is a reasonable expectation of escalation. Keep your hands off until you have no choice. A guiding hand is a lot different from a strike. Be prepared to explain why you chose your level of contact.
- **Impact Weapon**—A baton strike to the forearm is more than

hands and less than deadly force. A full blow to the head with a big, rechargeable flashlight falls into deadly force. Cops have off-limit zones for normal use of impact weapons: head, spine, kidneys, genitals, and in some cases, knees and elbows. Don't assume swinging a stick is automatically less than deadly force.

- **Deadly Force**—You have shouted commands or otherwise expressed yourself (ran or screamed), and you pushed the bad guy away. When he came back at you, he got a whack with your purse or briefcase. Now he's got a knife. You need to draw your handgun. That's easy, but what if the attacker skips the textbook sequence? Let's say the attacker jumps out from behind a stanchion in a parking garage and grabs for you. Think about the Gold Standard. Are you in fear for your life? Do you have time for alternatives? If you're startled and pushed back against a car by an attacker, you don't have to keep losing the fight. But fear for your life is still the key. There's no trick here. If a person 3' shorter and 100 pounds lighter than you is your attacker, ask yourself the same question: Am I honestly in fear for my life? Depending on your own health, you may be in fear for your life at a much lower point than another person of your age, experience, and gender. Be prepared to explain your legitimate fear. Deadly force is any force likely to cause death, serious injury, or great bodily harm. A 300-pound strong man smacking an elderly woman in the head is likely to be considered as using deadly force. Similarly, an old woman pointing a shotgun trumps a 300-pound man at 10 yards. Don't get hung up on the weapon or lack of weapon. Weigh the totality of the facts in front of you.

---

**Control and Safety**

In the early 1990s, the FBI conducted a study of cop killers. They actually interviewed the murderers as well as cops who knew the deceased peace officers. The results were somewhat surprising at the time. Prior to the results of the study, it was assumed that police deaths were more apt to occur when the officer was young, inexperienced, or overbearing. It turned out that the deceased officers, who averaged approximately eight years of service, were considered intelligent, educated, and less likely to use force than most officers. Many of the deceased had considered themselves proficient at reading people. Most of the murderers stated that the killings were unplanned, but the opportunity presented itself due to the officer not taking control.

Control saves lives. If the good guy doesn't take charge, the bad guy will.

*FBI's Uniform Crime Reporting Program report "Killed in the Line of Duty" (September 1992)*

---

## Post-Incident Threat Evaluation by Law Enforcement

We know that deadly force actions are legally considered in light of local law, reasonable prudence, and some version of the Gold Standard. But at the nuts-and-bolts level, cops still have to reassemble the threat to determine if the degree of force used was justified. An essential element of that review will be an attempt to determine the defender's perspective at the time of the incident. What did the defender fear? How did the defender measure the threat *at the time of* the occurrence?

Investigator's checklist:

1. **Who is the defender?** This includes gender, size, physical capacity, fitness, age, health, training, general mental state, and background.

2. **How did the defender assess the threat?** Investigators will want to know what the defender honestly thought immediately prior to using force. In other words, they care less about whether the attacker's gun was actually a toy and more about whether the defender *knew* it was a toy. What could the defender see and hear? What *specifically* did the defender fear about the attack? If a defender claims to *not* have been in fear

of the knife-wielding attacker, but rather was agitated at the possibility the encounter would make him late for an appointment, he's going to have some legal trouble, despite the presence of the attacker's weapon. For instance, a guy holding a knife in his hand and cleaning his fingernails, which the defender claims was not perceived as threatening, is in essence an unarmed person. Again, it probably doesn't legally matter whether the attacker was an expert kickboxer, but it does matter whether the victim honestly believed that the attacker had great superiority in physical skill.

Those first two criteria give investigators a general idea of the balance of power as *perceived by the defender*.

3. **What was the sequence of events between the threat and the use of deadly force?** One person may have threatened an acquaintance with a machete, but afterward both parties sat and watched a movie. During the movie an argument arose, and the acquaintance shot the machete guy. Obviously, imminent threat within the sequence of events is going to be a concern in that case. It is common for officers to become aware of witness insincerity through sequence irregularities. If a woman shoots her ex-husband during a reported domestic-violence restraining-order violation and then claims to have been terrified of the deceased man, police will be suspicious if they find she had repeatedly telephoned the man immediately prior to the shooting.

4. **What were the constraints of time in relation to the immediacy of the threat?** All other elements being in accordance with law, did the shooter have sufficient time for an alternative? An attacker beats a victim to the ground with his fists and then falls to the ground gasping for breath. Did the victim have time to do more than draw a concealed weapon? Could the victim have left the scene? Investigators must compare what occurred to any opportunity that existed to use a non-deadly or even non-violent alternative.

The above two criteria give investigators an understanding of the moment of opportunity in which the deadly force decision was made.

5. **Who was the attacker? What was the attacker's physical, mental, and emotional state?** Professional fighters divide

into weight classes because size matters. Did the attacker have special abilities, or was he historically prone to violence? What weapons did the attacker possess? A gun is usually a gun for legal purposes, but a .22 derringer and a center-fire rifle vary greatly in their ability to threaten people at 400 yards.

6. **Where did the event occur and at what time? Was help nearby? Was the scene open to the public?** I recall taking a police report from a young girl who emphatically stated she had been raped in a nearby field during the late afternoon. Through my investigation I discovered the field had been clear-cut just prior to the alleged rape and was open to view by commuter traffic. The girl confessed to making a false report to influence her mother's behavior. Cops need to know if the scene will support the allegation.

The last two criteria give investigators facts against which a defender's reported perceptions may be matched to assist in determining truthfulness. If a shooter reports being fearful because the assailant demonstrated his martial-arts prowess with a spinning back kick, investigators will want to know if the attacker is literally capable of such a feat. If it turns out the attacker was lame at the time of the incident, there's obviously a problem with the defender's honesty or competence.

## Incident Dissection

Let's take a couple of incidents and break them down from a cop's point of view. We'll be the cops, and our goal will be to determine if a deadly force incident was self-defense or unjustifiable homicide.

*Incident Summary #1: A man calls 911 to report that he shot and killed an attacker in a public park during a lunchtime walk.*

We learn from witnesses that the attacker tightly embraced the shooter in a bear hug, forcing him to the ground. On the ground the attacker continued to keep his arms wrapped around the shooter. After being unable to extricate himself from the grip of the attacker, the shooter drew a pistol from his belt and fired two quick shots into the side of the attacker's torso. After a few seconds the attacker sighed and fell limp.

The shooter rolled the attacker onto the ground without resistance and rose to a kneeling position. He discovered the attacker was unresponsive and showed no sign of life. The shooter immediately called *911*.

Force was certainly used by the attacker. The shooter was knocked off his feet during the assault. Did the actions of the attacker merit a deadly force response by the victim? No, not even close. The shooter was restrained and could have continued in that state until help arrived. If the attacker had escalated force, the victim would have been within his rights to escalate to a higher level. Verbal commands should have been given. There was no threat of serious injury and no urgency. This case would likely result in prosecution of the shooter.

*Incident Summary #2: A woman reports shooting her estranged boyfriend inside her home.*

The woman tells us that her ex-boyfriend entered her home without knocking. He told her that he wanted to discuss their breakup. She told him to leave. He sat on the couch and began to shout at her. She left the room, used the bathroom, and got a bottle of water from the kitchen. When she returned, he was watching television. She turned off the TV and told him to leave for the second time. He agreed to leave if she'd talk to him. She sat down and they talked for a few minutes.

Afterward she got up and walked to the door and ordered him to leave for the third time. He followed her but, instead of leaving, leaned toward her and kissed her face. She shoved him back. He punched her, knocking her to the floor. She got up and ran into the bathroom, locking the door. After applying a washcloth to her face, she walked to the kitchen, passing him, who still stood at the doorway. He was crying and told her that he was sorry. She went to the refrigerator and got some ice for her face. The man followed her. When he put his hand on her shoulder, she shrugged it off. He slapped her on the back of the head, knocking her to the floor a second time. She walked through the house into her bedroom. After a few minutes, he followed her, accusing her of provoking him. She told him to get out of her bedroom, and he moved back into the hallway but continued to shout at her.

The woman squeezed past the man and went to the garage.

She retrieved a loaded revolver from a storage trunk and tucked the handgun into her waistband. As she walked back toward her bedroom, the man stood in front of her, blocking her way and demanding to be allowed to explain himself. She ordered him to leave the apartment for a fourth time. He stepped forward, put his hand on her shoulder, spit on her, and called her a vulgar name. She ducked past him and went into the bedroom. He followed as far as the bedroom doorway. She drew her handgun, told the man again that he was trespassing and, for the fifth time, ordered him to leave the home or be shot. He responded by making an obscene sign, refusing to leave, and daring her to shoot him. She shot him, causing his immediate death.

I took the last call, so you take this one. Do we arrest the shooter, or is this a justifiable homicide? Here are some facts:

- The shooter was violently assaulted two times during this incident in addition to being kissed, touched, and spit upon. She was knocked to the floor twice.
- She had attempted to use hands to force the man back after he committed an assault by kissing her. Her shove was met with greater force. She had shrugged to remove his hand from her shoulder and was met again with greater force.
- Her clear and repeated legal commands for him to leave the apartment were not obeyed.
- The man, who had just demonstrated violence, refused to leave even though he saw she was armed.

What do you think?

In real life, it's anybody's guess how a jury will decide or what will motivate a prosecutor or judge. However, we can make a pretty good guess about the above case: She's getting arrested and likely charged with some form of manslaughter or murder. No doubt her lawyer would attempt to make the case that she retreated to her room and issued an ultimatum in fear for her life before firing, in the belief that deadly violence was upon her. The reality is that she avoided reasonable alternatives prior to the shooting but, most importantly, used deadly force in a moment when deadly force was not specifically justified. A stationary, unarmed person standing apart from the defender and shouting bad words does not, of itself, merit the use of a firearm. If the man had advanced into the bedroom, she could have had a legitimate fear of a physical assault but would still be accountable for not choosing previously available alternatives.

The shooter had sufficient freedom of movement and action to be able to leave, summon aid, call the police, or lock herself in another room. Any fear she may have had did not extend to trying to stay out of the man's reach. Instead, she squeezed past the victim—who did not impede or follow her when she went into the garage, got a gun, again walked past the man, and repositioned herself in the bedroom. When he refused to leave (though he did not advance), she shot him, purportedly for trespassing.

The man's acts of violence were *interspersed with opportunities for her to seek alternatives*, if she had been genuinely fearful. The punch was the worst of it, and that was followed by two decreasingly violent slaps. His violence is significant, but her behavior suggests she wasn't afraid for her life—she acted with malice. The killer orchestrated the final circumstances that resulted in the man's death. We don't shoot people for justice, revenge, minor assault, or misdemeanor crimes.

When considering deadly force, the circumstances surrounding the incident must be measured by the Practics Gold Standard. It is easy to become distracted by all the emotion and extraneous information in these cases, but the elements of the Practics Gold Standard are simple to understand and can save you a lifetime of misery.

If you become embroiled in a confrontation, your emotion—and even the "moral rightness" of your situation—have no bearing on the legal use of deadly force. If you refuse any reasonable opportunity to diffuse the situation, expect to be held accountable for your use of deadly force.

## Malice

Malice, or malice aforethought, is an element always considered in murder cases. This is not of great concern to the honest defender, because the defender is acting from a reasonable fear, not malice. Check yourself. If you're baiting traps, manipulating conditions, or creating your own crisis, you may be on your way to committing murder.

## After the Shooting

Friend, a criminal investigation is not your opportunity for a dramatic audition. Many people get themselves into a great deal of trouble through pointless verbal declarations to the police. Please be quiet. Honest people seem to feel compelled to tell the police every detail of their lives, and I don't expect I will talk anyone out of that with this book. Give the police your identifying information and answer immediate questions about fleeing suspects, injuries, and ongoing dangers, such as outstanding armed suspects. If you cannot resist speaking further to the police, they'll need some kind of statement to *not* arrest you. Keep it concise: "I woke when I heard my front door breaking. I got my gun. He attacked me with a knife. I was afraid he was going to kill me, so I fired my gun." Then you can tell the police you want to cooperate but are confused and frightened and would like to have your lawyer present before you say anything else. There are worse things than being booked into county jail. The less you say without legal counsel, the better.

Keep the following Dos and Don'ts list in mind when speaking to the police about a deadly force encounter:

- **Do request an attorney.** If anything is untoward or likely to be inflammatory, get a lawyer. If you live in an Idaho county and shoot an armed home invader, a straightforward statement to the deputies *may* be fine. In Southern California, I'd be a little less confident speaking to the local PD. It is better to go to county jail for a few hours and have to make bail than it is to inadvertently incriminate yourself. If you have the discipline to limit yourself to giving only your identifying information, indicating you acted in self-defense, and then invoking your right to an attorney, you will be better off in the long run. The point is if you can afford an attorney, hire a good one. Know in advance which attorney you will use. Don't sit in jail, flipping through the yellow pages. Ask around. If you know local cops, ask them. Don't ask them whom they *like*, ask them whom they'd *hire*. All lawyers are not equal. A person may pass the bar and still offer clients a combination of laziness, inattentiveness to detail, and bad courtroom behavior. A good lawyer is serious and discreet. It's not like the movies where the nut-job lawyer wins a hopeless case through street smarts, personality, and emotional attachment. Good lawyers are like every other successfully employed person: hardworking and diligent. The best ones can be socially exhausting because they love minutiae and won't give an opinion without qualifying it (no doubt making them a joy in marriage). The work of the law is always in the details. A sloppy lawyer is as desirable as a drunken airline pilot.

- **Don't give estimates.** Say "I don't know" when you are not willing to risk your life on the accuracy of your memory. Acts committed under duress or excitement can be difficult to recall with accuracy. Officers who fire more than a single round are often uncertain of the number of rounds discharged. (Later on we'll look at an efficient method for keeping track of ammo.) We are all susceptible to diminished capacity during life-threatening events. Complete recollection may take hours, days, or weeks. Hasty statements may have to be amended later, casting doubt on your credibility.

- **Do not guess in an attempt to be helpful to police.** Today's well-intentioned guess may be tomorrow's false statement. If you know you fired more than one round, say "I fired more than once." They'll ask you if you fired more than two times. If you bite, they'll go to five times and then 10 times. Or they'll go the other way and ask if you fired 20 times. Then they'll work you back down. Don't participate in that parlor game. If you don't know, say so and refuse to say more. This isn't lying; it's refusing to be forced into speculation. Ideally, you will demand an attorney before answering any questions, even it means having to bail out of a city or county jail.

- **Don't befriend the police.** The police aren't your friends. They aren't your enemies either, but they don't have a dog in your fight. Whatever you tell a cop, you should expect to hear repeated at the most inopportune time. Remember, the police have to determine if you are a murderer. Many murderers claim self-defense. The police don't know you, and they don't know what you may have done. A peace officer worthy of the name must be professionally skeptical.

There is no moral argument to be made against an honest citizen exercising constitutional rights. If the police ask to search your home or vehicle, you should politely but firmly decline. If they have the right to search, they won't need your permission. It's not a question of having something to hide. It's a question of exposing yourself to thousands of obscure laws that may be used against you. Granting permission for a search exposes you to the interpretive whims of officers either willing to exceed constitutional restraint or give a broad reading to ambiguously written law. I am not referring to criminal acts by police. In fact, there is no real punishment for police who openly try to stretch a criminal statute because they are not committing a crime. Even if they are unsuccessful, you may be tied up in court for years. An example of this would be the discovery of some item not typically considered illegal but, combined with other circumstances, might induce confiscation, arrest, and forwarding to the prosecutor's office. For instance, your state may prohibit the concealed carrying of folding knives with blades over a certain length (let's use 4" for this example), but the law may not instruct officers in how blades are to be measured. Such a law may send you to jail if your 3.8-inch blade is measured along the outside of the blade's curve, bringing the length to 4.1". Don't expose yourself to that risk. When I worked in California, the law allowed for the arrest of a person based on the confession of a felony crime if the statute of limitations for that crime had not been reached. This meant a casual statement during a traffic stop about something relatively minor, which occurred years earlier, could land an upright citizen in jail. You may be surprised what constitutes a felony in some states. Our forefathers legally recognized our right to be free from unreasonable search, seizure, and self-incrimination. Assert your rights.

Many of us have heard stories from an old relative or friend about a defender who shot an attacker back in the 1960s or 1970s and was coached by the responding police officers on what to say and what to omit. Those incidents certainly happened in the past, but—believe me when I tell you—the past has passed. Much of the discretion that enabled officers to uphold the spirit of the law, as opposed to the letter of the law, has been legislatively withdrawn. Very often your local police officers work in a mild state of fear of their employing municipalities. Additionally, prosecutors make their bones by getting at least one good "bad cop" case. The U.S. government *loves* to initiate federal cases regarding "under color of authority" violations of constitutional rights against local police. The reporting officer who interviews you is not going to risk termination, lawsuits, or imprisonment in order to advise you. You're a suspect until you're not, and then, for the next few years, you're a potential lawsuit defendant. Know what you're doing and watch your mouth around the police.

- **Don't be a tough guy.** "In fear for my life" loses a lot of its meaning when accompanied by "I'm glad I was at home. I wanted that punk to get a taste of his own medicine." Nobody cares about how tough you are, nor are they likely to be impressed by any movie-cliché statements. But they will take note of your bravado as it relates to the possible absence of fear, which may also reflect a pre-existing desire to shoot someone.

- **Don't speak about the attacker.** Don't mention his race, religion, or family. Keep any answers specific. Police will look for any overriding ill will on your part that may have unduly influenced your actions. Always be honest, never foolish. It is better to say "We always disagreed on our property boundary" than to say "That thieving scum spent years trying to steal 10 feet of my pasture." Don't lie and don't grandstand.

- **Don't volunteer anything.** Everybody does silly things that investigators can present as outrageous and obvious signs of unreasonable behavior. Many people talk to themselves. Others dance in their bedrooms at night. Some tell their cats things they would never say in public. Your words and actions occur within a context that you may not be able to properly express. Every word you speak is going to be examined. Keep your answers concise. It is not your responsibility to help the police ask the right questions. If you want to talk, hire a lawyer. Otherwise, shut up, shut up, and shut up.

- **Don't become a celebrity.** Judges and prosecutors are going to make you pay for going on a news talk show and running your mouth. There are times when you need to alert the public.

Get a sane, competent, discreet, levelheaded lawyer to guide your public statements. Avoid grandstanding lawyers, particularly those who jump in front of cameras dressed like Buffalo Bill or those who earnestly believe an earring and ponytail are appropriate for a middle-aged man to wear in the presence of a superior court judge or in front of a TV camera. Your lawyer represents you, your interests, and your intentions. How do you want to be perceived by people who can throw you into prison?

- **Do be honest.** If you attempt a deception, there must be a reason for it. No one in authority is going to assume that reason to be insignificant. The whole theory of lawful self-defense rests on goodwill. If honest, reasonable actions follow an honest, reasonable decision to use force, there's no need to tell lies.

## Arrival of Police

The manner in which you prepare for the arrival of police after a deadly force incident greatly depends on your immediate circumstances. If you took a shot at a man who forcibly entered your home, resulting in the wounded man fleeing the area, you may be able to unload your weapon and place it on your kitchen table while you wait on the porch for the police. On the other hand, if you're forcing the detention of two violent criminals, you can't very well disarm. When the police are present, do not manipulate a firearm without being told to do so. Here are a few more recommendations concerning police contact:

- If you're in phone contact, let *911* dispatch know you're armed and the location of the weapon.
- If you're in a public place and have a CCW handgun, holster and conceal it. When the police arrive, allow the officers to approach or summon you. Keep your hands free and to the front. Tell the officers "I have a CCW permit and am carrying a holstered pistol on my belt." Keep your CCW permit and driver's license in your hand, shirt pocket, or jacket pocket to prevent having to reach toward your hips. Don't assault the cops with the permit. If they want to see it, they'll let you know. Allow police to direct you or ask you questions. Avoid

bombarding the officers with needless information. Let the police lead the conversation and action.

- When police arrive on a scene with one unknown person holding a gun on another unknown person, they will point their guns at everybody. You can't explain that you're a good guy while being shouted at, and it's foolish and dangerous to try. If the cops have their guns pointed at you and order you to put your gun on the ground—obey. It'll all get worked out.

- Do not have a gun in your hand unless your life depends on it. Let the officers acclimatize themselves to the scene, and then you can explain the presence of your firearm. If a cop comes around a corner and sees you holding a gun, he will fear the worst. Mitigate his fears by giving him time to access and control the scene before introducing a firearm. On your initial contact, unless there is an immediate emergency, such as shots being fired at the officers, tell the police that you are carrying a gun or have control over one. Never surprise the police by physically presenting an unexpected weapon.

- In the midst of chaos, get your hands up but don't walk toward the police unless specifically ordered. Walking toward the police escalates their treatment of you toward greater caution. If you can't hear them, stand there and let them adjust. They can use a bullhorn or external public-address speaker in a patrol car. Walking toward police with your hands up while shouting "I can't hear you" is dangerous. The more time and space you give the cops, the more civilly they will treat you. Mitigate their fears, and you will have some control over what happens to you.

- If you have to leave a scene after an incident, then leave. Make no more delay to contact the police than necessary for safety. Here's an example, one that is often misadvised by the support-your-local-police enthusiasts: You're involved in a minor traffic accident in a bad part of town. The other driver attacks you with a hammer, and you draw your weapon and fire a shot. Almost immediately residents come onto the porches of nearby houses and shout obscenities at you. You are an idiot if you stay there waving a gun or wait for police while barricaded inside your car. Get in your car and drive to safety and then call the cops. If the police catch you leaving the scene, might they suspect you of fleeing? Of course, but fleeing what? You're not a criminal. The police will understand actions that are reasonable and consistent with the facts. If you tell the police that you feared greater violence if you stayed and that you only traveled as far as necessary to safely contact the police, they will weigh your words against your actions. Again, staying put for the convenience of the police is good only as far as it is safe. Use reasonable, honest judgment.

- When circumstances permit, leave your handgun intact for the police. For example, you fired a shot inside your house, the bad guy may have been struck but is verifiably gone, and you are able to place the handgun on the kitchen table of your unoccupied and secured home while you wait outside for the police. In such a case the handgun should not be unloaded, and, as a general rule, it is inadvisable to unload a handgun after an incident for reasons of safety and control. Most unintentional discharges occur during loading and unloading, and the stress of a recent attack will only make it worse for the marginally trained shooter. On the other hand, there are rare but real exceptions. Let's say you're a jeweler in a major city who has been professionally trained and have maintained your gun-handling competence. You were just in a shooting in the middle of the street after a robbery and kidnapping attempt, which began inside your store. Someone has died, and people are running and hiding behind cars as they take cell phone pictures of you and monitor your actions. You have no contact with *911*, and you have no holster on you. The police cars can be seen speeding toward you from a couple blocks away. If the circumstances permit, kneel down and remove your magazine, empty your chamber with the muzzle pointed downward, place the handgun on the ground, stand and discard your sweater or jacket, and then take a few steps away with your hands above your head. In such a case, it would be advantageous to have witnesses report to *911* operators that the gunman has unloaded the pistol. The police will prefer to have the handgun intact after a shooting for evidentiary purposes, but a handgun that appears unloaded in a completely safe condition will be perceived to be less of a threat than an apparently loaded handgun within reach of a possibly violent person. Do you want to be quickly judged to be a non-threat, or do you want to posthumously win a junior evidence tech badge? Ninety-nine percent of the time defenders should NOT manipulate the handgun beyond engaging the safety, but it is incumbent upon the individual defender to realistically assess circumstances and evaluate risk. In short, less firearm handling is *usually* better, but the lawful defender always has the burden for intelligent thought and reasonable action.

- Be as calm as possible when encountering the police. Cops work off initial impressions. Don't talk about your gun, don't give an opinion, and don't praise the police. Listen for instructions and answer questions with concise statements. Think about what cops are trying to accomplish and don't obstruct the pursuit of those objectives. It's that simple.

## Evidence

There's a lot of talk about criminal evidence in our culture, some of which probably stems from TV police dramas. Much of the popular information on the topic of physical criminal evidence as it relates to the legal use of deadly force by a private citizen appears to be right out of a police explorer's study guide or propaganda from the local PD's public affairs officer.

Unfortunately, some of it comes from defensive tactics instructors who ought to know better, so let's consider evidence preservation for a moment. Even the police don't make evidence the primary concern until the scene is clear. Many times I have moved potential evidence or weapons before I knew for certain a person was deceased or incapacitated. We have to be reasonable. Evidence goes hand in hand with police reports. Many officers have to handle evidence during an incident and later explain it in the report. The same reporting must be done when evidence is handled by a private person:

> Smith claimed that he was unaware whether the suspect was seriously injured and, fearing for his own safety, took the pistol from underneath the suspect's right shoulder and placed it on the coffee table.

The result would be that both Smith's and the suspect's fingerprints might be found on the pistol. The evidence and the report narrative will explain the course of events. The preservation of life is always the priority. Evidence is important, but evidence is not your job. Certainly, physical evidence can be important to you because, after a use-of-force incident, physical evidence may demonstrate your innocence. Nonetheless, evidence is not your primary concern, and in most cases, it's none of your business. Law enforcement personnel are responsible to collect evidence. Of course, if you deliberately tamper with evidence, you will be guilty of a crime and utterly discredit yourself. I'm not suggesting that you should hold potential evidence in a nonchalant disregard, but let your actions be motivated by your legitimate defense requirements and not what you imagine to be the convenience of the police. Get your priorities right.

## Preparation

Long before you are involved in a deadly force encounter, you are laying a trail of statements and publicly defining yourself. You may recall that the Zimmerman case dug up the criminal justice courses the shooter had attended. Deadly force cases involve a backward look at the shooter. Now is the time to prepare your image and control your public statements. Here are a few suggestions:

- Don't have a skull and crossbones engraved on your pistol grips, at least not unless you keep a parrot on your shoulder and make your living through robbery on the high seas. A gun is a constitutional right and a somber responsibility, not a toy for a wannabe tough guy. Make sure your gear is not evidence of something you don't intend. Likewise, you don't need a handgun from a manufacturer who marked the slide or barrel with a childishly provocative model name. Bear in mind that your weapon, ammo, and related gear will be taken as evidence and shown in court.
- Avoid kill-or-be-killed nonsense on cars, on posters, and in conversation. Here are a few examples of bumper-sticker idiocy:
  Kill 'em all, let god sort 'em out.
  Insured by Glock
  Honk again. I'm reloading.

I'd rather be judged by twelve than carried by six.

- Are we 10 years old? Get that childish nonsense off your car or be prepared to eat it later. Yeah, I know you have a right to say what you want, but I also know lawyers have the right to make inferences from your pre-incident statements. *Bumper stickers are self-declarations.* I wish good sense was the judicial standard in admissible evidence, but it is not. Don't make things harder on yourself for no good reason. After a self-defense shooting occurs, resulting in the death or serious injury of a criminal, ambulance-chasing vermin will flock to the criminal's family if any opportunity exists for a payoff. Your mature, good sense is shyster repellant.

- Clean up your Web sites and Internet presence. Police routinely check social media pages. It is amazing how many people will reveal crimes or indiscreet actions online. You can bet a lawyer in a civil case will examine everything you have written. Watch what you say and with whom you associate. This is too easy a precaution not to be done immediately. If you're keeping or carrying a gun, your public persona needs to be professional, or at least at a socially acceptable 1950s' standard. Keep a little formality and distance in your online presence. Be polite, never vulgar or crude. Consider yourself to be a lady or gentleman attending a black-tie event—not every person in the ballroom needs to know your innermost thoughts.

- Your outward face should be clean and prudent because it may be presented to a hate-filled jury or a politically motivated judge. See yourself in that light through the personal advertising you've placed in the public sphere. Consider limiting your social media presence to work-related activities.

## Use-Of-Force Summary

The legal use of force against another human being is a terrible responsibility. It is your duty to know the laws that govern its use within your jurisdiction(s). Know the Practics Gold Standard. Always be prepared to articulate the reasoning behind your actions.

**Question: When do you shoot?**

**Answer: When it would be absolutely unreasonable to do anything else.**

## Use-Of-Force Knowledge and Training

The legal use of deadly force requires knowledge. Everything in this book is based on a moral and lawful response to an illegal threat to life. We cannot act lawfully if we choose to be ignorant of what the law permits. More importantly, our moral judgments require sufficient forethought to keep our actions based on reason rather than on emotion. The below requirements are as important as any training in this book.

Knowledge-Installation Requirement:

1. Find your state's last change in statutory gun laws. In some cases changes will be recent; for others, changes may not occur for some years. If you know how to locate the most recent changes to your jurisdiction's laws, you will have no difficulty staying informed.

2. Get three informed, personal recommendations for a good criminal lawyer in your area. Seek out one good reference for a civil attorney in your area. Go to your local superior court and check the docket for any criminal attorneys you are considering. Attend one trial or pretrial hearing to see if your candidate(s) is prompt, prepared, and professional. Check with your state's bar association; in some cases they act similar to a Better Business Bureau and can advise you of complaints against an attorney.

3. Research your state's laws pertaining to self-defense. Select an adjoining state and do the same. You will better grasp your own state's laws when you can distinguish between your state's and other states' laws.

4. Research your state's gun laws relating to permissible

firearms, storage requirements, ammunition limitations, transportation, and statutorily gun-prohibited areas.

5. Find at least one news article on a shooting by a private citizen. Notice what information the news organization has chosen to include and what questions the article attempts to answer.
6. Memorize the Practics Gold Standard.
   Knowledge-Maintenance Requirement:
1. Know when your state legislature tends to put new laws into effect. Every year you must learn of any change to existing self-defense and gun laws. Your state attorney general's office would be a good source for this information.
2. Keep a copy of the Practics Gold Standard in your range kit and read it at every range visit or gun-cleaning session.

**Command Drill**—This drill requires the training partner to act as an attacker. The attacker will need a simulated weapon; a rolled-up magazine or a toy knife can serve as a weapon. The student defender will need a toy gun. Begin with the attacker facing the defender from about 20' away. The training partner will charge the student at a jog. The student will respond by sighting the toy gun onto the upper chest of the attacker and issuing a command to "Stop!" If the command is loud and clear, the attacker will stop. If the command is timid or confused, the attacker will continue. The student has one second to issue the command "Drop the weapon!" Failing to properly issue the command or not doing so within one second will cause the attacker to continue forward at a jog until a proper command to "Stop!" is again given. After the attacker has been stopped and disarmed, the command will be given to "Turn around!" The last two commands are "Lie down!" and "Spread your arms and legs!" Any failure to give a command within one second causes the training partner to resume the attack. If the attacker closes the gap sufficiently to be able to lightly touch the torso of the defender with the rolled-up magazine, the student has failed. Commands are an exercise in control. Timid, confused, half-hearted commands tell an attacker that the matter of control is still undecided. It is essential that the defender never leave the sights while issuing commands. If the sights are abandoned, the defender has failed the drill.

Some variation of this exercise is performed in police academies across America. A little pressure is more than some people can bear. Admittedly, this drill is a relatively easy one, and if it's easy for you, do it with an audience or use multiple attackers. When your blood is pumping and you're concerned about your well-being, it is no small thing to speak clear, direct, and forceful commands while maintaining sight control.

Verbal commands require training.

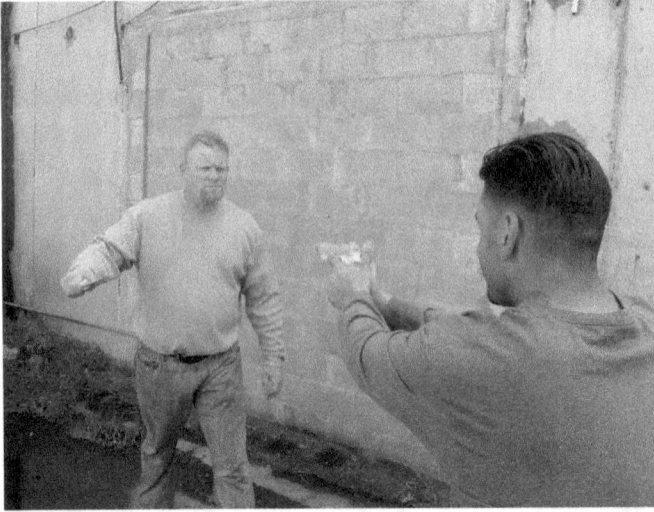

Make your commands loud and clear. They are not requests.

When the suspect is turned away, his attack may be slowed and his sense of your location diminished.

Skill-Installation Requirement: 20 consecutive reps without error

Maintenance Requirement: Include verbal commands as part

of your normal range training. Easy does not mean pointless. The more you say the commands, the easier it will be to recall them.

Now that we know the *why* and the *when*, let's talk about the *how*.

# Chapter Three: Marksmanship Reminder

*It is far more important to be able to hit the target than it is to haggle over who makes a weapon or who pulls a trigger.*

Dwight D. Eisenhower

*Fast is fine, but accuracy is everything.*

Wyatt Earp

*Where is all the knowledge we lost with information?*

T. S. Eliot

In 2011 Paladin Press published my fundamentals-of-marksmanship book, *The Perfect Pistol Shot.* That book was derived largely from the hour-and-a-half lecture that always preceded my live-fire instruction, primarily for law enforcement classes, though originally for U.S. Marines. I knew the material was sound, having witnessed dramatic changes in shooters during single range sessions.

Still, I didn't know whether the book would be well received. The meat of the book was old, proven material that had been fairly well-known a few decades back and universally accepted a hundred years ago. I didn't know if I was beating a dead horse. Just prior to writing *The Perfect Pistol Shot*, I hadn't been paying much attention to the changes in the firearm and shooter-training industries. My biggest surprise after the success of the book was how "new" the information was to current shooters. What I had thought to be common knowledge, at least among professional instructors, turned out to be virtually unknown. The serious study of marksmanship is all but gone. Marksmanship is not only unpopular; it isn't taken seriously by most of today's shooting students.

Many readers may be frustrated that I'm even mentioning

marksmanship in the introduction to a defense-tactics book. Please bear with me for a moment. Marksmanship is the intellectual understanding and physical skill needed to hit your aiming point under diverse conditions. Either you can hit what you aim at through application of specific knowledge and skill or you cannot. There is no successful alternative to marksmanship. Accuracy is not hard, but it does require understanding and effort. Since all pistols come from the manufacturers with sights, it ought to be no surprise that mastery of the sights is critical to successful handgun operation. Point shooting— that is, shooting without the use of the sights—has a place in defensive shooting, but point shooting cannot replace marksmanship any more than penicillin can replace surgery. If you want to box, you'll have to learn how to stand. If you want to be an astronaut, take algebra. If you want to shoot the spinning wheel out of a spider's rear-end, learn the fundamentals of marksmanship.

Let's pretend I'm wrong about marksmanship. How do I know that you, dear reader, if you are a right-handed shooter, probably shoot low and to the left? If you're a southpaw, you're probably shooting low and to the right. Where did I get that secret knowledge? If I can successfully make such a claim concerning the majority of shooters, there must be some fact-based principles that inform my knowledge. Those principles are referred to as the Fundamentals of Marksmanship. I do not mean to presume or suggest on our brief acquaintance that I know the degree of your firearm competence, but most shooters who claim to know the fundamentals actually know no such thing. Most of us can't shoot well, and most of us don't know why. The Fundamentals of Marksmanship are NOT "line up the sights and squeeze the trigger." You can't learn the fundamentals in 15 minutes. At least, I can't teach them that quickly.

By the way, the reason you're shooting low and inside is because you're over gripping your handgun—don't crush the grip. That particular fault is so widespread that a popular handgun manufacturer's blog recently hosted a thread wherein owners of a certain model pistol had convinced themselves that the weapon had an inherent low-left fault. Sadly, those shooters all seemed to consider themselves to be fairly competent.

Competition shooting, which has brought us advancements in equipment and training, may have caused some of the current overgrip mischief. Some top-of-the-food-chain competitors appear to use a tight grip. (I wish they would speak more openly about the diligence they use in sighting.) Thoughtful students take all information in context. Professional shooters may *appear* to over grip, but they never grip harder than they can sight. Additionally, many competitions are done at similar distances and elevations with standardized targets, making hasty sighting a reliable possibility.

Bullseye shooters, on the other hand, are still shooting unobtrusively, and that's where we ought to be starting. During my years as a shooting instructor, I witnessed many shooters *instantly* improve through a lightened grip. I never witnessed the opposite. When push comes to shove and a shooter is required to exceed normal personal limits, the knowledge required to obtain accuracy has no substitute. Marksmanship alone meets that need.

No gimmick or shortcut to understanding what is required for a successful shot exists. Either you know or you don't know. Most don't and, based on the instruction popularly available, aren't very likely to learn. Which brings us to the real culprit—you. Today's students are too much like the martial-arts students of the 1970s. During the Asian-martial-arts boom of the 1970s, many students chose drive-up-window black-belt factories over rigorous training. After the *Rocky* movies came out in the 1980s, there was great interest in pain-free, ineffectual boxing lessons. Likewise, current students of pistolcraft spend a great deal of money on training and materials that promise instant success without the work of acquiring knowledge-based skill. Instead of achieving understanding, a student can get an embossed certificate with crossed pistols and an American flag. Hang it on your wall. You're qualified to shoot less accurately than your mom can spit. Nothing of value comes cheaply. Firearms mastery demands study and work.

I don't mean to alarm my readers. Practics is NOT about marksmanship, *though it assumes the reader is already a legitimate marksman.* (This book contains a very brief refresher, but it is insufficient for acquiring baseline competence.) Marksmanship and defensive shooting are interrelated. You need formal safety and marksmanship training before you can master tactical training. The always-dramatic kill-or-be-killed crowd continually argues for realism on the target range—an oxymoron. I'll concede the point: They're absolutely right—at least in theory. But if you train, as is popular, to hit a *realistic* man-size silhouette at five to 10 yards, *and that is all you train to do*, you are endangering innocent people.

Let's say your typical training is done on a "realistic combat target," which is about 15" across and maybe 30" high. You have a 10-shot pistol and can dump all your rounds into the black at five yards within three seconds. Let's say it's a couple days before Christmas and you take the kids to the mall. You have a CCW (Carrying a Concealed Weapon) permit and carry your pistol. After leaving the mall, you herd the kids along the snow and ice through a crowded parking lot. You enter the row where you parked your car. A guy steps in front of you and orders you to lie on the ground. He's waving a gun, and your kids are between him and you. The bad man is a *realistic* two car lengths' away, over 12 yards. The height of your gangly 12-year-old has made your available target area a *realistic* 8" tall. The bad guy angled his body away from you so he can watch anyone coming from the mall entrance. Your target width is now perceived as a *realistic* 5" wide. He's shaking badly and shifting his weight forward and backward, reducing your *realistic* target area to a perceived 6" high and 3" wide at 13 yards. Go ahead, yank your gun, and rip off half a dozen *realistic* shots. Your normal low, left rounds will strike your children, and your usual 8" group at five yards will open to over 1,000" by the time they travel across the parking lot. Now you're the public menace.

If you want to carry a gun, learn to shoot. Marksmanship is not only practical, it's a moral imperative. Having said all that, I'll shamelessly refer you to *The Perfect Pistol Shot*, and we'll press on.

## Overview of The Four Fundamentals of Marksmanship

Marksmanship is like brain surgery: a good amount of standing, some controlled movement, and a whole lot of deliberate effort. The rules for being a good shot are simple; success is completely in the application. There are four fundamentals of marksmanship:

1. **Sighting (Eyes)**—The human eye can only focus to one depth at a time. When the sights are properly aligned and placed on the desired aiming point, the rear sight *must* appear out of focus. The target *must also* appear out of focus. The front sight must appear crystal clear. If you cannot find your worn handgun from among several guns of the same make and model by viewing the front sight tip alone, you are not

properly focusing on the front sight tip when aiming.

2. **Trigger Control and Grip (Hands)**—The trigger must move rearward in a straight path. The trigger finger naturally closes at an angle, like a swinging gate. The hand must be placed high enough on the backstrap to allow the trigger finger to be kept level. This will also give the finger leverage necessary for a smooth, controlled trigger press. The great folly in marksmanship is too much pressure on the handgun. That truth used to be understood as common sense.

Today, instructors teach students to over grip. Of course, this nonsense is hidden beneath a veneer of practical effectiveness. Forget hitting your mark. Just trying to hold a handgun on target with a crushing grip for 10 minutes is exhausting. Fifteen minutes is common for police officers during felony car stops, and it is also a realistic length of time for home defenders who are detaining attackers until the arrival of police. So grip easy.

The trigger finger can fight good sight alignment.

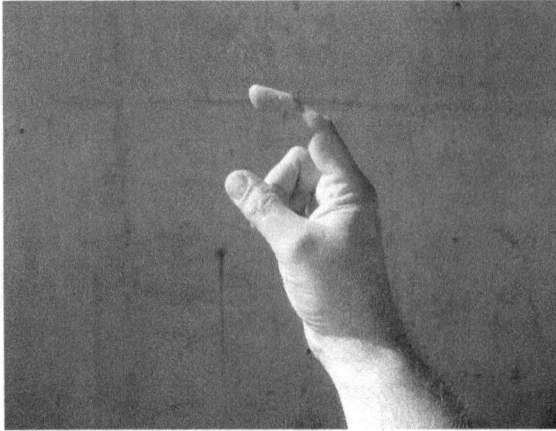

Press with the intention of bringing the trigger as straight to the rear as your finger will allow.

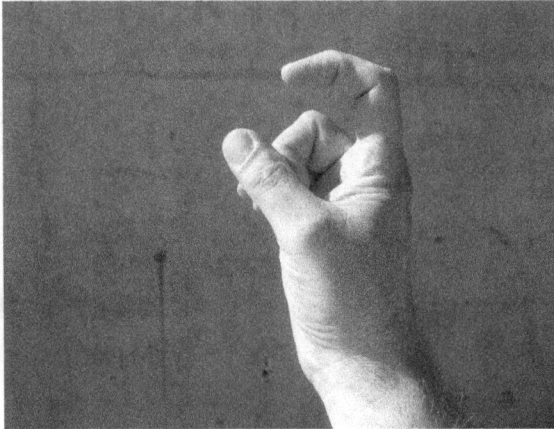

This is the final position for a neutral trigger press. Conform to the handgun.

3.  **Muscular Tension and Natural Point of Aim (Body)**—The body is comprised of muscles. When one muscle pushes, an opposing muscle pulls. The body is "sprung" to always seek a neutral position without muscular tension. Every physical action requires muscular tension, which is movement.

    Extraneous movement is the enemy of marksmanship. Shooters may limit extraneous movement and advantageously use the body's tendency to seek a neutral position by aiming and firing in a natural stance. The key element of a muscle-neutral stance is the complete absence of any muscular influence that seeks to pull the shooter off target. If your toes are pointed toward the target at a 30° angle, your shoulders should be pointed toward the target at the exact same angle. The easiest natural position to acquire a neutral muscular influence is to face the target directly.

The method for testing your Natural Point of Aim is sighting on your target and closing your eyes for five seconds. Open your eyes and see if your sights have drifted off to the left or right. Do not twist the body to correct but ensure there is no muscle pull in your stance and shuffle your feet to the left or right to naturally orient the body onto the target. That is your Natural Point of Aim—learn it.

A precise natural stance. Relaxed and alert.

4. **Breathing (Circulatory and Respiratory Systems)**—You cannot align the sights to within the required hundredths of an inch when your body is denied oxygen. Likewise, you can't align the sights for best accuracy while the chest is rising and dropping. Controlled breathing can slow the heart rate and the

lungs. The preferred method is to breathe normally, pausing the breathing cycle in the middle of the exhale. After no more than a two-second pause, the exhale is completed and normal breathing resumes. If, after firing a shot, you so much as sigh, you will know that you were denying your body oxygen through improper breathing technique.

During rapid fire this technique adapts to multiple shots. While the practicality of this technique may seem dubious to defensive shooters, many peace officers who have tried to hold sighting on suspects during lengthy felon car stops have found themselves shaking and light-headed through undisciplined breathing. Perfection in practice is needed for *good enough* under duress.

Friend, it took an entire book for me to satisfactorily explain the above four principles. This brief reminder is not enough if you have not received formal marksmanship training from someone *qualified* to teach marksmanship. Please seek additional instruction. You will get much more enjoyment out of your shooting, get greater service from your handguns and rifles, and enhance the safety of those around you.

## Minimum Standards

Marksmanship is a pursuit rather than a destination. All marksmen undergo shooting education until retiring from the use of firearms. Nonetheless, marksmanship is science, not art. There is a *minimum* competency level necessary to have safe operational control of a full-size, defensive handgun:

- Three shots in one ragged hole at seven yards
- Five shots in a palm-size cluster at 25 yards
- Consistent hits on a silhouette target at 100 yards

If you are able to perform the above, you are a practical marksman ready to develop greater shooting skill. If you cannot achieve the above standard of accuracy, don't feel bad. Nobody is born a marksman. The good news is anyone in reasonably good health and with no major physical impairments is capable of becoming a marksman.

The argument between marksmen and point shooters is moot. Defensive shooters need both skills, but marksmanship is the platform on which handgun mastery is built. No reason exists to *not* study marksmanship. The pursuit of accuracy will not hurt other defense skills, and the instruction is very unlikely to confuse students who are also pursuing point shooting. It serves no practical purpose to argue between two essential and non-exclusive skill sets. Laziness and ignorance are poor excuses.

I have successfully trained many shooters from a variety of backgrounds. Willingness, patience, knowledge, and structured experience are required for shooting success, but that's all the student needs to begin learning. You are a marksman waiting to happen. Using a handgun for self-defense and not being capable of reliably hitting our mark at stone-throwing distance suggests we ought to dump the guns and grab some rocks. It does us no good to have tools we are incapable of properly using. Marksmanship is a study, a never-ending pursuit of knowledge. Ballistics, distance, weather, light, firearms, physiology, and self-discipline are your subjects. A future of shooting success and enjoyment is waiting for you. Master marksmanship!

**Dry Fire**—There is no better training for the marksman than dry-fire training. Many marksmanship competitors spend more time in dry fire than live fire. Dry fire—pulling the trigger on a verified-to-be-empty handgun—is the method by which we get the purest view into our marksmanship skills. During live fire we have recoil, a degree of stress, additional safety concerns, and many other minor but present influences. In dry fire nothing distorts the shooter's view of the sights the instant after the hammer has fallen. The training value comes through the absence of the above-mentioned live-fire influences and distractions. By shooting in a more pure, undiluted way, the average student can quickly begin to experience perfect "shots."

Dry fire requires the absolute assurance of safety prior to training. Begin with a completely safe handgun in storage-safe mode. This means you have verified that the handgun and magazine are unloaded by touch and sight. Likewise, you must verify your revolver cylinder is empty by touch and sight. Take a second and slowly turn the cylinder for your inspection. More than a few shooters have overlooked a round in a cylinder. If you are not dry firing on a proper firearms range, you must inspect the area for ammunition. You can't dry fire in a room where you keep boxes of ammo. You have to be a petty, insecure nut when it comes to safety. Petty, insecure safety nuts need never say "I don't know how the gun went off." Also, you need a real backstop. The basement wall may work, but the bedroom wall will not. The environment must be quiet, well lit with a no-glare lighting source, and away from any wind or vibration (you can't dry fire under the L-train).

Take a piece of paper and draw a 3" or 4" cross with a very fine black marker or quality ink pen. The junction of the cross must not appear any larger than the front sight tip during sighting. Securely fasten the paper to a flat background. Bumps or wrinkles must not be in the paper. Stand about 5' from the target. Index. Raise your weapon onto the target and cock the hammer on single-action pistols. Some weapons will require you to cycle the slide. (Double-action firearms should be dry fired in both action modes.) Find your Natural Point of Aim. Apply the Fundamentals of Marksmanship and achieve perfect sighting. Press the trigger for a perfect shot at the center of the cross. At that instant note the location of your front sight. That is where the bullet would have struck on the range—not *maybe*, not *probably*, but *absolutely* where the bullet would have struck the target. Obviously, at a distance of a few feet an actual bullet would strike slightly below where sighted because the front sight is an inch or so above the muzzle and it takes a couple of yards for the two trajectories to join. That has no impact on dry fire training.

Now you know your errors and can correct them. Also, you can train yourself to fire perfect shots before you ever get to the range. Reading and correcting errors is more than we have space for here and is a good reason for you to undergo competent marksmanship training.

Some handguns cannot be dry fired. Generally, rim-fire calibers can be damaged by dry fire. Some handguns may require dry-fire caps or inert rounds. Most handguns are fine for dry-fire training, but your owner's manual or manufacturer's helpline will be your best source of information.

Skill-Installation Requirement: eight reps · six sets with a three- to 10-minute break between sets

Maintenance Requirement: 10 perfect reps every week for the rest of your shooting career

Practics, as you can see, has a lot of training requirements. Some of them just have to be, well, endured to gain a needed skill. Dry fire is different. Learn to love this drill as a recreation. More is gained quickly through dry fire than any other type of firearms training. Everything relating to handgun operation boils down to two things: safety and accuracy—proper dry fire teaches both. Of course, you must dry fire with the weak hand, too.

# Chapter Four: Tools of the Trade

*The more complicated and powerful the job, the more rudimentary the preparation for it.*

William F. Buckley, Jr.

*Remember the first rule of gunfighting . . . "Have a gun."*

Jeff Cooper

A bowman needs more than a bow; he needs arrows and a quiver to hold them. The swordsman needs a scabbard. Every weapon requires supplemental equipment to be practically useful. In this chapter we'll review the equipment needed for the study of Practics and for the general application of the handgun as a defensive weapon.

Shooting a handgun requires the possession of a handgun. Carrying a handgun for self-defense requires a bit more. The original virtue of the handgun was portability; the pistol could be fired with one hand and carried near the waist or on the saddle. Rifles, even when slung, are cumbersome to users engaged in physical tasks other than shooting. The advent of the pistol was quickly followed by the birth of the gun belt. Absent belt and holster, the pistol has little convenience over the rifle, requiring one hand for carrying—same as the long gun. Serious situational handgun operations require a holster to be affixed to the shooter in order for the shooter to gain full advantage of the handgun. Otherwise, we'd do better to carry rifles.

## Gun Belt

The least-discussed piece of gear in the gun world is the platform on which it all stands. The gun belt is simplicity itself, but a bad belt can destroy defensive actions from drawing to re-holstering. A thin, soft belt that allows excessive movement can render quick draws from the holster impossible. When Hollywood became fascinated with quick-draw, cowboy gunfights from fashionably low riding holsters, leg ties were added to ensure a smooth draw. The holster, to be used properly, must remain stationary, and the only method we currently have for accomplishing that goal is to firmly affix the holster to a sturdy belt.

There are two different sets of belt requirements for use by the private defender, just as patrol officers have two different belts: duty and off-duty. The first is for home or property defense, and the second is for concealed-carry use. Most self-defense shootings by private citizens occur on private property where concealed carry is not involved. The concealed-carry belt is fairly easy: It fits through belt-loops; is rigid enough to properly hold a loaded, holstered handgun and pouches with full magazines; and is strong enough to resist some miscreant tugging on it. On the other hand, the home-defense belt has no concealment restrictions and ought to be geared toward a planned criminal assault of the property and occupants because having only a handgun and extra ammunition is not sufficient for a *best* defense.

Police use a two-belt system, which involves a slightly thicker trouser belt with a heavy duty belt placed over it. The duty belt is buckled through a post and two-prong system and affixed to the trouser belt by "keepers." Keepers are small straps that are wrapped over both belts and snapped in place. The whole thing is attached to the wearer by the trouser belt being normally threaded through the belt loops on the trousers. The result is a platform that will carry a lot of weight evenly distributed through the belt and keeper system. Holsters on duty belts don't move, and the belts don't lose their shape under movement.

All things being equal, I would recommend every defensive shooter use such equipment except for two insurmountable problems: First, it takes time to get the whole thing in place, and second, you have to be wearing pants. Cops put the duty belts on long before they need their handguns. The defender doesn't have that advantage when the window smashes at 1:00 AM. So we need a compromise that will provide holster stability without all the preparation required by duty belts.

Many of the leather-holster makers (and some laminate-gear manufacturers) make trouser belts specifically designed for holster use. These belts are often thicker and a slight bit taller than everyday trouser belts and, in some cases, are too big for certain belt loops. They close with either Velcro or traditional buckles. Laminate works well, sticks like glue to skin, and doesn't stretch as much as leather. In my opinion, laminate is tough enough, but while its service life can be extended through good maintenance, it won't outlast leather. Leather better survives nicks and cuts and, if not over-sealed with oils, will temporarily absorb sweat and body fluid rather than sliding across them. In the end it's simply a matter of preference; both will do the job admirably. Nylon gear, if reinforced to prevent collapsing, performs well, breathes, lasts a long time, and is extremely tough. I have found nylon a little tougher to keep clean, and it will fray over the years, but it's very comfortable as well as serviceable. Nylon also allows for home defenders to use a police-style belt because nylon duty belts tend to have a simple snap-type buckle that can be donned in a second without the need for a pants belt. Admittedly, it's bulkier than a trouser belt but will more evenly distribute the weight of a defender's gear than would a common trouser belt.

The belt needs to hold under the violent pull of a draw and the brutal shove of a quick re-holster, and it also has to fit your holster. The holster should not easily slide onto the belt unless it has adjustment screws. Rather, you should have to coax the holster and magazine/speed-loader pouches into place. If they're tough to get on, they'll be more likely to stay put.

As we discuss the rest of the belt gear, you will have a better idea of the qualities a good belt must have to meet your individual needs. Ideally, we want to use the same home-defense gear every time and the same concealed-carry gear every time. Changes in equipment require full training and may lead to confusion under duress. Think the gun belt through before choosing. The Practics gun belt holds in place even against bare skin, which is a result of the belt's contact surface area and interior lining. Know before buying that your belt will hold a loaded, non-collapsible holster and set of pouches without sagging. You must test it before you buy it. Finally, if you can't get the belt on *right now*, without having to fiddle with too many straps, buttons, and buckles, its defensive value is diminished to the point of worthlessness.

## Magazine Pouches

Practics recommends using only the standard one-piece double-magazine or speed-loader pouches to give the defender three sets of ammo, rigidly and consistently placed: one in the weapon and two in the pouches. Pouches with flaps or straps are Practics preferred. I confess that non-strapped magazines are quicker to draw and easier to access, but the time difference is miniscule. Tension-retained magazines are more likely to be lost or taken, and though they can be advantageous in certain concealed-carry circumstances, it is generally preferable to use strapped pouches. Practics is not a static-line-shooting skill; it is a self-defense system based on the assumption that things will not go the way of the defender. Cops carry strapped magazines because they know things will be pulled or knocked off the gun belt. There is no misery exemption for the home defender. If you fall down while running across your concrete driveway, you will not be permitted time to retrieve lost magazines. Forget the speed gear; secure those magazines.

## Setting Up the Ammunition Pouches by Handgun Type

There is a proper pattern for placing ammunition on a duty belt depending on whether you carry a pistol or revolver:

**Pistol**—The pistol is on the strong-hand side, and the magazine pouches are on the front of the support-hand side.

**Revolver**—The revolver is worn on the strong-hand side, and the speed-loader pouches are also worn on the strong-hand side.

The reasons for the above patterns are purely a matter of function. In the case of a pistol, the strong hand can eject the used magazine, and the support hand may drop naturally to the pouches for a fresh magazine. If the magazine pouches are worn on the strong side, the shooter will have to reach across the body to grab a magazine. Additionally, a prone shooter may roll slightly to the strong-hand side during reloading to gain access to support-hand pouches. The reverse would require a quarter roll onto the support side, and even then the support arm would be pinned to the ground.

Magazine pouches on the support side allow easier access on the ground or against obstructions.

Magazines must be stored in the pouch downward and with the rounds pointing toward the strong side or torso centerline. By storing magazines with the rounds pointed inward toward the strong side, the shooter need only grab the butt of the magazine, withdraw it from the pouch, roll the hand palm upward, and slam the magazine into the well. Otherwise, the magazine will have to be manipulated before being inserted into the pistol. At the instant the magazine enters the well, the fingers are lifted away, allowing the palm to drive the magazine home. It is the palm of the hand that cups the bottom of the magazine and fully seats it. The insertion action should be strong and decisive. When releasing the magazine from the pistol, hit the release button with the shooting finger, dropping the magazine. Allow the magazine to fall free—never touch the magazine unless it fails to drop. At the same time the support hand must retrieve a fresh magazine, which should be ready for insertion while the expelled magazine is still dropping to the ground.

Revolvers load quickest using a two-hand transfer. The revolver is transferred to the support-hand for brass ejection as the shooting hand drops straight down and collects a speed-loader. If the speed-loader pouch is on the opposite side, the shooter will have to reach across the body for ammunition. The prone revolver-reload position is a roll to the support side because the revolver is passed to the support hand during the reload. Therefore, the pouches must be on the strong side for access. Revolver operators load their pouches with rounds down and knobs up. (Later we'll look at an old method for speed loading a revolver without loaders.)

The best way to understand ammunition-pouch placement is to try it. Don't let anyone fool you. Many gray areas in shooting boil down to individual preference, but magazine and speed-loader placement is not one of them.

Proper magazine use always starts with proper magazine placement. I recognize that magazine-insertion training may seem like pretty basic stuff, but the truth is only a very small percentage of shooters properly coordinate magazine changes. If the fresh magazine is not moving to the well as the spent magazine is dropping to the earth, the shooter waited too long before moving to the magazine pouch. The real value of the pistol—the honest, practical value—is in the magazine. Single-action pistol shots are an improvement over double-action revolver shots, but many pistols fire at least the first shot double-action. The great Ed McGivern used Smith and Wesson revolvers for his record-breaking speed exhibitions because he could fire revolvers faster than pistols could cycle their slides. (Very few human beings are in danger of outshooting the cycling action of pistols.) The glory of the pistol is in the reload, meaning, if you aren't training hard on magazine reloads, you're throwing away an incredible technological advantage.

## Flashlight

A small battery-operated flashlight in a belt pouch is worth its weight in gold. Flashlights attached to handguns certainly have advantages, among which are the ability to keep both hands on the gun with a normal grip. Integrated flashlights also have disadvantages, such as requiring the muzzle of a loaded weapon to point wherever illumination is needed and not allowing use when the pistol is holstered. An independent flashlight can be used without the handgun or illuminate an area without pointing a loaded weapon at it.

Select the proper size and maintain the flashlight for emergency use. For defensive purposes a flashlight ought to be no more than 5" long, which won't interfere with your movement, and have a large rubberized on/off button located on the butt end of the flashlight. The butt switch will negate the shooter having to hunt for the button. Battery-operated flashlights stay ready in the holster instead of waiting in the charger. Change batteries at least every two months and bulbs every six months, and your light will be ready when you need it.

The flashlight should be worn on the support side in front of the hip and to the outside of any magazine pouches. When equipment is placed directly on the side of the body, it is difficult to reach with the opposite hand and is more likely to strike walls and doorways because it substantially increases the wearer's girth. Individuals with small waists may not have a choice but to carry gear on the extreme sides, but such an arrangement is never desirable. Also, keep gear off the back of your belt with the exception of the Practics hasty-aid kit. The home defender won't be wearing the belt enough to agitate the sciatic nerve, but patrol officers will do themselves a favor by getting attachments of any weight and size off the back of the belt. Defenders carrying flashlights in the center of the back expose themselves to injury during a rearward fall. By keeping equipment near the front, the shooter is able to press back against a wall and still have full access. Again, waist size will be a determining factor in equipment placement, but try to keep your gear off your hips and back.

Here's an example of a Practics style flashlight.

## Flashlight Support Grip

Using a flashlight while maintaining a two-handed grip on the weapon is impossible, but there is a compromise that is much better than a one-handed grip on the handgun. Through marksmanship we learn that the primary function of the support hand is to serve as a weight-bearing platform rather than a means of steadying the firearm. This technique will enable the shooter to fulfill the weight-bearing objective while keeping the light beam in line with the muzzle. Hold the handgun as you normally would with a proper one-handed shooting grip. Use the support hand to grip the flashlight with the butt of the flashlight at the thumb side of the fist. Bring the two hands back to back, which will align the muzzle and flashlight. Keep the supporting forearm at an angle and rest the shooting hand on the back of the support-hand wrist. Now you have the benefit of a proper two-handed grip with good use of your flashlight.

Light is an advertisement that screams "Here I am!" I was trained to never keep my flashlight on for more than two seconds in order to minimize my light exposure. That's not a bad rule, but I never found it universally workable, either. In a dark living room the bad guy already knew a cop was in the same room. He could hear me and, in some cases, see me. After turning the flashlight on, I would destroy my night vision, but the other guy might keep some of his if he avoided looking directly at the light. It takes several seconds to a few minutes to regain your night vision, depending on the light exposure from which you are recovering. So in a small room I found it better to either use the light constantly or abandon it completely, and in most cases I chose to use the flashlight. The opposite is true for open spaces. A shooter may aim for your light from some distance but may have no other way of locating you. In that case less light (or no flashlight) may be better. The Practics recommendation for the use of flashlights is whatever is best for your immediate situation. Reason it out before you hit the on/off switch.

The use of a flashlight does not need to deteriorate good hand position.

## Knife

I must tell a tale on myself. Regarding the knife as a backup weapon, I came to appreciate the value of a knife after managing to get the ring finger of my strong hand stuck in the mouth of an angry lunatic. Despite a genuinely Homeric effort, the poor soul was unable to sever the bone in my finger. For my part, I was certainly willing to consider the potential loss of a digit "serious injury or great bodily harm," but my attached friend and I had another person between us, who prohibited my discharging a firearm. Further, our body positions were such that reaching my holster with the weak hand was nearly impossible. Afterwards, I bought a quick-opening folding knife.

Of course, nothing is easy. I soon discovered that a knife clipped onto the trauma-plate pocket of my ballistic-vest cover would not stay in place during even moderate movement. Since I had enough junk on my duty belt and didn't want to compound the problem with a knife pouch, I used my support-side pocket with mixed results. The good news is the Practics belt setup has room for a knife pouch, which is preferable because a knife pouch placed to the outside of the flashlight pouch provides fixed accessibility to either hand.

Choosing a knife is fairly simple. See if your state places limits on concealed-blade length. There's no sense buying one that you can't legally carry outside of your home. A 4" blade is about right. Since we want a knife that can be flipped open by thumb pressure, longer blades should be tested for ease of opening. The Practics knife has two opposing knurled posts or knobs on each side of the blade near the hinge, making the knife ambidextrous. I prefer the knife's unlocking mechanism to be on the back of the handle and easily operated with a deliberate press of the thumb with no need for any part of the body to cross the blade's path. However, it is difficult to find knives that have both knurled knobs and a top-rear blade release. Colombia River Knife and Tool makes a few examples, and I'm certain there are others. However, the primary concern is an ambidextrously opening device that is quick and absolutely reliable with one hand. Each student will have to train to safely manipulate his particular blade release. Some knives will have holsters that aid in its opening. Be certain your state allows such sheaths or pouches before purchasing.

Of course, a strong blade is good, but the greatest concern is a strong locking mechanism. In fact, we want the blade to break before the locking mechanism fails. A knife that may close the blade on your fingers is a weapon carried on behalf of your attacker. Traditional fixed-blade sheath knives work well for defensive use but may restrict the torso from bending forward when worn toward the front. If you prefer a sheath knife, and yours doesn't impair torso flexibility and meets your legal requirements, absolutely nothing in Practics bars its use.

The grips of the knife should have some sort of sufficient tread to stick to the hand and allow sweat, blood, and body oils to escape inside the grip pattern rather than form a slippery seal between knife and hand. Most folding knives require routine tightening with a screwdriver or hex wrench, cleaning, and a drop of oil on the locking mechanism. A dull knife has little value. Sharpening your knife should be part of your normal range cleaning process. Treat your knife like a firearm and read the owner's manual or check the manufacturer's Web site. Keep in mind that a knife does more than serve as a backup weapon. It can disgorge swollen brass after a failure to extract, fill in for a screwdriver, and cut twine and rope, so keep it in serviceable shape. There are plenty of good values in knives but don't skimp on quality.

## Practics Knife-Closure Technique

Flicking open one of the quick-opening knives is easy to accomplish with one hand. After a few tries, flicking the blade into the open-and-locked position will be second nature.

Unfortunately, closing the knife with one hand is a different matter. Knives vary. The following is a technique that can be used with the Practics-recommended style of knife. The odds are your knife will be different and require you to train accordingly. Study the elements of the following technique and ensure that you maintain comparable safety measures suitable for your particular type of folding knife:

1. Begin with the knife locked open and in the support hand, blade forward in the normal use position.
2. Reverse the knife in the hand, pointing the blade to the rear.
3. Press the inside/sharpened side of the tip of the blade lightly against a non-slippery solid-surface blade block: brick wall, tree, etc. If kneeling, you may use the heel of your boot. (Do not use dirt if other choices are available. Dirt dulls blades.) The goal is to stop the blade from closing on your fingers when unlocked.
4. Use the thumb to press the lock release.
5. Keeping the blade tip firmly blocked, close the grip slightly toward the blade to ensure the knife does not relock.
6. Tuck the fingertips between the grip and the hand; straighten the thumb, removing all digits from the path of the blade.
7. Lay the back of the tip against the blade block and rotate the grips down to the blade until the knife is fully closed.
8. Pinch the knife between the thumb and finger and drop it back in the pouch.

The defender needs to be able to close the knife with one hand, without visual assistance, and without injury. Knives require dedicated training too.

A safe grip for closing the blade from the rear.

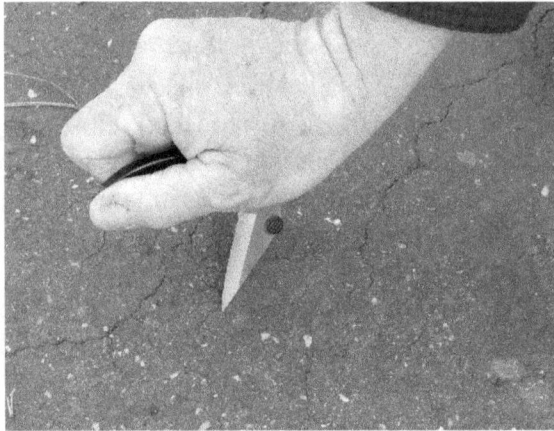

Train to close your knife with one hand.

## Cell Phone

The most powerful tool on a cop's belt is the radio. Communication brings help, directs forces, and collects intelligence. The defender needs communication too. When the door breaks open in the wee hours, there is no time to search for your phone or take it out of the charger— what you can grab is all that you have.

The Practics belt requires a cell phone, charged and in a belt pouch. If you cannot afford another cell phone, buy two prepaid phones at the local convenience store, which will give you two batteries and one serviceable phone for well under a hundred bucks.

Program the few emergency numbers that you will need (911, household members, and a good neighbor) and turn off the ringer and all alert tones. Charge the battery in the phone every two or three days. Completely drain one battery every six weeks to prevent development of a charge memory, which can prevent batteries from receiving a full recharge.

You will have to buy a cell-phone pouch from a belt maker. Several are available that police use on duty belts. The primary concerns are belt fit and durability. You cannot wear a pouch that can be torn away during a struggle. If all else fails, you can use a small nylon pouch like those sold as part of personal first-aid kits. Place the phone pouch between the flashlight and knife. In addition to convenient access the rectangular phone pouch will assist the wearer in distinguishing between the two similarly shaped flashlight and knife pouches.

A belt phone is a small inconvenience and an incredible weapon. It may also be the only means for separated household members to communicate. Not everyone in your home will likely need a gun, but almost all will benefit from an emergency phone.

## Hasty-Aid Pouch

Hands and faces get cut. If you get into a fight, particularly in very hot climates, you will have a problem contending with blood. Blood behaves like oil that doesn't stop leaking. It is extremely difficult to manipulate a handgun with bloody hands. In my experience it is also virtually impossible to get a bandage out of its paper pouch with bloody hands.

Realistically, self-defense confrontations will end quickly. Those are the odds, anyway. The defender needs a means of sufficiently controlling bleeding in order to continue the defense for a short time. Practics uses a hasty-aid kit for that purpose. This is not for first aid. You will need a first-aid kit also, but that's not the object of our concern for a belt pouch.

The hasty-aid kit is a roll, or partial roll, of medical tape 2" to 3" in diameter and 3/4" to 1" wide, with the metal canister removed and the running end folded back to make a 1" pull tab. Place the tape in a small, soft pouch on the back of your belt, in the very center. This pouch will be available to either hand and is too small to interfere with your movements or to cause injury to your back. Don't include scissors or blades in the pouch. You can rip or bite the tape. The tiny pouches used by paramedics to hold an extra pair of rubber gloves may work for your hasty-aid pouch.

When you cut your hands, fingers, wrists, or forehead, simply tape them. You won't have the tape on the wound for very long. When the event is over and you have sought professional medical treatment, the wound can be properly cleaned and treated. If you're delayed, the tape may be overcome with trapped blood. In such a case replace the tape and press onward.

If blood has made your grips slippery, use the medical tape to wrap the grips (yes, like in *The Godfather*). Medical tape is a wonderful thing, costs very little, and weighs next to nothing.

## Holster

The greatest advantage in law enforcement equipment is a good holster. The greatest equipment disadvantage to the private citizen is the absence of one. Defense competency is limited without a good holster. Everything works off the holster: quick draw; firearm security; and, most importantly, the ability to work with both hands and remain armed. Holsters are much more than carrying devices and ensure the handgun is held ready in the exact same position at every moment. We need that consistency in training to establish competence and speed. You can't throw your gun on the ground to render medical aid, carry your kid, or engage in a non-lethal struggle. The handgun must stay attached to you, whether you are tossed down the stairs or have your clothing torn to shreds. When the kitchen door gets jimmied at midnight, you need a belted holster to throw around your waist. The holster provides a platform for consistent hand-to-gun placement. Holsters are not optional.

Although an overwhelming majority of handguns made today are reliable and accurate, holsters run the gambit from junk to jewel. In order to choose an appropriate holster, we must first consider what purposes we expect the holster to serve. The first job of a holster is security, and the second function is to provide quick, convenient, one-handed operation of the firearm. Consider that early military holsters were designed to retain and protect the handgun, not to facilitate a quick draw. Defensive shooters certainly need a "fast" holster, but draw speed is still not the first purpose of a defensive holster. Most law enforcement encounters involving officer and suspects both reaching for weapons at the same time are relatively rare because officers tend to draw their weapons prior to the suspect becoming armed or before the officer enters the suspect's presence. Home defenders are similar in that they arm themselves due to a noise or visible movement rather than waiting for the final instant of armed confrontation. Cowboy-style quick draws and last-minute weapons races happen, but they are a small minority of defense encounters. A secure, available holster beats a fast holster with an unsecured handgun.

In addition to the variety of brands of available holsters, a smattering of function-types (such as belt, ankle, pack, and shoulder holsters) are available, and each has its shortcomings. The ankle holster is positioned too far away and compels the defender to drop when he may need to move. Even worse the ankle holster does not lend itself to quick, convenient re-holstering and drawing as may be needed during a home-defense incident. Ankle holsters are not adequate for anything more than backup weapons or concealed handguns during extraordinary and specialized circumstances. The shoulder holsters are better but do not re-holster as well as belt holsters, often requiring support from the weak hand. Additionally, the draw is always high, and the muzzle is not immediately pointing forward, which can be a problem with a close-range attack. Likewise, cross-draw belt holsters, though an improvement over shoulder holsters, also require the shooting arm to swing outward before firing. Fanny packs tend to lack the rigidity needed for good access. Since Practics requires immediate en motion firing, the belted, top-draw holster worn toward the strong side is the only practical choice.

The greatest improvement in holsters has been the advent of the retention holster, sometimes called a "security holster." These holsters are constructed to have an interior obstruction that prevents a straight-lift draw. The retention drawing motion varies from holster to holster but generally involves a subtle push-and-rock motion prior to the lift. An attacker can pull on a retention holster all day without success unless the holster is improperly fitted or defective or the attacker is strong enough to rip it apart, which would be extraordinary. Retention holsters are slow to use until proper training and practice have occurred, but a well-trained shooter with a retention holster can be blindingly fast. I'm not suggesting speed competitors will ever use retention holsters, but the speed difference in practical circumstances is slight. Retention holsters are evolving. Not that long ago these holsters were only available for full duty rigs. Today, leading manufacturers are making concealable retention holsters. Certainly the new breed of concealable, retention holsters are not as secure as some of the duty holsters, but they are a worthwhile improvement and a promise of better designs in the near future.

Retention holsters are generally rated by security level. A level II holster has an internal block and a thumb strap, while a level III adds an additional strap that is disengaged by the ring finger of the shooting hand. Whichever holster you choose, use it as it was designed. If you have two safety straps, use both of them. Keeping the "extra" strap on a retention holster unsnapped for speed's sake is dangerous. Like the external safety on some handguns, loose straps can be inadvertently engaged, making the holster dangerous for an unknowing defender. Train to use your holster properly. Ambidextrous operation of a retention holster is perfectly possible, but it requires dedicated training. In fact, weak-hand use of the retention holster requires more training than the overwhelming majority of Practics skills. In the end the security level of a retention holster is only as effective as the gun owner's proper use of it. The Practics home-defense belt will usually not support a retention holster because the belt is not secured by belt loops or keepers, which means the holster will shift with the handgun during the release movement, making the draw difficult. Fortunately, several good retention holsters are designed for concealed-carry use.

Holsters—good holsters—fit tightly. Whether leather or synthetic, holsters (and other gear) will stretch with use. Having a difficult holster will not be remedied by refusing to train with it. In some cases it may be extremely difficult to get the straps closed on your new holster. Leave your handgun in the holster when not in use and keep all straps ·closed to stretch the material. However, the best remedy for a tight holster is hard, continual use.

Let's examine the qualities necessary in a good defensive holster:

1. **Security**—If your handgun is not secure, it is a potential danger to you. Many peace officers have had an unwanted hand on their service weapon, which resulted in neither the loss of life nor gun because of a good retention holster.
2. **Reliability**—The job of a holster is to safely retain the

handgun in the exact spot the shooter left it and to facilitate a smooth, quick draw when the handgun is needed. Bad holsters lose their stitching, split under use, and fail to retain handguns. If your holster fails and your weapon is lost, your entire handgun defense is a failure.

3. **Access**—I know the current interest is in all things concealable, but the tail shouldn't wag the dog. Certainly, concealed carry imposes particular limitations on both the firearm and the holster. If you stick your small pistol into your underpants, it may be concealed, but it will most certainly be tactically worthless. Concealment must follow function. A holster that is inaccessible to the weak hand is a danger to the wearer. An elbow struck against a concrete floor may render the shooting arm numb, or a blow from a blunt object may break the strong-side arm. In such a case the shooter that cannot access the holster with the support-side hand would be better off if the handgun were in a plastic grocery bag tied around his neck. You must be able to draw your handgun with the weak hand. If your physical build doesn't permit you to reach your holster, you will have to experiment with wearing the holster slightly forward.

   Another concern with access is rigidity. Your holster, ammunition pouches, and knife pouch must not be collapsible. Holsters and pouches must stay open so that equipment may be inserted without the use of both hands and without the shooter looking at the belt. Poor access endangers the defender by occupying both hands with holster or pouch operation.

4. **Speed**—Draw time is a matter of an acceptable holster and an ongoing regimen of disciplined training. Your holster is as fast as you are willing to make it. A lazy defender is slow with a speed holster. A disciplined defender is amazingly fast with a retention holster. All holsters demand training, but most shooters refuse to train and practice specifically on the draw. Be excellent with the holster currently on your belt. If you replace your holster, train with the new one as if it were your first holster. Time spent on proper drawing and re-holstering is never wasted.

## Handguns and Magazines

Handguns are good. What I mean is currently manufactured handguns from major and custom gun makers are sufficiently serviceable. In the old days it was a mixed bag, but, like today's automobiles, airplanes, and dishwashers, firearms have achieved a standard of reliable performance.

Stainless steel has no appeal for me. I prefer blued or parkerized handguns. I like a handgun that shows wear from usage instead of a million little scratches. Blued handguns are beautiful; stainless steel handguns look like toasters. Now that's my preference, but my aesthetic preferences mean absolutely nothing to me when considering a handgun's defensive value. The truth is stainless steel handguns are fine. Hybrid-action handguns are fine. There is nothing wrong with polymer-framed handguns. Don't let the preferences of others or your own romantic notions cheat you out of a weapon that fits your hand, budget, and defensive needs. In the end, handguns are only tools. Romanticize tools, and you'll wind up throwing out your chainsaw and buying an antique axe. We must never forget the reason we have defensive firearms.

Today, technology and the love of the "next new thing" run the firearm industry, new guns replacing new guns. Never have Americans owned so many firearms, and never have so many firearm owners been such lousy shots. Technology, equipment, gear—stuff—doesn't foster skill. On the other hand, tradition is a comfort. It's a remembrance of quality and the honor of craftsmanship. However, the reason the 1911 pistol is still popular is because the 1911 is still competitive. Tradition for tradition's sake is foolish. If your child had a blood cancer, would you seek out a cancer specialist or an eighteenth-century practitioner with a jar full of leeches? Most of what is offered today is no improvement over the 1911 design. One might argue most new designs are not as good. We do enjoy increased choices in size, ergonomics, and caliber. Handguns are more reliable and effective than ever, but the pursuit of things only results in more things of dubious improvement being offered. In the end it's still a matter of skill. Shooting well is never about the gun—it's always about the shooter.

Handguns are like tuxedos and wedding dresses: A person doesn't need a great deal of experience to recognize when one doesn't fit. Your handgun fits if you can properly reach the trigger with a centered grip, can operate safety or de-cocking levers with the shooting-hand thumb, and are able to encircle the grips with enough room for your thumb to touch the top joint of your middle finger. If you cannot do the above, get another handgun because you are headed for failure or disaster. Conversely, if your hand is too large for the handgun, you will not be able to repeatedly fire the weapon without infringing on the movement of the slide or cylinder, or you won't be able to bring the trigger straight to the rear with a normal grip. Either way, an ill-fitted handgun doesn't serve the shooter. Nothing else is close in importance as hand-to-gun fit when selecting a firearm. A .22 revolver that you can shoot well beats *any pistol* that is too large for you to safely and accurately fire. After 9/11, a three-letter federal agency headquartered near D.C. insisted on its contract guard force carrying the HK USP pistol. The USP is a magnificent pistol, but it is too large for general-force issue. Some smaller men and many women don't have the finger length to properly use the USP. In the case of the guards with the HK, some could only get the tips of their index fingers onto the trigger. The results were, of course, disastrous. Some of those guards would have been safer and more effective carrying a good carpenter's hammer. If it can't be safely used, it's not a gun—just a very small club. No handgun, regardless of quality, is worth a bad fit. Don't buy a handgun without first ensuring it fits you. The Practics goal for handgun fit is a medium-size handgun based on the individual shooter's hand. Don't seek the biggest gun you can carry. Back down in size a bit, and you'll be a faster shot with better gun-retention potential.

This beautiful HK pistol is much too large for this shooter's hand.

Practics requires the shooter to hit the mark. In order to better use the sights, we need some distance between them, which is a result of barrel length. Shorter barrels are quicker to sight. Longer barrels allow for better discrimination of the sights but are slower to bring onto the target. The Practics suggested minimum barrel length for a pistol is 4" and the maximum is 5". Revolver barrel length should stay between 3" and 4".

True target pistols are not acceptable for Practics use. I am not referring to a service pistol with target sights but to a specifically designed target pistol. Such pistols have tighter tolerances and are sensitive to ammunition choices, dirt, and wrist movement while firing. Practics requires use of a service pistol, which is designed to operate when fouled through extended firing or the accumulation of dirt and debris from use in rough environments. Target pistols are wonderful for training and recreation but are the wrong tools for the job of self-defense.

If your handgun will allow dual controls for ambidextrous use, as on the 1911 design, have them installed. Make certain that lever surfaces (de-cocking, safety, slide release, magazine release) are wide enough and at a sufficient angle to be used under sweaty duress. If you can't replace difficult-to-use levers, you need a different handgun.

Grips need to be sticky. Sweat, water, and blood can easily overrun even good, heavily checkered grips. I despise the look of rubber grips on any handgun, but defense is not about looks, is it? Put a little vegetable oil on your hands and test your grips. Blood is oily as sin until it turns into crust. If you get into fights, your hands will perspire and bleed. You need grips that will seal to your flesh but also allow some runoff for blood and sweat. Smooth (worn or un-checkered) rubber grips trap fluids and prevent a seal with the hand. Many shooters use rubber grips that were excellent when new but have since worn bald. Wood can be made into decent grips but depends on the "points" of the checkering to hold onto the hand. Those points will eventually wear and push down into the valleys of the checkering, making the grips more prone to squirm in the hand. Grips are the tires of the handgun; you have to routinely replace them. The Practics shooter demands grips of a good, sticky material with a sufficiently deep tread. In other words, snow tires for the hand.

Capacity is ridiculously over-emphasized. I am still waiting to hear of a gunfight that actually involved more than 10 rounds from a single handgun. Police and defensive shootings tend to involve less than four rounds. There are cases where multiple officers have a shooting frenzy and expend a large amount of ammunition, but it always turns out to have been unnecessary and grossly ineffective. Single officers and defenders just don't fire that many rounds, statistically speaking. Let me clarify that I have no gripe with a handgun holding a lot of ammunition. If the gun fits your hand and the weight isn't a problem—load up. However, capacity should never be a major discriminator in choosing a handgun. Practics recommends pistols that have a minimum of eight rounds with the maximum being determined by hand-to-gun fit, not round capacity. Revolvers ought to hold six rounds. The seven-shot and nine-shot revolvers from Smith and Wesson are acceptable provided the shooter has very large hands. You don't want to carry a handgun that seems large in your hand. You want a handgun that is medium size by the standard of *your* hand. Some excellent five-shot revolvers are available but are not Practics-preferred due to ammunition management goals, which we'll discuss later in the book.

Caliber used to be a bigger deal than it is today. Advances in bullet design have made lighter calibers more viable. A larger caliber is generally more effective than a smaller one with the same type of ammunition, though the comparison must stay apples to apples. When shooters select a large-bore handgun but load it down to smaller caliber ballistics, a straight caliber comparison is no longer valid. In such a case there is no advantage to the larger caliber. There is also a point where handguns become too powerful for defensive use, and, of course, some handguns are not sufficiently powerful for personal protection. Generally, the following calibers can be adequate in power, ammunition choices, handgun size, penetration control, and recoil management:

9mm
.38 Special
.38 Super
.357 Magnum
.40 S&W
10mm
.45 ACP

Calibers such as .44 Special and .45 Colt are excellent defense calibers with proper ammunition, but the handguns chambered for those calibers tend be larger than most of the shooting population would find reasonable or are restricted to five-shot revolvers. Smaller calibers, such as the .380 and .25, have recently become more viable due to improved ammunition but still lack sufficient power, capacity, and sight radius to serve as primary defense weapons. A reasonably sized 9mm with mild loads is easy on the shooter and still more powerful than the traditional pocket calibers, and in some cases, less perceived recoil could be had with a larger caliber shooting mild loads in heavier weapons. Variations of popular defense calibers such as the .357 Sig and the .45 Glock meet all Practics requirements but are not readily available in many stores, potentially limiting, or even preventing, their use.

All major pistol design types—single action, double action, hybrid actions, and all their variants—are adequate for self-defense. Personal preference matters here. I have a favorite type of pistol, which should hold no significance to any other shooter. I also never really enjoyed shooting a particular brand of popular pistol, but that too is a personal preference, of no objective value to anyone else. Go to a local gun shop or range and rent the pistols you're considering. If the handgun is of recent manufacture from a reliable builder and meets all other Practics requirements, it comes down to comfort, cost, and personal preference. If after a little use a handgun still feels awkward in your hand, how well it performs doesn't matter. Enough good pistols are available to find one *you* enjoy shooting. Regarding revolvers, we only want the traditional double action for defensive use, leaving the single action to hunters and recreational shooters. Medium-framed revolvers tend to fit the Practics ideal better than small or large examples.

Sights must be upright, visible, and crisp around the edges, preferably rounded on the exterior corners, and sturdy with a rear sight that at least allows for windage adjustments. Fixed sights with a rear sight that can be tapped left or right are adequate. Front sight blades may be reduced or replaced if needed. Illumination dots can help with a hasty sight picture during low-light situations but, like many things, tend to give way after years of hard use and will likely require replacement. Smith and Wesson's medium and large revolvers have had excellent sights for decades; they've been tough enough for law enforcement service. I don't know why they never made it over to general pistol use.

Magazines die. They get tired and worn out and need replacement. Cracks, deep cuts, bent lips, wobbly guides, weak or unresponsive springs, and failure to insert smoothly or drop freely are reasons to replace magazines. Your ammo holders (magazines or speed loaders) need to be the *best you can afford*. A thin rubber bumper on the bottom of the magazine can reduce the chance of damage during dropping. Magazines with bumpers need to fit in the pouches, but a thin rubber piece will provide substantial drop protection. The only place for cheap magazines in Practics is during training, which we'll discuss in the training section. Another good source for training magazines is old service mags. Once they're not good enough for service, they're just right for practice. Ask around for a bloated or bent magazine. Defective, junk magazines can be great for malfunction training. The serious defender has to train hard with magazines, but damaged service magazines are deadly. When magazines fail, you are back in the 1700s with a single-shot pistol, or, even worse, your handgun may not fire without a magazine, which leaves you holding a really bad boomerang. Magazines are certainly made to withstand empty drops, particularly on dirt, but the more care you take in protecting your magazines, the more likely they will never fail when needed.

Occasionally good magazines will fail to eject. Often the

85

failure is due to dirt or fouling. The variety of magazines and pistols prevents me from giving you an exact method of positioning your fingers to remove your stuck magazine. In most cases, the magazine will drop slightly, allowing a support-hand pinch between the thumb and fingers. It is your responsibility to determine the most efficient method for grabbing hold of a stuck magazine in your pistol; some have pronounced bases, some don't. Once the magazine has been grasped, it is simply yanked free and released. Don't throw the magazine when removing it. Don't touch it one millisecond longer than needed, because your support hand must immediately insert a fresh magazine. The advantage of the pistol is in the reload. We don't want to lose our advantage even when a magazine gets stuck.

## Practics Sequence for Clearing a Stuck Magazine:

1. The support hand moves to the pouch for a fresh magazine, as in a normal reload.
2. The fresh magazine is raised to the support side but slightly ahead of the stuck magazine.
3. The fresh magazine rests along the web of the thumb and index finger of the support-hand. The result is that the thumb, index finger, and middle finger, are able to pinch the stuck magazine while still holding the fresh magazine up and slanted forward in the support hand.
4. The stuck magazine is yanked and dropped (immediate release, not thrown).
5. The support hand is tilted back, orienting the fresh magazine in an upright position, and drives it upward into the well with the palm as the fingers and thumb lift away.

The only delay in dealing with a stuck magazine is the time it takes to pinch, pull, and release. Your stuck-magazine reload time won't take a full second longer than a normal reload.

Stuck magazine is pulled by the lower fingers while the fresh mag is already in hand.

A quick movement to insert a fresh mag while keeping control of the other.

The above equipment recommendations are sincerely offered to guide the reader toward an effective defensive handgun. However, some readers don't have the capacity or means to own a Practics gun. There are defenders who cannot physically manage a full-size weapon or one with noticeable recoil. Arthritis is reality. Likewise, there are defenders who own a .22 and simply can't afford to buy another handgun. (I am NOT endorsing the defensive use of the .22, but economics are reality too.) If you can acquire a weapon within the suggested Practics parameters, you'll be properly equipped. If not, you have even more incentive to become an accomplished marksman and proficient point shooter. (Bullet placement is also a reality.) You'll also have to be more diligent when researching potential ammunition choices. Stay within your handgun manufacturer's maximum limits and find the most effective rounds you can afford and handle, perhaps choosing close-range effectiveness over mid-range performance if your environment tends to be indoors and crowded. Practics means knowing what we have to use, mastering our tools and equipment, developing intellect-based skill and muscle memory in using our chosen implements, maintaining our gear, and exploiting each piece's inherent advantages. In other words, we will try to acquire good equipment but must be determined to do the very best with the tools we have.

Finally, whichever service handgun you currently possess is probably adequate. The performance you attain with any acceptable handgun will have much more to do with the degree of discipline and dedication you bring to your ongoing shooter education. Constantly switching guns destroys all the knowledge you acquired regarding the previous gun's accuracy quirks and performance issues. If you've got a good defensive handgun, stick with it. If you choose to acquire a new handgun, it is your duty to complete a break-in period before relying on the handgun for defense. Five hundred rounds will typically be enough to get your handgun where it needs to be in terms of trigger pull, accuracy, reliability, and lubricant requirements. Until then, you're shooting an unprepared weapon.

## Ammunition

The future of ballistics is in bullets, not propellants. Yesterday's favorite defense calibers were replaced for better ballistics by more powerful choices, the thought being that more energy, within limits, would provide better bullet expansion and, therefore, better stopping power. Many of the old calibers were discarded, supplemented, or surpassed by new additions. The interesting thing for us to remember is that the old police calibers were not the largest available calibers even for their time, nor were they the most powerful. Law enforcement has always recognized the need for a good mid-caliber handgun possessing sufficient power without over-penetration. The good news is that we can now go back and rediscover some of the great law enforcement calibers of previous decades due to improvements in bullet efficiency. Advancements in bullet design are providing excellent expansion at less energy. What police were trying to achieve in the old days can now be realized. The .38 Special and the 9mm (and their numerous variants) are more viable than was thought possible 30 years ago. Less recoil, less expense, less wear, and a manageable size are the benefits of the old defense calibers, though price has disproportionately risen for revolver ammunition since the rise of the pistol. Penetration of a heavily clothed human body is necessary, but passing through the body of a grizzly bear is not.

Bullet size and velocity requirements vary by caliber. Practics defenders need jacketed hollow-point bullets (though JHPs are evolving too) in rounds with sufficient energy to penetrate and expand the bullet. Fortunately, most major ammo makers offer law enforcement or defense product lines. The shooter must be responsible to never exceed the handgun manufacturer's pressure limits for ammunition. Old handguns weren't designed for new, hotter ammunition. You only need enough. It does you no good to carry an 18-shot pistol that you can't fire quickly due to recoil.

The gun press routinely tests new bullets and ammunition; no shortage of independent information is available. The old adage "practice with what you carry" is a Practics rule. You may use reloaded ammunition or lighter loads for some of your practice, but skills training must be completed using your defense ammo. Routine skills maintenance also requires firing your "duty" ammo.

Computers changed ammunition forever. Now all major manufacturers make reliable ammunition with staggering consistency. They also assume some civil liability for the performance of their products. Don't sit down at the reloading press and load your own defense rounds unless you are a legitimate expert. Reloading is a great benefit to an active shooter, but come race day, it's not a good idea to try to make your own gasoline.

Above all, ammunition, like a handgun, is only as effective as the person using it.

## Body Armor

I haven't mentioned soft body armor simply because it is beyond the reach of most readers. Some jurisdictions restrict the use of bullet-resistant vests, and soft armor costs about as much as a service-grade handgun. Truly I understand that the average defender cannot go on a security-equipment shopping spree just because some book-writing yahoo recommends it. (I already asked you to buy a good holster belt.) If it is within your means, financially and legally, to acquire a vest, there is no better security investment outside of a good firearm. I know of officers who are working and going about their lives today that would otherwise be dead or severely disabled were it not for a department-issued vest. You can throw a vest on about as quickly as throwing on a pair of pants. Why not do it, if you can? The National Law Enforcement and Corrections Technology Center (NLECTC) claims that during the more than 30 years that soft body armor has been available to police, more than 3,000 lives have been saved.

National Institute of Justice (NIJ) rates body armor by levels based on effectiveness. These standards and rating levels change as technology improves. Today, levels IIA, II, and IIIA would all be worthy of defender consideration. Levels of protection are assigned by which calibers and rounds the vest can stop and the amount of blunt-force trauma that the vest can prevent. Trauma occurs when the vest stops a round but allows the force to continue inward against the wearer. Blunt-force trauma can kill by rupturing organs and causing internal bleeding. If you will be wearing your vest frequently, consider buying an extra carrier, which is the garment that holds the front and back ballistic panels. Carriers are ridiculously expensive for glorified underwear, but vests can cause heavy perspiration, and you'll need to wash the carriers frequently. Follow manufacturers' guidelines for cleaning the panels and protecting them from premature wear. Once struck, a ballistic panel must be discarded even if penetration was successfully prevented. Body armor requires maintenance and replacement to be effective. Some carriers will accept an extra trauma plate covering the heart. A trauma plate protects against heart stoppage due to blunt-force trauma to the chest. All major manufacturers make vests specifically designed for women and available in custom and standard sizes for both genders. Many vest wearers have died because their vests didn't properly fit, particularly on the sides. Learn what the fit should be and then ensure that your vest properly fits you. Putting on weight requires a new vest. Body armor has a lifespan and needs occasional replacement; bear that in mind before buying a used vest. Vests are bullet resistant, not bulletproof. The presence of body armor does not change tactics. Acquiring body armor demands study prior to purchase. Be diligent in your research.

## Gun-Belt Order of Placement

### Pistol:

1. Holster on the strong side, slightly forward of the hip as needed for weak hand reach
2. Double magazine pouch immediately on the support side of the torso's centerline
3. Small flashlight pouch about 1" or 2" to the support side of the magazine pouch
4. Cell-phone pouch immediately to the support side of the flashlight pouch
5. Knife pouch immediately to the support side of the cell-phone pouch
6. Hasty-aid-kit pouch centered in the small of the back

### Revolver:

1. Holster on the strong side, at or slightly forward of the hip as needed for weak-hand reach
2. Double speed-loader pouches immediately on the strong side of the torso's centerline
3. Small flashlight pouch under but slightly to the outside of the support-side pectoral
4. Cell-phone pouch immediately to the support side of the flashlight pouch
5. Knife pouch immediately to the support side of the cell-phone pouch
6. Hasty-aid-kit pouch centered in the small of the back

## Gun-Belt Equipment Training

Police officers don't train to master gun-belt equipment. They become familiar with the belt by wearing it every workday. Unfortunately, many police trainees have difficulty accessing specific tools on the belt, particularly under duress, due to the lack of gun-belt training. Often the belts worn in police academies do not mirror the future officers' duty belts. The following exercises and knowledge-research requirements are designed to quickly give you practical familiarity and, ultimately, muscle memory with your Practics gun belt.

<u>Gun-Belt Knowledge Requirements:</u>

1. Set up your gun belt as described above. Check to see if your belt supports the equipment without rolling or sagging. Test the belt by wearing it without shirt and trousers. Your gun belt should provide sufficient friction to allow forceful draws and re-holsters. If it doesn't work without clothing, you may need a different belt, possibly with a wider contact area or less slippery interior lining, or your belt may require the addition of a lining with greater friction.

2. While wearing your gun belt, try to reach the holster with your weak hand. Slide the holster slightly forward if needed.

3. Gear requires maintenance. Manufacturers provide care information for their products. Using the maker's recommendations, acquire any necessary cleaning and preservative products and schedule routine maintenance for the next 12 months.

4. Learn how to sharpen a knife. Acquire the tools necessary to keep your knife sharp and properly oiled.

The following drills are designed for use with a storage-safe weapon. No ammunition should be present during gun-belt training that is not conducted on a range.

1. **Walking the Belt**—While wearing your gun belt, walk normally toward a pre-determined point approximately 15 yards away, where you will turn and walk back. At the turnaround point, you will increase your speed for the next leg. By the fourth leg you should be moving at a slow jog. During each leg the training partner will command you to draw a piece of gear with your weak hand, lift it to chest level, and then re-place it in the pouch. During this drill the training partner will not call "gun," but limit the commands to "magazine one," "magazine two," (or "speed loader one, two") "flashlight," "knife," "phone," or "tape." The training partner will ensure the trainee does not look at the belt or fumble when reaching for pieces. Failure to successfully complete a leg requires the leg to be repeated correctly. Students who can't jog should limit themselves to walking at a brisk speed. This drill is not intended to be strenuous physical activity. The training partner should not give commands

quicker than the trainee can react.

At the completion of the four legs of the drill, the student may take a short break.

Walking the belt

Skill-Installation Requirement: three complete exercises, monthly for the first year

Maintenance Requirement: one complete exercise each quarter unless the belt is worn for duty or *fully* used in monthly training; in either case maintenance training will not be necessary.

Repeat the above training using the opposite hand.

2. **Four-Position Drill**—This drill will assist you with using your gun belt while contending with belt-line access challenges such as when seated, prone, or with limited balance. The training partner will give random commands for the defender to retrieve a specific piece of gear from the belt. The defender will bring the piece to chest level and then return it to the pouch. Each position will have 10 random commands. The handgun will not be present during this drill. The four positions are:

1. lying facedown on the ground
2. sitting in a non-upholstered chair that has a back but no arms
3. kneeling on the left knee with the right foot no more than 6" to the side
4. kneeling on the right knee with the left foot no more than 6" to the side

Skill-Installation Requirement: three complete exercises, monthly for the first year

Maintenance Requirement: one complete exercise each quarter unless the belt is worn for duty or *fully* used in monthly training; in either case maintenance training will not be necessary.

3. **Flashlight Two-Hand-Grip Drill**—The best way to learn how to use this technique is to do it. No ammunition or magazines may be present, and the handgun must be storage-safe without a magazine. The student will select an interior space that allows sufficient space for a few minutes of uninterrupted movement. A full basement will work well. Inspect the area for trip hazards prior to training. The safety officer will make the space dark and give the command for the student to move slowly through the space while using the Flashlight Two-Hand Grip. Student training objectives will be to use the sights by keeping the beam pointed inline with the muzzle. The sights should appear in silhouette against the lit area. The safety officer will follow behind the student and within arm's reach. Every two seconds the student will stop and turn the flashlight off using his shooting thumb. After a three count, the flashlight will be turned on using the shooting thumb, and movement will continue for a total of 10 minutes.

Skill-Installation Requirement: three times

Maintenance Requirement: one 10-minute drill monthly for the first year

Repeat the above requirements for the weak hand.

4. **Knife Drill**—While standing near a wall or tree (not an interior wall that may be cut), draw your knife from the pouch and open it using only your weak hand. Close the knife using the Practics method (explained in the "Practics Knife-Closure Technique" earlier in this chapter) with the wall or tree serving as a knife block. From a kneeling position draw your knife and then close it using the boot heel as a knife block. This two-position cycle must be conducted in two stages: a safety stage where the student is allowed to look at the knife during the drill, and a tactical stage where the student is prohibited from watching the knife and must keep visual focus downrange. The training partner will ensure that the student is focusing downrange during the second stage and the movement is not unduly rushed. During the safety stage, the training partner will ensure that the movement is slow and deliberate and the student is properly

positioning the fingers.

Skill-Installation Requirement: two-position cycle (safety stage) eight times, two-position cycle (tactical stage) eight times

Maintenance Requirement: two-position cycle (safety stage) eight times, two-position cycle (tactical stage) eight times, monthly for six months

Repeat the above requirements in their entirety with the strong hand.

5. **Hasty-Aid Drill**—This drill simulates a minor wound to the first knuckle of the index finger. The drill can, and should, be done while addressing other fingers, hand, wrist, and forehead, but the purpose of the drill is to learn how to manipulate the tape with the hand and mouth. (Under heavy perspiration it may be necessary to wrap the entire head to secure the tape to the forehead—not a recommended training drill for students with hair.) Defenders in sufficiently good health will get additional benefit from doing this drill immediately after exercise.

This exercise will require the substitution of your hasty-aid pouch's medical tape with that of a "training" roll. You will get oil on the tape, rendering it unserviceable, so set your service roll off to the side for this training. Be certain to replace the training roll with the service roll at the completion of the exercise.

First, *lightly* coat your support hand with oil in order to simulate blood and sweat. Holding an object in your shooting hand to simulate a handgun and keeping it pointed "downrange," draw the medical tape from the hasty-aid pouch using only your support hand. Bring the tape to your mouth, bite the free end, and unroll approximately 10" of the tape. Spit the tab and use your teeth and support hand to tear the tape near the roll. This will leave you with the 10" strand of tape dangling from your mouth. Place your index finger, just below the first knuckle, against the adhesive side of the tape at the bottom of the strand. Point the finger upward and make a twirling motion that will wrap the tape around the finger. Pinch the tape between the thumb and finger as you go and give a *very light* tug against the mouth to take slack out of the strand and ensure a tight fit. Using your thumb as an aid, continue wrapping the finger by moving it upward, causing the tape to wrap higher on the finger. When you've used most of the length of tape, ensure that the free end is pressed surface-to-surface against wrapped tape, not skin. The training partner will ensure that the defender keeps focus downrange and will determine whether the finger was wrapped securely enough to conceal the oil and provide a stable gripping surface. The wrap must not cut off circulation; it need only be tight enough to allow the hand to function without interference from blood.

Skill-Installation Requirement: 10 repetitions

Maintenance Requirement: twice semi-annually

Naturally, you'll repeat the above training for the strong hand.

6. **New-Holster Drill**—This drill is designed only to improve your holster manipulation. We will train for the draw later. A storage-safe handgun must be used for this training, in a safe area and absent any ammunition. Begin by ensuring your holstered handgun is completely secure in the holster; every strap and every snap must be secured as intended by the manufacturer. Then grasp your holstered handgun with your strong hand, simultaneously releasing the security straps, and draw the handgun no more than an inch above the holster. Immediately re-holster the handgun and secure all the straps. Don't look down during the exercise. If you need eyes to draw or holster, you are not training properly. The training partner will ensure that your eyes are downrange and the holster snaps are properly secured when the handgun is holstered.

Remember, jab those retention snaps as you assume your grip.

Skill-Installation Requirement: 20 reps · five sets (Student may take a 90-second break between sets, as needed.)

Maintenance Requirement: This drill will only be repeated

when a new holster is acquired. Maintenance of this skill will be accomplished during drawing exercises and live fire. The Practics holster drill is invaluable at developing muscle memory for drawing and holstering with a new holster, but partial movements are never used in Practics maintenance training due to the possibility of training the student to improperly hesitate.

7. **Magazine-Slam Drill**—The practical advantage of the defensive pistol over the defensive revolver is reload speed. But in order to enjoy that advantage, the pistol shooter must train for the reload. A well-trained revolver shooter will reload more quickly than the average pistol shooter. But when done properly, magazine reloading can enable almost-continuous pistol fire. I mentioned earlier that there was a place in Practics for cheap magazines—here we are. You will get much more out of training with additional magazines, and plenty of cheap magazines are available. Whenever you have a few dollars to spend toward your defense supplies, include a cheap magazine or two. Service magazines must be kept free from cracks and even slightly damaged lips. As mentioned, modest-size rubber magazine bumpers, which assist in gripping the magazine, are a worthwhile investment and can prevent or lessen damage caused by dropping the service magazines. The more training that can be done with cheap magazines, the longer your service magazines will last.

The goal of this drill is to train the shooter to make a quick, fluid magazine change. Proper magazine use starts with proper magazine placement. As previously mentioned, most shooters will never spend any time on specific magazine training, and that's the point: A very small percentage of shooters can properly coordinate magazine changes.

Let's review magazine placement inside the pouches one more time. Make certain that your magazines are inserted in the pouches with the feed end down. The rounds inside the magazines must be pointing toward the belt buckle, or the centerline of the torso. After you unsnap the magazine pouch, lifting the retaining strap upward with the support hand, grab the bottom of the magazine and lift it from the pouch. Once clear of the pouch, rotate the fist to the outside until the magazine is pointed upward. Slam the magazine into the empty magazine well of your pistol, lifting the fingers away as soon as the end of the magazine is inside the well. The palm of the hand cups the bottom of the magazine and fully seats it. The insertion action should be strong and decisive. I don't know of anyone who ever lost a magazine because it was seated too firmly. When releasing the magazine, hit the release button with the shooting thumb, dropping the magazine. Always use the inside magazine (closest to the torso centerline) first and the outer magazine second. Make it your permanent, unwaverable practice and you will never reach for the empty pouch. Train for it.

This non-firing drill involves heavy repetition of ejecting and inserting magazines. No ammunition should be present, and only a storage-safe weapon and empty magazines may be used. The more magazines you can use, the more benefit you will get from this training. If you have sufficient practice magazines, you won't have to use your service magazines, extending their service life. Place a waist-high table in front of you, or use a firing-line range table, and cover the table with a protective mat. The training partner plays a very active role in this exercise. As you pull magazines from your pouches, the training partner will stand beside you and refill the pouches with additional magazines from the table. The training partner must snap the pouch straps after loading the pouches. The speed of the drill should be brisk but not fast enough to overrun the training partner. It is the rhythm and repetition that instructs the shooter.

The student will draw the pistol with empty magazine inserted, keeping it pointed downrange. Release the magazine using the shooting thumb as you draw a magazine from the innerrmost pouch. Insert the new magazine and then drop it, replacing it with a fresh magazine from the outermost pouch. Continue the repetition. The training partner will keep the pouches filled and snapped closed and ensure the muzzle is always downrange. The goal of this training is to have both expelled and fresh magazines in motion at the same time.

Once the magazine is in the well, flatten out the support hand and slam it home.

Slam magazine into the magazine well with a flat hand.

Skill Installment Requirement: 100 magazine changes
Maintenance Requirement: 10 magazine changes weekly (first four weeks), 20 magazine changes per month (first year)
The above training is not completed until performed with the

99

pistol in the weak hand, which includes making the initial draw with the weak hand. You don't want a functioning handgun and a healthy hand and still not be able to competently defend yourself due to a failure to train.

8. **Stuck-Magazine Drill**—Stuck-magazine training involves two elements: awareness that magazines will fail to drop and a removal action. You can feel, and hear in some cases, whether your magazine was cleanly dropped. Many shooters hesitate to act on a stuck magazine. The reason is simply because they did not train with the assumption that magazine-drop failures are part of pistol shooting. We can overcome that hesitation by including a small amount of magazine-clearance training as part of our normal range training.

You will need to prepare two or three practice magazines to make them fail to drop. An easy method is a couple of wraps of electrician's tape around the middle of the magazine. The tape should be kept thin enough for the magazine to go fully into the well without force but of sufficient thickness to prevent the magazine from freely dropping when released. Overwrapping will leave electrical tape shavings inside your magazine well. Replace the tape after each session to keep it intact. Non-taped mags will be needed during this drill to serve as fresh pouch magazines to replace the stuck magazines.

Ensure no ammunition is present. Gently insert a taped magazine into your storage-safe weapon. Press the magazine release and move to collect a fresh magazine. When you notice the magazine has failed to drop, conduct the stuck-magazine reload as previously described.

A single wrap of tape is often sufficient to simulate a bulging or dirty magazine.

Skill-Installation Requirement: 100 stuck magazine reloads

Maintenance Requirement: five stuck-magazine reloads every range visit

Switch hands and repeat the entire training.

9. **Ammunition-Selection Experiment**—Buy three boxes of JHP defense loads from three different reputable manufacturers whose products are *readily available in your area*. Test the ammunition with your broken-in handgun. Whichever functions best while having good accuracy and reasonable recoil is your defense load choice.

Now we have a stable intellectual and equipment platform from which we can begin shooter training . . .

# Chapter Five: Elemental Skills

*Owning a handgun doesn't make you armed any more than owning a guitar makes you a musician.*

Jeff Cooper

*To begin, begin.*

William Wordsworth

Before a boxer learns to throw combinations of punches, he first learns how to throw proper jabs, hooks, crosses, and uppercuts. The defensive shooter needs to master the shot before moving on to situational techniques and tactics. In this chapter we'll lay the foundation for Practics defensive shooting.

The reader will notice that I use law enforcement statistics to illustrate defensive shooting principles. Unfortunately, no reliable or comprehensive source exists, of which I am aware, for shooting statistics involving private defenders. However, police statistics are a good match for Practics students because single-officer deadly force encounters tend to mirror shooting distances in self-defense shootings by private persons.

Preliminary numbers (January to June) for 2014 law enforcement in-service deaths show a 56% increase in gunfire deaths over the same period for 2013. I do not claim that increase in deaths is a result of failed doctrine. Rather, criminal violence is increasingly spontaneous. During the last 40 years significant changes in officer-safety practices have been universally adopted. Today's police officer maintains greater distance during contacts, positions patrol cars for increased cover, and postpones suspect contacts until supporting units are present. Additionally, in recent years, police have been taught to shoot to completion, rather than the old practice of predetermined fire-and-reevaluate. Nonetheless, as violent crime declines in America, shooting incidents are becoming more deadly for police. Whatever we're doing isn't working. Under the best possible circumstances police shootings are always going to include misses because shootings will continue to involve surprise, adrenaline, fear, officer injury, diminished vision, breathlessness, and a limitless variety of unforeseen circumstances. Nothing is going to cure reality. Deadly force incidents will never go perfectly for the good guys—cop or private defender—but we must not accept the current failure rate as inevitable.

Point shooting has failed in two areas: accuracy and speed. Police miss half their shots at close range. Of course, missed shots are the product of failed aiming practices. But close range speaks to the matter of speed. We've had 50 years of point shooting as a law enforcement-trained skill, and neither accuracy nor speed have been satisfactory.

Practics has substantial differences from traditional point shooting. To begin with, Practics does not use the popular body-triangulation method for "instinctively" pointing a handgun. Squaring the body onto a target; centering the arms by feel, forming a triangle between the arms and torso; and discharging toward the target has been point-shooting orthodoxy since the 1950s. It dominates law enforcement training despite the popular myth that police are taught marksmanship. Marksmanship—proper marksmanship—hasn't been taught in most police academies for decades. Police have been point shooting using the triangulation method for more than a generation, and the results have been abysmal. According to New York Police Department's report on officer deaths during gunfights (1854–1979), 82% occurred within 6' of the shooter. Most police shootings involve far more misses than hits. Close-range fire by officers will probably miss the intended target. General estimates of police close-range accuracy hovers around 40%. We're missing six out of every 10 shots inside an elevator. Continuing to train for triangulation point shooting is a losing bet. As mentioned at the beginning of this book, twentieth-century innovators such as Fairbairn and Applegate recognized that traditional one-handed marksmanship training was insufficient for close-range self-defense. Short-range fire needs to be accurate, extremely fast, and sufficiently instinctual for a defender under severe duress. Triangulating the body seems to make sense—center on the target and the bullet will travel straight toward the target.

Unfortunately, what seems good in theory has, over the last 60 years, killed a lot of good guys. The failure of the common point-shooting technique is due to four problems. The first problem is the reliance on muscle memory for accurate fire. Muscle memory has a place in defensive shooting. For instance, it is the foundation for quick no-peek reloading. But muscle memory depends on continuity, everything being exactly the same each time. Point shooting requires the memorization of arm position because the arms float freely and have no reference point beyond "feel." So targets that are higher, lower, or off-center may exceed the skills that can be gained through muscle memory. Muscle-memory training demands firing in exactly the same way each time; otherwise, there is nothing for the muscles to "memorize."

The second problem is the amount of training required and the training frequency needed to retain muscle-memory skills. Muscle memory has an expiration date. Once a shooter spends the time to get a feel for where his arms are placed during point shooting, he must have continuous maintenance well beyond that required for sighted fire because triangulation shooting cannot be intellectualized. The arms are where the arms are placed; there is no independent measuring device such as sights. The shooter has no reference at the time of firing beyond what has already been acquired through repetitive practice.

The third problem is in the mechanics of triangulation fire. We humans can point instinctively with a straight arm and hand. However, when the hands are brought together, grasping the handgun, triangulation of the arms naturally bends both wrists outward (at slightly different angles), forcing the arm and the hand to point at different angles, which is not an accurate method of aiming unless the shooter has some external physical reference as we will discuss later in the Practics Architectural Firing chapter.

The fourth, and probably worst of the triangulation-shooting problems, is the fact that it survives through a training bait-and-switch. Shooters train for point shooting by standing on static firing lines and drawing the handgun all the way within peripheral vision. Then they use their eyesight to guide the handgun. If shooters can raise a handgun to chin level, they can certainly raise it to eye level for a hasty-sighted fire technique. The real need for point shooting is when there is no chance to raise the handgun beyond the line of the chest. If training is conducted with vision-guided fire while the actual use of point shooting occurs without the aid of visual alignment, then the entire point-shooting training regimen is pointless and even dangerous to those who depend on it. Vision restricts under emotional duress, and awareness of surroundings is reduced to a narrow focus on the threat (tunnel vision), meaning in real life point shooting is unlikely to be visually assisted. When students are required to point shoot at a lower point in the draw using the triangulation method, the results tend to be unsatisfactory. Point shooting has been getting by as a lazy man's version of marksmanship while it was intended for quicker, closer confrontations.

Practics answers these four problems with "balance shooting." Unlike triangulation fire, successful balance shooting requires a combination of grip, draw, trigger control, and stance. Later in this section we will examine each element needed for successful balance shooting.

The first thing to consider is the scope of work required of a handgun user when attempting self-defense. Or, to put it plainly, what is the defender's fire responsibility with a handgun? We have to know what we're trying to accomplish, in the broadest sense, before we can train to meet that responsibility.

## Sphere of Responsibility

Imagine a defender within perfect space: no obstructions, no walls, no ceiling or floor, simply an armed person floating in space. Now imagine a transparent sphere encapsulating the defender. Every fraction of an inch of the encapsulating sphere's surface represents a possible bullet path from the defender outward. Those thousands and thousands of angles-of-fire represent the defender's Sphere of Responsibility. In other words the defender must be capable of sending a bullet through every fraction of space on the Sphere of Responsibility. A person defending life with a handgun may have to fire overhead or underfoot, to either side, or to the rear. People get attacked on catwalks; through driver and passenger windows; from balconies, underpasses, overpasses, the bottoms of stairwells, the tops of ladders, the doorway they just left, the doorway to which they are heading, and every point of direction within existence. I think it is fair to say that standing on a firing line, crouching, and shooting straight ahead is not sufficient to achieve directional mastery. Any point at which a bullet may enter your Sphere of Responsibility requires you to be capable of accurate fire along the same bullet path. So if you may be vulnerable to fire descending from above, you must also be able to accurately and efficiently shoot upward. The tactical basis for intelligent defense with a handgun must begin with the defender's scope of responsibility. Think about it. What must you be able to do with a handgun in order to have tactical control of your surroundings? Forget about ground fighting and special situations for the moment. Think in terms of an armed defender in pure, open space. No walls, ceiling, or floor, just unobstructed space. Imagine the defender firing a handgun with each bullet leaving a visible line of travel from the defender outward. The defender is responsible for fire covering every bullet's width of space within the invisible sphere that surrounds him. Every point of the Sphere of Responsibility is a possible pathway for incoming and outgoing fire for which you must attain mastery.

To make it easier for us to train for firing within the sphere, the shooting hemisphere is divided into quadrants: low left, high left, low right, high right. The sphere also has an axis with two unchanging points: straight up and straight down. Generally, the lower quadrants will *tend* to be point-shooting targets. The higher quadrants will *tend* to be sighted-fire targets. The defender must ensure that training is adequate for competence at all six points of the shooting hemisphere, the means of which we will examine during the course of this book. Training requires disciplined and successful fire into each of the quadrants, sighted and unsighted. During training, targets within each quadrant should be moved to prevent the shooter from lazy spot shooting, which is firing at a predetermined fixed target that never requires an adjustment of the shooter's position. Simply moving the targets within each quadrant will force the shooter into a fresh body-and-target alignment, preventing an unintended skill handicap.

Now that we know the scope of our defense responsibility, we can begin the nuts-and-bolts construction of a holistic firing defense.

## Beating the Triangle

When time and space permit, sighted fire is always desired. Quick-draw contests do occur, but those occurrences are the exception. Practics differs from traditional point shooting in several ways, but none is more significant than the shooting stance and method of body aiming. I will confess to the reader that I think *most* point shooting, or shooting without the sights, is completely unnecessary. If you can raise the weapon to your chest with two hands, you probably have time to raise it to eye level. Under extreme time constraints, hasty sighting may be required, but such techniques still utilize the sights. Time and space are the interrelated determiners of defensive shooting techniques. In most cases police and private defenders will have drawn their weapons prior to confrontation. Police are rarely caught unprepared when doing a high-risk vehicle stop. The suspect who exits the vehicle will already have weapons pointed at him. That doesn't mean it all works out well for the police, but disaster won't be due to losing a quick-draw contest.

Every day across this country students are taught to point shoot at close-range, non-moving targets. The shooters learn to adjust fire using the bullet holes made in the target, which has no similarity to real-life. In many cases the shooters take a moment to position their arms prior to the start whistle. Drawing-and-firing drills are little better, because the handguns are raised high enough to be guided by peripheral vision, which, as stated earlier, is just a bad form of marksmanship. Remember, during an actual confrontation the defender will not have peripheral vision on the handgun, because the field of vision shrinks during a fight-or-flight response. Even when students are required to keep the weapons at the beltline, they only learn to shoot straight ahead at an unvarying target, temporarily memorizing a function instead of acquiring a permanent skill.

Let's not throw out the baby with the bathwater, however— point shooting is a critical defensive skill. I believe that most instruction on point shooting, unfortunately, is the result of the blind leading the blind. Pointing and jerking at a stationary, close-range target is easy to teach. Train for a day and become an "expert." Marksmanship is an intellectual pursuit; point shooting is a physical skill. Marksmanship is science; point shooting is art. Marksmanship is reason; point shooting is muscle memory. Despite my unwavering belief in the above, I consider point shooting an invaluable skill in specific circumstances. Though often misused, point shooting meets a need that cannot be met by sighted fire. *Defenders who cannot accurately fire without the sights are helpless when the time or distance threshold for action precludes bringing the handgun to eye level.* Abuse or misrepresentation of point-shooting techniques and capabilities do not diminish the legitimacy of this important skill.

Triangulation of the shooting arms does tend to get the shots moving in the right direction, but defenders must remember that despite the popularity of this technique, most shots fired by police at close range miss the target. Arm triangulation has value to the Practics defender but only when engaging in Practics Architectural Firing techniques, which we'll examine in another chapter. However, the successful use of the triangulation method depends on it not being immediate and spontaneous nor used apart from some corroborating physical support, which, of course, would entirely eliminate how triangulation is currently being used in law enforcement. Finally, the current typical use of triangulation requires an alignment, a posing of the entire body, which is rarely practical. Practics accepts that point shooting will be done in whatever position the defender is in at the time of firing. A good natural shooting stance has a place in defensive shooting, but genuine point shooting cannot be "set-up," because the entire purpose of using point shooting is to accurately fire when a quick, close-range attack is underway. If you have time to pose your body, you probably don't need point shooting.

Practics offers a relatively simple and effective alternative to traditional, body-oriented triangulation firing: Linear-Balance Shooting. This technique is the closest thing Practics has to a static firing position, though there are almost no strict stance requirements beyond good footing and general body direction. We'll add even fewer restrictive techniques throughout the book, but the principle of shooting in concert with our physiology (rather than trying to conform it) is common to all Practics elements.

## Practics Linear-Balance Shooting

Imagine a line running from underneath your shooting foot to the centerline of your target. Now imagine a draw, wherein the muzzle of your handgun follows that running line to the base of the target and straight up the target's centerline. That's the linear firing path. Everything works off the shooting-side foot from low to high. Why? Well, a majority of shooters can successfully execute linear aiming and achieve quick draws and close-range accuracy with very little effort. I am aware that forswearing arm triangulation is an act of defensive-shooter blasphemy, so let's test the general theory before we go any further.

---

**The Linear-Foot Test**

Stand in the center of a room and single out an object no bigger than the width of a human torso. Without looking, point your shooting-side foot at the object by stepping. Look down to see if you accurately aimed your foot at the target. It's that easy.

---

The reason the above demonstration works is because you have been accurately pointing with your feet all your life. Little kids learn to control the angle at which they kick balls by the angle at which their feet contact the ball. More to the point we all learn to "aim" our feet in the direction we wish to travel. For some it takes a little sensitizing, which can easily be done through Practics training, but for most pointing the toe at a target can be immediately done with just a little extra pressure on the foot to increase sensitivity. Eventually, accomplished practitioners won't even need the feel of the ground once full-foot sensitivity has been acquired.

---

**The Foot-to-Hand Test**

Close your eyes and vigorously stamp your shooting-side foot with the toe pointing outward. At the same time, point your shooting-side fist (as if holding a handgun) in the same direction of your shooting-foot toe with the intent to mimic the exact line of the foot. The goal is to position the hand approximately over the toe. Open your eyes and look down at your hand and foot. Were you able to aim the hand based on where you *felt* the shooting-side foot pressed against the ground?

---

The hand knows where the foot is and the foot knows the target angle.

Aim with the foot. It couldn't be easier.

The degree of accuracy that can be had with the above technique in a very short period of time is astounding. Initially the shooter will need to exaggerate the pressure on the foot to increase feel but very soon will develop an awareness of foot position. Step naturally toward the target, and the hand will follow the foot.

The five greatest differences between linear aiming and arm triangulation follow:

1. Linear benefits from good body position but does not require it. Arm triangulation cannot be used without pre-positioning the body.
2. Linear does not require muscle memory for aiming. The ground under the foot serves as an independent guide on which the position of the foot can be immediately and constantly verified. Triangulation floats the arms without a means of subjective measure.
3. Linear may be used as soon as the muzzle has cleared the holster. Triangulation requires the handgun to "center" in front of the body for aiming.
4. Linear is fully accurate for one-handed shooting. Triangulation is based on two-handed shooting. One-handed triangulation firing is certainly possible but with dramatically different aiming dynamics.
5. A linear draw brings the handgun in line with the dominant

eye, whereas triangulation draw brings the sights equally between the eyes.

The advantages of linear aiming over triangulation aiming are speed and accuracy. What else matters?

Now that we understand the mechanics of the aim, we'll consider how the body can be positioned to enhance speed, accuracy, and movement. The balance portion of Linear-Balance Shooting is very simple. The shooter shifts more than half the body weight onto the shooting foot. This redistribution of weight will increase accuracy by increasing awareness through pressure on the foot. Additionally, the vertical centerline of the torso will move slightly behind the handgun, which will assist unsighted accuracy, particularly during rapid fire from low, unsighted fire transitioning up to high, sighted fire. Perfect marksmanship is easily obtained when the body returns to a 50/50 weight distribution at the end of the upward drawing movement. This slight shifting of weight is all that is required for accurate, fast, Linear-Balance Shooting. The shifting of body weight is subtle and almost imperceptible to the casual training partner. Firing accurately while the weight is shifted over the shooting foot is certainly possible, but returning the body weight to a 50/50 distribution will ensure the best possible marksmanship platform, which may be necessary to maintain for several minutes to make shots at long distances. Shifting the body over the foot has more importance for those learning this skill than it will for those who have mastered it. Additionally, the body tends to crouch a bit during stress—it needn't be exaggerated or encouraged—and moves slightly toward the holster during the draw, which will naturally bring the body over the shooting foot. All in all, Linear-Balance is more intuitive than triangulation.

Don't lock the joints. Easy grip.

As previously mentioned, the Natural Stance is preferred in Practics because it is already known to every human with the power to stand, is perfect for both Linear-Balance Shooting and marksmanship, and accommodates all body types, unlike the excellent but often improperly executed Bladed Stance. The Natural Stance faces the target with feet naturally apart and the weight evenly distributed. The shoulders are rolled forward slightly, simulating a position of fatigue. When the shoulders are slightly forward of the hips, recoil is minimized and multi-shot speed is dramatically increased. The arms are raised to eye level for aimed fire without locking the elbows. Legs maintain the natural bend at the knees and are never locked. The head is naturally upright, which includes an extremely slight downward cant. Muscular tension is limited to only the force needed to keep the body upright and the arms raised for firing. Point shooting must be done from whatever position the defender is in at the time deadly force is required, but adopting the Natural Stance will provide the defender with the most advantageous shooting stance for executing Practics techniques, from firing from just above the holster to using the sights.

**Balanced Weight-Distribution Test**
Stand with your weight evenly distributed over both feet. Close your eyes. Shift your weight onto the shooting foot. The sensation will be of "coming over" the shooting foot with your torso. Raise your shooting fist out in front of you with the intention of matching the line of your shooting foot. Open your eyes and check your aim by comparing the position of the hand and foot. Repeat the test a few times, varying the angle of your foot. You will notice that having more than half your body weight over the shooting foot dramatically increases sensitivity and aids in your ability to reliably coordinate hand-to-foot alignment.

## Shifting and Reversing the Stance

Let's go back to the Sphere of Responsibility. There is an obvious problem when considering the defensive responsibilities of the sphere. We can only cover the space in front of us or immediately to either side, yet we can be attacked from behind. A Practics defender must be able to adjust position to meet all angles within the sphere.

Imagine again that you are inside that invisible sphere. Divide the sphere into two hemispheres: front and rear. The Shooting Plane is the 180° space to the front and sides of the shooter. Remaining behind the shooter is the 180° referred to as the Back Plane. These hemispheres are not fixed, and a full reversal in position will flip the shooting and back planes. The purpose of distinguishing these two areas is to make the defender conscious of the full 360° range of responsibility and the two movements necessary for controlling the entire sphere: pivot and reversal. A reversal is necessary to immediately switch hemispheres, whereas pivoting only shifts the planes as the shooter moves. If the shooter pivots 5° to the left, the back plane swings 5° to the right. A reversal flips the planes but a pivot only adjusts them. The following standing transition techniques are quick and controllable and will prevent stumbling.

## Pivot

The pivot depends on whether the defender is going toward the shooting side or the support side, but the footwork technique is the same:

**Shooting-Side Pivot**—Step forward with the support foot

toward the shooting side while pressing down with the shooting-side toe and lifting the heel. The result will be a pivot off the shooting-side toe. Pivot to align the toe onto the target. Nothing could be easier.

**Support-Side Pivot**—Step rearward with the support-side foot while pressing down with the shooting-side heel and lifting the shooting-side toe. This will provide a pivot motion of the shooting-side heel. When the desired pivot angle is reached, the shooting-side toe is dropped down in line with the target.

## Reversal

The quickest way to get pointed in the opposite direction is by doing a modified military about-face. The reversal can be done to the left or right. This is a simple maneuver but requires practice to know how to adjust the angle of turn, which will determine where the body is pointing at the end of the reversal.

**Reversal Movement**—Move one foot rearward beyond the line of the remaining foot. For instance, if the right foot is moved, the toe of the right foot must be placed to the rear and left of the left heel. Then the shooter turns using the heel of the left foot and the toe of the right foot. The farther back and to the side the moving foot is placed will determine the degree of the reversal. This sounds far more complex than it is, and after a couple of tries you'll discover you can easily control your ending position. Done well, this is an extremely fast maneuver.

Up to this point we've recognized the scope of our fire responsibility and have acquired a good stance, body aiming, and the ability to change directions from a stationary position within the sphere. Now let's get the gun in hand and on target.

## Grip

We won't belabor the obvious, but we must make certain that hand-to-gun fit facilitates point shooting. Practics depends on knowing where your muzzle is located once outside the holster. You already know the handgun grip must be high, to the top of the backstrap, in order to minimize muzzle flip (the upward rise of the muzzle during discharge) and increase follow-up shot speed. Practics also requires alignment of the barrel with the forearm. I certainly did not invent barrel-forearm alignment. It has long been a staple of traditional marksmanship technique. However, a substantial percentage of shooters tend to slightly cant their handguns when gripping, while another group's handguns simply do not fit their hands. During sighted fire imperfections in grip can be detected by watching the front sight tip; however, unsighted fire has no such assurance mechanism. The grip must be made perfect every time the hand and gun come together.

The goal in grip placement is to obtain a position that allows the shooter to point with the arm and fist and, by extension, the handgun while maintaining a straight line from elbow to muzzle. As previously mentioned, no shooter can accurately point a handgun without knowing the exact position of the muzzle at the instant of discharge.

Every handgun manufactured today is balanced right and left, which means the barrel is situated in the center of the frame; likewise, the grips are equally spaced on the right and left sides of the handgun. Even target grips that are asymmetrical fill the hand in such a manner as to ensure the handgun can be centered in the grip.

The shooter's responsibility in achieving good grip is to ensure that the center of the web of the shooting hand (between thumb and trigger finger) is placed exactly on the center of the handgun's backstrap. When you look at your hand, you will see that when the wrist is straight and the hand is in line with the arm, the web of the thumb and trigger finger is directly in line with the elbow. *The handgun, if properly centered, will become a perfect extension of the line originating at the elbow, allowing the shooter to point the fist and hit the target.* Some shooters will discover that their handguns are too large or too small for a true centerline fit. A good measure of handgun fit is the ability of the shooter to operate shooting-hand levers, such as de-cocking and slide release, with the shooting hand. In a perfect world the shooting thumb would always reach the slide release without adjustment. In reality, that doesn't often happen. A slight canting of the handgun to accommodate lever operation is acceptable provided the backstrap does not have to be repositioned to resume firing. If the shooter can bring the handgun back to a perfect centerline grip simply by straightening the wrist, the handgun fit is acceptable. Grip panels and sleeves may be replaced to gain or lose a fraction of an inch, but otherwise the only cure is to find a handgun that fits your hand. No handgun made today is sufficiently superior to any other handgun as to be worth the cost of a bad fit. While proper grip is critical in marksmanship, in point shooting the hand-to-gun fit is a primary determiner of accuracy and consistency in shot placement. A bad grip during point shooting means missed shots.

In the marksmanship-reminder section of this book I mentioned the most common marksmanship error: overgrip. Whether you are point shooting or using the sights, a shaking handgun does you no good. What's the point? I suppose it would not matter a great deal if the choice was genuinely between marksmanship and point shooting, but these two skills are not a decisive choice. In fact, they're not really a choice at all. Point shooting and marksmanship are two skills at different points on the firing timeline. To be clear, we always want the accuracy of marksmanship, but we recognize that time and space may not permit it. Practics is always preparing for aimed fire while using point shooting. Grip your handgun for perfectly aimed shots, and you'll have the right grip for point shooting. The opposite is never true. Grip will tighten under duress, undoubtedly, but there is no need to intentionally preclude yourself from the possibility of accurate fire by training to over grip. You will not need a reminder to grab your handgun tightly during a close encounter, but you will not be able to talk yourself into a non-destructive grip for a quick shot at 10 yards if you don't train for it. Stress exaggerates the shooter's trained responses, but it does not completely reverse them, provided skills are actually "trained in" to the shooter's subconscious. Good grip and good trigger control will be lessened under duress, but if the shooter trains to over grip and jerk the trigger, the lessening effect will be severely worse. Let's train toward our best in order to make our worst "good enough."

So what is a good grip? A proper grip doesn't require the shooter to drain the blood from the fingertips. Defensive handguns, even magnum revolvers, need no more grip to fire than the trigger finger and the web of the shooting hand—you won't drop the gun. The other fingers simply prevent the handgun from moving between shots. Thumbs tend to increase overgrip by providing leverage for the rest of the hand. The cure is to keep the thumbs off the weapon. If your handgun weighs 40 ounces, then hold it like a 40-ounce object. Any pressure beyond that is dispersed through muzzle movement. Master grip and you will see a remarkable increase in your ability to control shot placement. Again, I am fully aware that things change under duress, which is all the more reason to raise the bar of competency during training. The goal of shooting, whether point shooting or marksmanship, is to hit your target. Practics has one grip in order to execute two different but consecutive skills. Responsible defenders must plan and train to use accurate aimed fire, should the opportunity present itself.

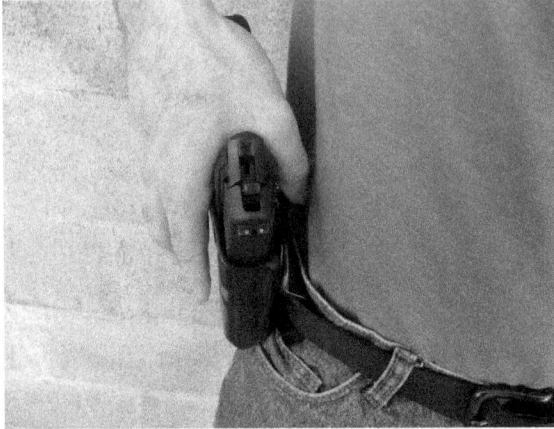

Clear interior snaps as part of your initial grip.

## Trigger-Finger Placement and Movement

The old rule of trigger-finger placement is to position the first joint of the trigger finger for a revolver and to use the first pad of the trigger finger for a pistol. How-to rules are always compromises for the sake of clarity, the truth being a bit more complicated. Proper placement of the trigger finger is one that allows the shooter to bring the trigger straight to the rear. The finger naturally closes at a 45° angle, which pushes the handgun to the non-shooting side. Position your hand to achieve a straight rearward travel of the trigger. Bigger hands will require the trigger finger to be withdrawn from the weapon to allow the top half of the finger to bend at the knuckle. Each shooter must experiment for best fit, but always remember the goal is a neutral influence on the rearward-moving trigger, never pulling the trigger to the shooting side nor pushing it to the support side. Neutral influence. The point shooter must be able to accurately point and then fire without pulling the muzzle off target. Don't let bad trigger-finger placement or trigger movement cause you to miss. Many think that trigger manipulation doesn't matter in practical shooting. They are mistaken. The trigger is part of the hand, and if you train your hand to muscle your weapon off-target, it will certainly do that. Nothing is free. Nothing is a given in point shooting. Mastery of non-sighted fire takes the same diligence as required to become a proficient marksman. Every detail matters until the bullet leaves the gun.

Control of the trigger through trigger reset can reduce multiple-shot string time by half. Proper trigger reset is not allowing the trigger to go any farther forward after firing than is necessary to reset the trigger for the next shot. Triggers often have double the forward travel needed for reset, obviously a waste of time and movement. Trigger-reset mastery is an eminently desirable skill, but not without some risk. Preventing the trigger from moving forward far enough to reset can cause a trigger stoppage. Such a delay would require the shooter to allow the trigger to go all the way forward before the rearward press could be retried. The problem is greater in revolvers but worth mentioning for handguns in general. I believe this to be a legitimate concern but not one that should dissuade the student from acquiring the reset skill. The best protection against a short trigger press is to train for the "click." Do not focus on speed when training but rather focus on finding the reset point. This may seem to be splitting hairs, but the emphasis in training matters. Those students who focus solely on achieving the fastest possible trigger press are much more likely to bind the weapon because they will invariably train by using one fast movement, yanking the trigger as quickly as possible without regard to the reset point. Until those students have achieved great speed during trigger press, they won't notice any problems. However, as those students become faster through elimination of trigger over-travel, they will begin to press the trigger too early. On the other hand, students who focus on deliberately crossing the reset point will have little trouble as they become quicker and more proficient. Train slowly for a faster trigger press.

Another trigger challenge is over-travel, which is excess rearward trigger movement. In other words, the trigger will go back farther than is necessary to fire the handgun. Again, training to overcome this fault is fairly easy, but it must be done with deliberation.

## Draw from the Holster

The late Jeff Cooper wrote, referring to the double-action

pistol, "It is an answer to a question no one asked." That statement perfectly describes my view of the three-point draw. Practics, as previously mentioned, includes firing en motion and firing at ranges close enough to compress the attacker's flesh with the muzzle. Therefore, it is essential that the handgun be ready to fire as soon as the muzzle clears the holster and is pointed at some portion of the attacker. The average defensive shooter will likely agree with the above statement but will strongly disagree with the following: *The common and popular three-point draw does not lend itself to extreme close-range firing, nor is it the most efficient method of bringing a handgun on target.* I'll go further and say that the three-point draw does nothing of value without doing something detrimental to good shooting and defensive technique. I am, of course, referring to the "new and improved" method of drawing a handgun that all the cool kids have flocked to over the last 20 years. This drawing method requires the shooter to pull the handgun straight up, all the way to the armpit, and then thrust it forward into a locked arm and iron grip (of course, scowling is very important when doing this method, being a tough guy and all). Early on when the three-point draw was becoming popular with law enforcement, I was told that it prevented an officer from raising his handgun to the front and having it blocked by an evildoer. The answer in such a case, of course, is to fire the handgun. Additionally, the three-point draw takes longer and is therefore at greater risk of interference. A bear hug by one bad guy *may* stop a three-point draw, but trying to stop the upward swing of a Practics Draw is more likely to earn the attacker a shattered pelvis. My point is that wild and woolly "what-ifs" don't justify the three-point draw.

Let's reason this out together. The shortest distance between two points is a direct line. When your muzzle clears your holster, your arm should be moving up and out at an angle toward the target. Going to the armpit is a wasted movement. You will not acquire the sights any faster. Sight alignment is a matter of hundredths of an inch. You're not achieving that while thrusting your arms outward to hyperextended elbows. (I certainly hope no legitimate handgun instructor is teaching that sighting is occurring during that violent outward thrust.) As far as locating the sights, raising the handgun from a direct angle is an advantage to thrusting the weapon straight outward and lowering the head. Three-point practitioners always drop the head to the sights, altering natural eye relief. The primary complaint that

Practics has with the three-point draw is the vertical movement from holster to armpit. The muzzle is kept downward during the lift portion of the draw, which presents a problem with close-range firing and makes en motion firing impossible. Remember what point shooting is intended to provide—quick, close-range fire. Why would we want to wait for the pistol to reach the armpit before engaging a closing target? Later we'll discuss how the handgun may be used to deliver low shots immediately from the holster and continue firing en motion or until sighted firing is possible.

Practics uses the traditional draw movement. In fact, unlike some Practics techniques, the traditional draw is an essential element because it is necessary for en motion firing from the holster. You will hear this proven draw method disparaged as "plowing" or "dragging" or a host of other descriptions that seem to suggest that the handgun will become tangled up in the air if not bounced off a nearby armpit.

Competition shooters may have helped popularize the three-point draw. Some shooting sports require longer length barrels and often some form of optical apparatus on the gun. Naturally, where there is more handgun to get out of the holster, more vertical lift is needed. From this observation, the general shooting population may incorrectly assume that speed is enhanced by the three-point draw.

The fastest of all shooting sports is the quick-draw event. Those competitors draw and fire a single round as quickly as possible. Sometimes a target is used, sometimes not, but speed is always the primary concern. Watch one of those events, and you will clearly see that no exaggerated travel is used. No movement is wasted. The round is fired as soon as the muzzle is clear and forward of the holster. Why wouldn't defensive shooters want that advantage?

The Practics Draw is simplicity itself. Engage the handgun with a proper grip and lift it clear of the holster as you raise it on target. The muzzle sweeps the ground toward the target as it moves upward, lending itself to additional firing opportunity. The three-point draw forfeits this advantage by keeping the muzzle pointed at the holster until it reaches the armpit, making the "second point" of the three-point draw doubly wasteful. Practics requires the support hand to join the grip during the early portion of the forward motion of the draw (over the shooting foot), unlike the three-point draw, which requires the hand to cross to the top of the torso. In Practics the support hand should join with the shooting hand about 10" or so in front of the

121

shooter and near mid-abdomen level. The shooting hand does not wait for the support hand.

Imagine how the popular three-point draw would adversely impact low to high shooting.

The Practics Draw includes the immediate disengaging of external safeties. It is a common practice for double-action shooters with traditional safety levers to leave them in the fire position for the purpose of keeping the handgun in a more ready state. Single-action pistols, of course, must have the safety engaged in order to safely carry them. If you carry a traditional double-action handgun with the safety off over a long period of time, you will certainly experience the safety lever being engaged without your knowledge. If you have a de-cocking/safety lever such as that on the Beretta 92F, you must always jab the lever with your thumb during every draw. Officers carrying a 92F with the safety in the fire position learned that lesson the hard way. The reason many choose to carry double-action handguns with the safety lever in the fire position is to make the gun as readily usable as a revolver. Disengaging the safety lever is then one less thing the shooter has to worry about, or so it would seem. When the pistol is new, the lever is too stiff to move without shooter action, but as it is broken in with use, the lever becomes more relaxed. Eventually the lever is easily moved by contact with the patrol car, the holster safety strap, or anything else the wearer bumps into or rubs against. Drawing your weapon and finding it won't fire when the trigger is pressed is rather disconcerting. By sweeping your double-action external safety off each and every time you draw, you will prevent the possible disaster of an unintentionally engaged safety. *If you have an external safety, use it as it was designed or expect it to become your enemy without warning.* The thumb can disengage the safety as the hand draws the weapon. No time is lost in delivering the first shot.

The "armpit" technique is yet another example of some law enforcement instructor coming up with a new thing to sell and a bunch of young SWAT cops deciding it looks too cool and sophisticated not to be worthwhile. Don't fall for it.

## Draw from The Holster with the Weak Hand

Practics demands full use of the weak hand. Hands and arms break; there is a reason human beings have two of each. A defender not being able to use the shooting hand when drawing the handgun is a real possibility. The strong arm may be occupied during a close encounter. Throwing one's hands up in the air and declaring "I can't shoot with my left hand" won't stop the fight. Ambidextrous operation is a mandatory skill for anyone who purports to keep a firearm for self-defense. The only acceptable excuse for not acquiring weak-hand mastery is a severe physical handicap. Learning to accurately fire with the weak hand is relatively easy. Over the years I taught many peace officers to fire accurately with either hand. However, drawing with the weak hand requires a little more effort. In part the problem is self-discipline. Students *may* be willing to practice weak-hand firing on their own time, but it takes a stupendous effort to get students to practice the weak-hand draw at all. Yet this is a skill that truly may save your life. The movements aren't hard, just awkward. A shooter can't wait until an incident occurs to work out the physical sequence of the weak-hand draw. Friends, you've got to train for this skill *now*.

Holsters vary and so does physical ability. The safer the holster, the more effort is required for a weak-hand draw. Safety/retention holsters are designed to prevent an adversary from drawing the defender's handgun—and the adversary will often use the exact same grip as a shooter using a weak-hand draw. Safety holsters can be accessed quickly with the weak hand, but not without training. Simple sheath holsters with a single retaining snap are the easiest to use for a weak-hand draw. They're also the easiest for attackers that want to steal your gun. Safety holsters are like gun safes; they'll protect you but you'd better know how to get them open in a hurry.

A minority of shooters will be able to grab the handgun with the firing grip and draw it without having to change the position of the gun in the hand. Women tend to have much greater flexibility than men and are more likely to be able to do a straight draw. Double-jointed shooters may find they can use the normal shooting grip too. Some of this has to do with where the holster is worn. The farther forward the holster is positioned on the belt, the easier it is to draw with the weak hand. The belly-circumference-to-arm-length ratio also matters. Even shooters who are able to twist their wrists to the most severe angle will still have to contend with straps and snaps pointing in the opposite direction.

The majority of shooters will not be able to turn their weak-hand palm outward and grab the holstered handgun in the normal shooting grip. For those shooters Practics offers three alternatives, but first, let's settle the matter of snaps and straps. The problem with straps and snaps is that they are designed to be engaged from the outside with the thumb forward. Weak-hand access is done in exactly the opposite manner—with the exception of those very flexible shooters. But even in those cases the thumb and fingers will be pointing in the wrong direction to engage the snaps. So regardless of whether you can grab the handgun in the firing position while it is still in the holster or not, the first thing that all shooters must do is a snap break. How this is done depends on your holster. Generally, the thumb and one finger can be used to stab the snaps on a safety holster. Here's where the practice comes in, giving the shooter familiarity through muscle memory and preventing fumbling under duress. Most straps will be brushed aside as the handgun is pulled from the holster. If your holster has straps that prevent you from gripping your handgun after they have been unsnapped, you will have to sweep them aside after hitting the snaps. In some cases sweeping won't be possible due to the form of the straps. Those holsters require finger sweeping during the draw. Again, I can't speak to the specifics of every holster, but the following Practics techniques can be adapted to clear troublesome straps.

**Reverse Grip**—This is the technique used by those shooters with greater flexibility and does not require the handgun to be transitioned from the drawing position to the firing position. The weak hand is brought palm inward across the body to the holster. The thumb and fingers disengage the snaps with a single stabbing motion. If the holster doesn't have a second snap (safety holster), stabbing with the finger will not be necessary. Typically the thumb will disengage the main strap, and any lower straps/snaps will be stabbed by either the little finger or the middle finger. Once the snap or snaps are disengaged, the palm is turned outward, and the hand assumes a normal shooting grip on the handgun. During this movement the thumb may sweep the thumb strap to the outside if needed. The handgun is drawn, and the arm rotates the hand and gun upward and to the outside, bringing them into a normal upright shooting position while traveling across the body to the weak-side firing position. This is the preferred method of drawing with the weak hand, but most simply cannot twist their hands sufficiently to grip the weapon. I certainly can't execute a Reverse-Grip Draw without bringing the holster much farther forward on the belt. If you have the ability, the Reverse Grip is the quickest, surest method of a weak-hand draw to target.

## Grip Transitions

*Armpit Transition:* This technique is necessary for all shooters because it is the only one that can be done when the shooter is standing between two closely parked semi-trucks or wedged into a broom closet. The weak hand comes across the body, palm inward. The thumb (and finger if needed) is used to stab the snaps. All fingers can naturally brush the strap aside by being inserted between the disengaged strap and the handgun, if necessary. The weak hand grabs the grips with the thumb toward the butt and draws the handgun. As the gun is lifted, it will be butt up and muzzle rearward. Sliding the handgun up and into the strong-side armpit, the gun will be held in place by squeezing it between the upper arm and body. The weak hand will reposition into a proper shooting grip and draw the handgun from the armpit onto the target while twisting it into a normal upright position. Other than the inverted grip position this is very much like a shoulder-holster draw. Those who have lost use of the strong hand but retain some use of the strong-side upper arm may use the Armpit Transition. During this movement the shooting hand barely leaves the weapon, and this can be a very quick method of transition.

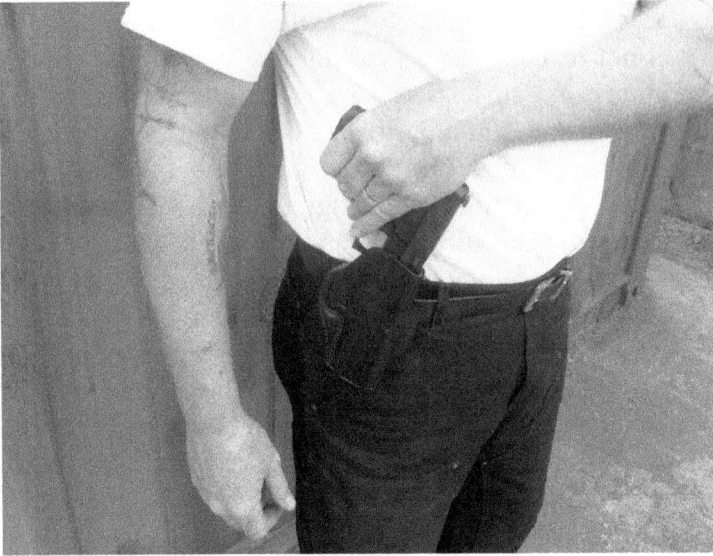

Support hand grabs the pistol for a transition.

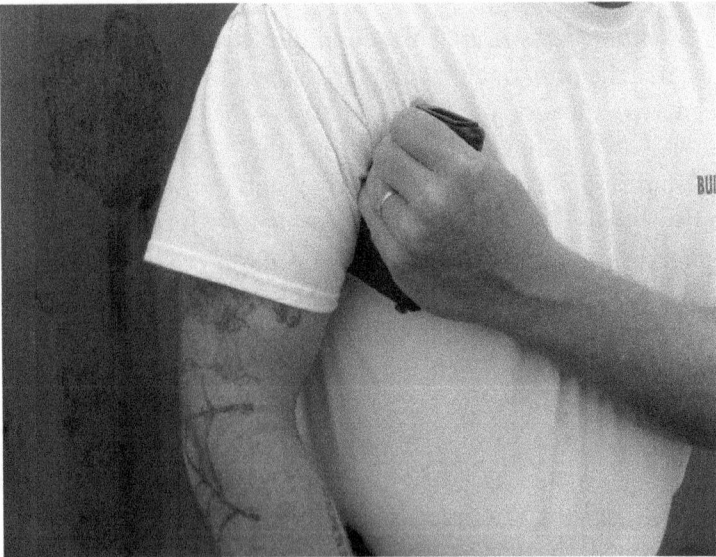

Top of the armpit for security.

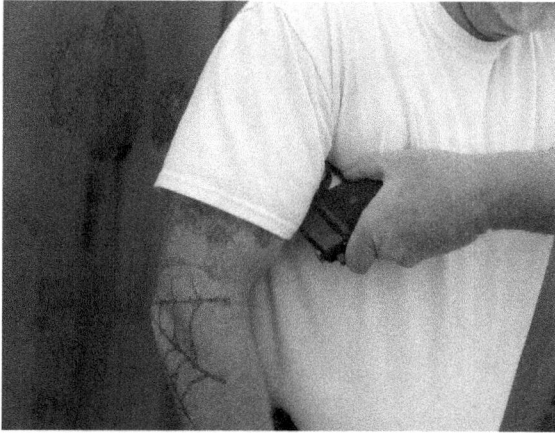

Simply twist the butt downward.

Assume a proper grip and the transition is complete.

*Platform Transition:* This is the safest and slowest of the three transitions. The Platform mirrors the Armpit Transition up to the moment the handgun is drawn. Instead of holding the handgun with arm pressure, the gun is laid on a stable surface and re-gripped. This is a great technique for a kneeling shooter who can use a thigh as a platform. Of course, the handgun can be placed on the ground or some raised surface. The speed of this technique depends heavily on where the platform is located. The Platform is the easiest of the three transitions.

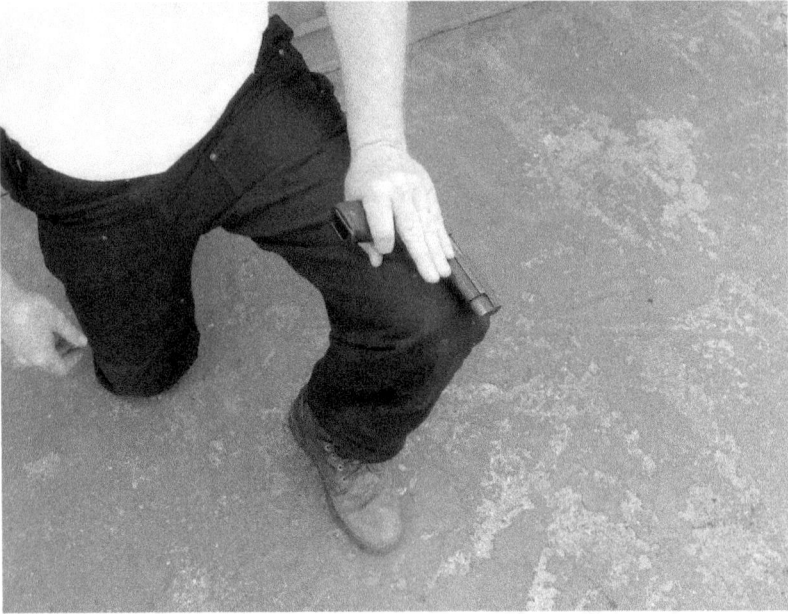

Platform transition: knees, ground, stairs, etc

Release and re-grip the weapon with a proper grip.

The Platform transition completed.

*Cowboy Toss:* This is the quickest of the three transition techniques and, I am sure, the one most likely to offend the overwrought safety sensibilities of fellow instructors. I could have named it the "Safety Flip." As the name implies, the handgun is separated from the hand while in the air, albeit for a very brief time. The maneuver begins exactly as the Armpit and Platform transitions but differs after the draw has been completed. Once the hand is moving upward, grasping the upside-down handgun by the grips, the wrist gives a quick jerking motion upward and to the weak side (direction of travel) while releasing the handgun. The handgun will turn right-side up in midair, and the hand will be in a drawing position slightly underneath it. The gun actually turns partially within the bowl of the palm. All that is required is for the hand to rise slightly and grip the handgun. It's very fast and the ergonomics of gun and hand make this an easy maneuver for the vast majority of shooters.

The time the handgun is in the air is minimal, and it is never beyond the reach of the hand. The Rambo crowd will insist that such a technique is dangerous because the shooter may be shoved during an execution and miss the catch. In reality a shove would likely dislodge the handgun from the armpit as well as separate the shooter from a handgun on a platform. Despite appearances the Cowboy Toss poses no greater risk from a shove than do the other grip-transition methods. I do realize that no one will want to teach this technique in an institutional setting, but it has a place in Practics. When a defender needs any weak-hand draw, circumstances are approaching the moment of last resort.

Cowboy Toss begins with the handgun upside down.

A quick upward and outward flip of the wrist and a proper grip may be assumed.

130

The Cowboy Toss is the quickest of transitions.

Cowboy Toss starting position.

Cowboy Toss in mid-air.

## Practics Malfunction/Reload Method

When I was coming up in law enforcement, we were taught two primary malfunction remedies: the military's Tap, Rack, and Bang, which encompasses tapping the magazine to ensure it is fully seated, racking the slide to clear any auto-loading malfunctions or bad rounds, and pressing the trigger for a "bang" and a second technique that used a rearward-sweeping movement with the forward edge of the support hand for clearing stovepipe jams in a pistol. Later on it became orthodoxy to turn the pistol chamber downward to better ensure that ejected rounds would not drop into the pistol, causing a second malfunction during Tap, Rack, and Bang. For a time we had a mini-drill wherein we pressed the back of the slide to ensure it was fully seated. Then some instructors began to teach students to pull the slide open and rotate the pistol downward as a surer method for clearing stovepipes than using a hand sweep.

All these remedies have value, and all worked well enough, allowing, of course, that no remedy is perfect. The problem for students was that the malfunction drills weren't sufficiently practiced to become an instinctual or muscle-memory response. Stovepipe-sweep training requires some setup to simulate a round sticking up through the slide. Tap, Rack, and Bang requires repetition, and most range sessions are allotted to actual firing time. The result has been that the average police officer or home defender doesn't have sufficient repetitive training to make the traditional malfunction drills a reflexive response.

The Practics cure for the malfunction-drill-training deficit is to abandon the above techniques, replacing all of them with a modified reload. Every shooter practices reloading during each range session. Even without specific reloading, which is necessary to avoid wasted movement, shooters will develop instinctual reloading skills due to a steady stream of normal reloads during a career of shooting. Purposeful training and practice will expedite and improve reloading skill. The student who has successfully developed effective, instinctual malfunction-clearing skills through means other than the Practics method ought to stay with what has already been acquired. But let's be honest—only a small percentage of defenders will train to acquire and maintain those skills to the level of reflexive response. The Practics malfunction remedy is not mandatory in order to use the

Practics system, but it is highly recommended for the overwhelming majority of defenders.

I anticipate some readers may be concerned that each malfunction remedy requires a change of magazine. However, the truth is that no defender is ever likely to use an entire magazine for self-defense, much less three magazines. The magazines are on the Practics gun belt because of the possibility of malfunction, not because 45 rounds are needed for self-defense. Additionally, if there is a fixable malfunction with the handgun, the problem will be in the ammunition or magazine because a broken handgun is a feet-don't-fail-me-now problem that no malfunction remedy will cure. In other words, there is a good chance that you'll need to swap the magazine anyway.

Let's examine the two methods used for bringing the slide to the rear and the reasoning behind the Practics preferred method. The popular technique (Top Rack) is the Practics *alternative method*. It requires the shooter to grasp the rear of the slide from the top with the non-shooting hand. The thumb is toward the shooter. The advantages of this technique are a full hand on the weapon, which provides better grip and requires less hand strength; a slight canting of the muzzle, which assists shooters with shorter fingers or larger pistols in reaching the slide release; and less likelihood of the hand slipping or unintentionally manipulating a de-cocking/safety lever because much of the gripping force is placed farther forward on the slide. The disadvantages are a greater tendency to "ride home" the slide due to the pistol's closer proximity to the shooter and the presence of more fingers on the pistol, which can cause a failure to fire; a dangerous tendency for many shooters to point the pistol to the side during manipulation; and a requirement for compromised grip on the slide or an excessively bent shooting elbow during sighted fire because the support hand is turned inward, reducing the reach of the support arm. Finally, Top Rack does not lend itself to working the slide during an inward rotation of the pistol for the purpose of clearing the chamber. Rotation can be done, but it is extremely awkward.

Top Rack method is useful in confined spaces.

The Top Rack method requires the non-shooting hand to continue rearward to avoid riding the slide forward.

The primary Practics load/reload/clearance technique uses the Modified-Slingshot method for working the slide, which requires the shooter to grasp the rear of the slide between the thumb and middle knuckle of the support-hand index finger (the other fingers provide increased pressure). As the shooter sharply pulls the slide to the rear, the pistol is rotated toward the support side to at least 90°. The rotation has two benefits: Most importantly, the tilt to the support side will ensure that most rounds that fail to feed or fully eject are dropped to the ground rather than back into the weapon, and secondly, the torque motion toward the support arm will assist the shooter in pulling the slide to the rear. The advantages of this technique are a natural downrange pointing of the muzzle, a fast slide pull and release (because this technique requires less hand movement and allows a sharp, fast pull from the shoulder instead of isolated hand strength), a greater likelihood of a clean slide release as the pulling hand may continue rearward instead of stopping at the release, and allowance of slide manipulation below the sighting, which is less disruptive to sighted fire. The disadvantage of the slingshot is a possibility of pinching the de-cocking/safety lever and thereby unintentionally engaging the safety. The "pinch" has less gripping surface than an overhand technique. Also the movement of the slide must be sharp in order to "break the seal" of slide to frame, which can be difficult for some shooters.

Practics Universal Malfunction Remedy is an enhanced reload.

Rotate the pistol upside down to empty chamber obstructions.

Both Top Rack and Modified Slingshot work well enough, and some of the advantages and disadvantages depend on individual shooters and their pistols. For instance, a Glock shooter has no worries about unintentionally engaging a de-cocking/safety lever, and a shooter with a good hand-to-gun-size ratio has no problem reaching the slide release. Practics shooters must train with both techniques because simple hand or arm injuries may require the defender to use the alternative Top-Rack method. Also Top Rack lends itself better to extremely confined spaces. The Modified Slingshot gives us speed, keeps the muzzle on target, and integrates well with other Practics actions. When we add a change of magazines and proper indexing to the Modified Slingshot, we've got the Practics Universal Malfunction Remedy.

## Practics Universal Malfunction Remedy

1. Move the support hand toward the pouches to retrieve a fresh magazine as the shooting-hand trigger finger indexes and the thumb ejects the stale magazine.
2. Slam the fresh magazine into the pistol with the support hand.
3. Pinch the rear of the slide (Modified-Slingshot method) and crisply yank the slide to the rear in a fluid movement while rotating the handgun more than 90° to the support side. Release the slide at the end of its travel without hesitation or assistance in moving forward. A clean break is mandatory to

prevent another possible malfunction. Return the handgun to its upright position. The muzzle must stay on target during this exercise.

4. Sweep the safety (if your handgun has an external safety) and return the trigger finger to the trigger and press.

Malfunctions may cause the slide to lock open, but even here the Practics method works because it includes a slide pull and release. Some manufacturers recommend shooters not use the slide release lever, preferring instead for the slide to be cycled. Regardless of which pistol you own, the Universal Malfunction Remedy will work for both open and closed slide malfunctions.

## Slide Rack

Life is full of exceptions and so is this book. I wish the Practics Universal Malfunction Remedy could be used for 100% of pistol malfunctions. Unfortunately it can't. Later in the text we will take a look at sub-contact firing, which involves extremely close distances between attacker and defender. During those confrontations both parties will want control of the gun, meaning an attacker will grab the slide of the defender's pistol. The pistol will still fire but the slide may not fully cycle. In such a case the slide must be brought straight to the rear and released. While I have great respect for the Tap-Rack-and-Bang technique, it requires too much time for sub-contact ranges, when a defender may be kicked or punched in the head. The Slide Rack is a simple working of the slide, paying particular attention to not "ride the slide home" with the operating hand. We'll put off slide-rack training until a later chapter, where it will be combined with other skills.

## Revolver Reloads

The revolver shooter has no Practics method per se because the best revolver-malfunction remedy is to press the trigger. The proper use of speed loaders is all Practics requires for a basic revolver reload. Practics recommends that shooters using loaders with twist-type release knobs use two fingers and a thumb to pinch or grasp the speed-loader knob. This method is more secure than a two-finger pinch and gives a faster release due to the thumb being able to roll the knob off the indented space between the tips of the two fingers. Push-button knobs may use the same method, though it is not as critical to the quick and secure operation of those loaders.

The use of half- and full-moon clips is an option for revolvers in traditional "rimless" pistol calibers. These clips are flat metal or plastic springs that hold ammo similar to a speed loader. Unlike speed loaders the clips stay affixed to the brass, making loading a matter of simply dropping the collected rounds in place and closing the cylinder. There are gunsmiths who now machine traditional-caliber revolvers to also use clips. Undeniably, the use of full-moon clips (half-moon clips require twice the handling) is the fastest method for loading a revolver, but it's a close race between clips and speed loaders. The quality of clips has greatly increased since the 1970s, and steel clips are very resilient, but even so, they remain far more susceptible to deformation than speed loaders. Many of the pouches available for full-moon clips are intended for sport shooters and are insufficiently secure or sacrifice the inherent speed advantage for the benefit of security. The pouch must protect the shape of the clip under kicks, falls, and the bodyweight of a defender in the prone position. I am certain the pouch issue and perhaps even durability will be sufficiently addressed by equipment manufacturers as the popularity of full-moon clips increases, but for now speed loaders remain the better, more reliable choice. Further, single-round loading is virtually impossible with a full-moon clip in place. The absence of clips also allows the revolver shooter the important option of tactical reloading, which we will discuss in a later chapter.

Revolver shooters have the world's best malfunction remedy: Six-gunners just press the trigger a second time. If the trigger press fails to fire a round, they press again, only conducting a reload when the revolver's ammunition is exhausted. This is one of the reasons revolvers remain worthy of consideration by anyone considering a handgun as a defensive weapon. Unfortunately, training to develop muscle memory with speed-loader operation requires far more speed loaders than pistol shooters need magazines because, unlike magazines, speed loaders must contain rounds in order to be used for training. This causes a logistical problem for the revolver student with only a couple of loaders. So if you have a revolver, acquire all the speed loaders you can reasonably afford. Yet another difference in teaching revolver and pistol operation is that all modern service pistols have a magazine release button, but some cylinder releases push while others pull. In general, however, modern revolver defensive loading is fairly standardized, though the procedures differ based on right- or left-handed operation.

## Right-Handed Shooting Hand

A. R/H thumb hits the cylinder release as the L/H separates from the grip and comes palm upward under the revolver. The L/H fingers push the cylinder open from the right side, taking control of the open revolver.

B. R/H drops to the speed-loader pouches to retrieve a fresh loader, using the thumb-and-two-finger method, as the L/H turns the revolver muzzle up and the L/H thumb plunges the extractor rod, expelling spent brass.

C. R/H returns with the fresh loader as the L/H releases the extractor rod and turns the revolver muzzle down.

D. While L/H fingertips keep the cylinder in place, the R/H inserts the speed loader and releases the rounds using the thumb and two fingers to turn the knob (or the thumb to push plunger-type loaders). The speed loader, which is positioned over open air, is immediately dropped by the R/H.

E. L/H closes the cylinder using the left side of the palm and thumb. The closure is decisive, not a slam. The R/H retakes the grips, and the L/H follows, completing a proper two-handed grip.

F. Firing may resume.

## Left-Handed Shooting Hand

*The first step requires an awkward movement, but it will prevent the southpaw from having to transfer the revolver hand-to-hand more than one time.*

A. Bring the L/H thumb from the right side of the revolver to operate the cylinder release on the left side of the revolver. Push the cylinder open with the right thumb as the R/H slips under the frame to take control of the open revolver.

B. L/H drops to the speed-loader pouches to retrieve a fresh loader using the thumb-and-two-finger method as the R/H turns the revolver muzzle up and the R/H index finger plunges the extractor rod, expelling spent brass.

C. L/H returns with the fresh loader as the R/H releases the extractor rod and turns the revolver muzzle down.

D. While R/H thumb and middle finger keep the cylinder in place, the L/H inserts the speed loader and releases the rounds using the thumb and two fingers to turn the knob (or the thumb to push plunger-type loaders). The speed loader, which is positioned over open air, is immediately dropped by the L/H.

E. R/H closes the cylinder using the fingertips. The closure is decisive, not a slam. The L/H retakes the grips, and the R/H follows, completing a proper two-handed grip.

F. Firing may resume.

## The Old Marine Corps Speed Loader

The federal government as a whole wastes more money than the GDP of most countries, while the United States Marine Corps will spend a penny and ask for change. Good Marine Corps logistics doctrine requires picking through the army's trash. Nothing gets wasted with Marines, nor does that organization commit itself recklessly to newfangled and unproven equipment—like foot-shaped boots.

In the 1980s the Marine Corps still issued revolvers to some Marines. These ancient six-guns were kept very clean, of course. However the Green Gun Club was not going to be suckered into purchasing revolver speed loaders. Instead they invented a method for speed loading with the bare hand (Marine hands are free), and—God bless them—it actually worked.

Friends, with just a little conscientious training, the following method can enable even a novice to reload a six-shot revolver with loose rounds in three seconds. The premise for this action is that the shooter has loose rounds and needs to conduct a reload after retrieving a few rounds from a pocket.

When grabbing loose rounds from a pocket or bag, it's important not to take too many rounds, which will prevent you from successfully doing the Old Marine Corps Speed Load. Don't bother to actually count rounds either. Time is critical. Only practice will teach you what five to seven rounds feel like. For brevity's sake we'll assume the shooter has the rounds in the shooting hand and the revolver in the support hand:

A. The shooting hand, which is holding the rounds, is held downward, the fingers loosely curled. The thumb tip is pressed against the second pad of the index finger. The thumb is the lid and controls the flow of the rounds; the index finger second pad is the feed ramp.

B. Close the back of the hand by pressing the little finger against the palm. Using a short, quick movement, jerk the shooting forearm up (pivoting at the elbow) and snap it back down over the waiting revolver. During this movement the hand and wrist must be loose, the fingers lightly curled. Open the little finger to allow greater space inside the hand during the downward movement of the forearm. It is imperative that the downward snap ends with the hand at a clear downward angle, as if grasping a railing while walking down steps. The rounds inside the hand will move back as the hand is raised during the upward forearm movement. When the forearm whips the hand forward, the rounds will come back to the front of the hand, heavy ends first, which means that the bullets will be pointed toward the thumb.

C. Using a forward rolling motion with the thumb and a vibrating motion with the curled fingers, feed rounds into the chambers as the support hand rotates the cylinder.

D. Resume normal operations as you would with a speed-loader.

The Marine Corps also used flap holsters for speed drills, but I think we can omit that particular innovation. Truthfully, there is much to recommend the revolver to defenders, simplicity of operation and reliability being near the top of that list. Sport shooting and its influence on high-capacity "practical-shooting" range scenarios killed the revolver, not self-defense failures. If you have a revolver, don't consider yourself under-armed—keep building and perfecting six-gun skills.

USMC Speedloader starting position.

Cartridge length and hand size determine if a shooter can use this method.

## Twelve and Six Firing Positions

So far we've discussed shooting in terms of the Linear-Balance method, which serves as the basic platform for Practics shooting. Later we'll look at free-arm firing that can be done outside of the Linear-Balance platform and is necessary particularly when more than one attacker is assaulting the defender.

While Linear-Balance Shooting can address almost the entire sphere, it cannot facilitate shooting straight up and straight down. Firing straight up dissociates the foot from the hand because the hand cannot stay in line with the foot while aiming at the target. Generally speaking, firing straight up is sighted fire because the gun has to pass the head in order to be brought onto target, and, therefore, point shooting loses any speed advantage over sighted fire. Firing downward also dissociates the hand from the foot and has the added safety challenge of not hitting the feet and legs. Straight-down shots are also likely to be sighted fire because the sights will be in line with eyes as the head is turned toward the target. Here are the two supplemental positions that will complete your Sphere of Responsibility requirements:

**Straight Up**—Think of this position as a Natural-Stance, two-handed shooting position with the shooting arms and face turned upward. This is an easy position from which to fire for short periods. However, balance can be a problem, particularly if the shooter must adjust fire to the side or rear. In order to provide a stronger base, place the support leg slightly to the rear. The toe of the support foot should be past the vertical line of the buttocks. In this position the shooter may walk forward or backward or execute a pivot toward the support side.

Firing upward is a question of balancing against the upward and rearward transfer of weight.

Shooting straight upward requires an easy balance adjustment.

**Straight Down**—The goal here is to get the muzzle far enough down to prevent any chance of shooting oneself. The Practics method for safely getting shots straight down is to assume a wider-than-normal stance with the support foot just beyond the vertical line of the support shoulder. By flexing the support knee inward and bending the shooting knee, the shooter will be able to lower the body and keep the muzzle away from the feet. Aiming the handgun in a two-hand grip between the legs can then be done with the muzzle lower than the support knee and less than one foot above the ground. The shooter may continue the descent into a one-knee kneeling position if a stationary position is needed for a longer period of time.

The downward firing position is about staying between the feet and using the legs instead of the back to preserve a natural firing position.

## Shooter Shuffle

Targets change and move, obstructions occur, and shooters must adjust while firing. The key to successfully moving from front to rear, rear to front, and side to side while firing is to not fall down. Really, that's it. Shooters won't be able to look down while firing and may have to fire in environments with which they are not familiar. The Shooter Shuffle is as good a means of moving as any I have encountered. Based partially on what the Marine Corps used to teach for bayonet training, the Shooter Shuffle is a means of walking blind while minimizing trip hazards. Defenders who need to cover distances in perfect darkness can use this same method. The Shooter Shuffle is done in the following manner:

- The direction of travel determines the lead foot. Moving to the right requires the right foot to step and the left foot to close. When moving sideways, the feet must never cross. Stay within the same step pattern, moving the lead foot and then drawing in the trailing foot. If the shooter is in a Natural Stance and has to move forward or rearward, the support-side foot will be the lead foot and the shooting-side foot will trail. Even when moving forward or rearward, the step pattern must be maintained, as if limping.
- Most obstacles that will trip you are low rather than high. You probably won't tumble over an office chair, but you may fall over a rumpled throw rug. When stepping, lift each foot 8" to 10" off the ground and you'll clear most curbs, ramps, and stairs.
- Keep your body weight on the stationary foot. If you are moving your lead foot, shift your weight to the trailing foot. Then shift your weight back onto the lead foot as the trailing foot steps. By controlling your weight distribution, you will have a better chance to prevent falling. For instance, if you step into a hole with your lead foot and have your weight evenly divided between your feet, you will likely not be able to prevent dropping into the hole. By keeping your weight on the stationary foot, you will be able to feel whether it is safe to commit your body weight onto the area on which you have just stepped. This can be done quickly, but it can't be done without deliberation.

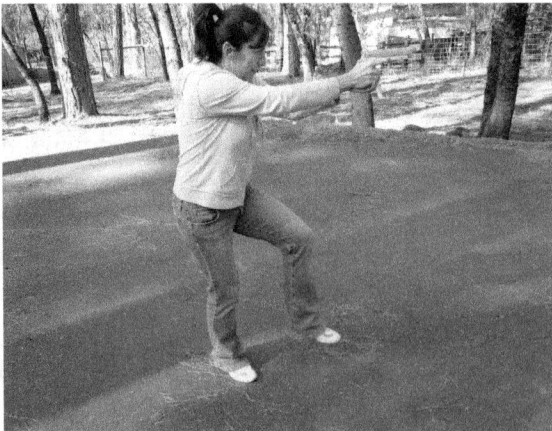

Shooter Shuffle: Keep bodyweight on the rear foot until the lead foot is stable.

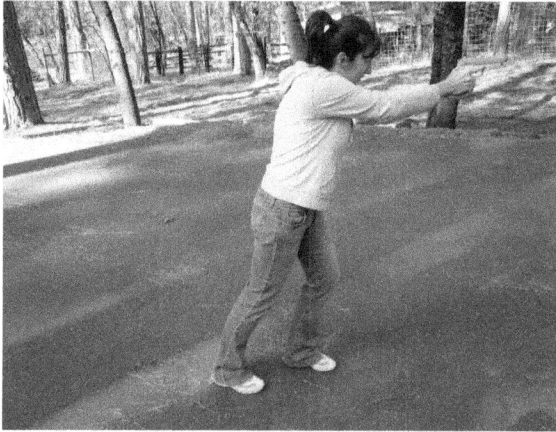

Shooter Shuffle step is completed by dragging the rear foot forward.

## Concealed-Carry Considerations

Everything that applies to unconcealed weapons applies to concealed guns. However, concealing a handgun requires two additional considerations: the appearance of not carrying a gun and the ability to effectively access the hidden firearm and holster. Concealability includes a holster that stays close to the body, but the build of the defender may require some accommodation in the location of the holster. Collapsible concealment holsters are popular, but a defender must be able to holster the handgun without the use of the support hand. If your carry holster closes when emptied, you need a different holster. Those defenders who "blossom" over the sides of their trouser belts may need to wear the holster a bit farther to the front. Likewise, large bellies may require a holster moved farther to the side. Since Practics depends on accessing the gun with either hand, it may be necessary for an extremely overweight defender to use a shoulder holster. Shoulder holsters are not a Practics preference, but they may be the best choice for those whose bodies either roll over the weapon or force it outward to an angle greater than can be concealed by normal clothing or, worse, where the muzzle is pointing toward the leg. If the defender is exceptionally overweight, it may be advisable to carry extra magazines in strapless pouches because they are easier to draw when a jacket is hanging in front and the pouches are turned outward and downward to any appreciable degree. Strapless pouches are not Practics recommended for normal use, but they do increase accessibility for certain body types when wearing a cover garment. One of the biggest problems with concealment is this current Age of the Slob, wherein many men don't possess clothing that properly fits. A blazer that you cannot *properly* button is already too small for use with a concealed handgun. We don't want to button the blazer or zip the jacket, but they have to fit as if they could be buttoned. Standing upright in front of your bathroom mirror is not a sufficient test of your concealability effort. Clothing must conceal the weapon when bending, stretching, sitting, and walking.

## Covering Garments

Practics concealment prefers a belted holster and, therefore, requires a covering jacket or coat. The ideal garment will be no longer than a sport coat or blazer. The garment must fit properly and not be form-fitting. We want the jacket or coat to drape straight down from the armpit. If your jacket is tailored too tightly at the waist, you won't have concealment from a rear angle. The hardest angle to conceal a belted handgun is from a rear view. A full-cut jacket or coat will give you a curtain of material hanging from the muscles of the upper back and chest, which will, hopefully, bypass a holstered handgun at the waist. In other words, no one will know you're carrying a gun. If the length of a coat is too great, the draw can be hindered as the weight of the material hanging below holster level will provide a drag during the coat sweep, which we'll discuss in a minute.

Wearing a buttoned coat or a zipped jacket is the same as wearing a lock on your holster. Unbuttoning or unzipping a jacket, even with the use of the weak hand, significantly delays the draw. However, there are times when a jacket or coat must be closed in order to not draw attention to the wearer. The solution is a garment modification popular with detectives. The button of the blazer is removed and reattached within the buttonhole, giving the impression of a buttoned jacket. On the interior side of the jacket, under the button, a 1" square of Velcro is sewn. Another square of Velcro is sewn onto the original location of the button. Closing the jacket requires a hand movement that will appear very similar to that of a man buttoning his suit coat.

Before we discuss the technique for sweeping the garment

away from the holster, we ought to consider some of the mechanics of dealing with cover garments. Weight and bulk of the covering garment influences both speed and success when drawing. Sport coats are actually better for drawing from than are the shorter, waist-length, windbreaker-type jackets due to the momentum that the skirt of the sport coat provides during the garment-sweep portion of the draw. The following CCW-draw technique requires some momentum in order to get the garment away from the holster. In cases where the garment is slightly longer but made of a very light material, adding a small amount of weight below the level of the holster may be necessary. In such cases, the defender may have a few choices, depending on the fit and design of the jacket. A light linen suit coat can be modified toward a better draw by sewing a *very* small bead of lead to the interior of the bottom edge of the suit coat. In most cases permanently added weight is not necessary, but the remedy is easy enough. On very windy days, or when a larger coat is worn, a few coins or some other object in the holster-side pocket may work well enough, provided the bottom of the pocket is below the bottom of the holster. Added weight in the jacket above the beltline can prevent the skirt of the jacket from moving sufficiently rearward during the sweep. Shorter defenders need to keep the inside breast pockets as empty as possible to prevent limiting the movement of the sweep. Weight too far below the bottom of the holster causes resistance to the sweep, requiring a greater rearward extension of the sweeping arm to get the bottom of the garment moving with sufficient speed. Be judicious when applying extra weight to your cover garment. Remember that concealment is an objective, so don't use any amount of weight that distorts the fit of the garment, drawing unwanted attention.

## The CCW Sweep and Draw

The coat sweep is the single modification that separates the Practics concealed draws from Practics unconcealed draws. In order to execute a proper draw, the covering garment must be removed from over the holster. Fortunately, little additional movement is necessary, and the sweep is incorporated into the draw. There are two methods for sweeping a jacket with the strong hand: One uses the thumb to hook the garment, and the other uses the first three fingers of the strong hand. Practics prefers the three-finger-rake method because three fingers provide a more certain collection of the cover garment and are much less likely to miss the pickup. The advantage of the thumb drag is that it is considered to be a hand position more conducive to drawing at the end of the sweep, but the reality is that it probably doesn't matter in any measurable way. At the end of the sweep with either method, the hand will be in a natural draw position a few inches behind the holstered firearm. Any difference between the two sweeps in terms of speed is more likely a matter of individual performance. Therefore, Practics uses the three-finger rake as opposed to the thumb drag for the benefit of a surer pickup of the jacket. Missing the jacket or coat on the sweep means a missed draw.

The three-finger rake is done by placing the three fingers of the shooting hand at the centerline of the torso, slightly above the navel. If the jacket is closed using the Velcro modification described above, the fingers will contact the shirt immediately above the jacket closure. The three fingers should be placed firmly against the shirt, slightly depressing the flesh. Think of it as a light scratching. In one movement the arm is pulled rearward with the hand following the torso around to the holster. During this movement the three fingers are contacting the torso by the fingernails. Remember to hook the fingers and scratch the shirt with the nails all the way to the rear of the holster. The movement continues until the fingers have passed above the holster and off the body at the imaginary junction of the side and back. Only the thumb will contact the body at the end of the sweep because the hand will turn naturally knuckles downward during the movement, which lends itself to an almost perfect drawing position. The jacket that was gathered by the fingers will continue to fly away from the body, and it is at that moment that the hand rotates down and forward into a proper draw position as the arm lowers the hand to grip the handgun.

Shooter Shuffle step is completed by dragging the rear foot forward.

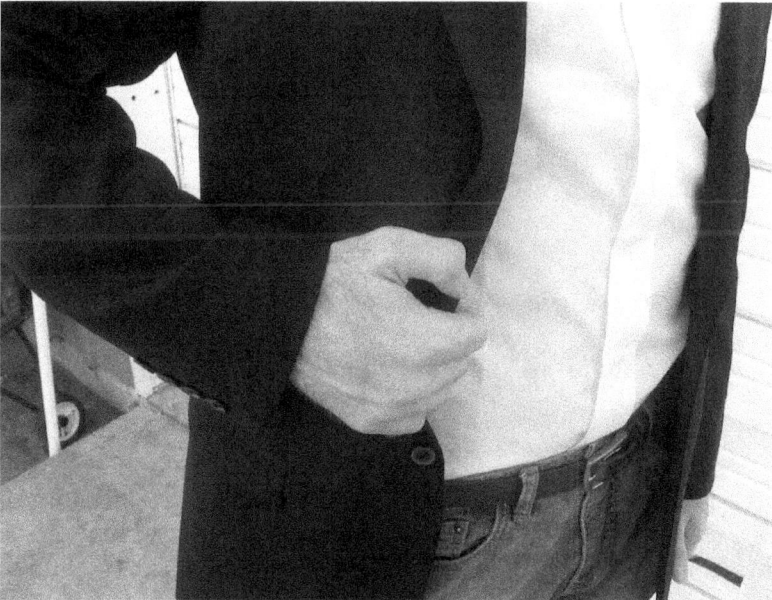

This is a fast, jerking movement.

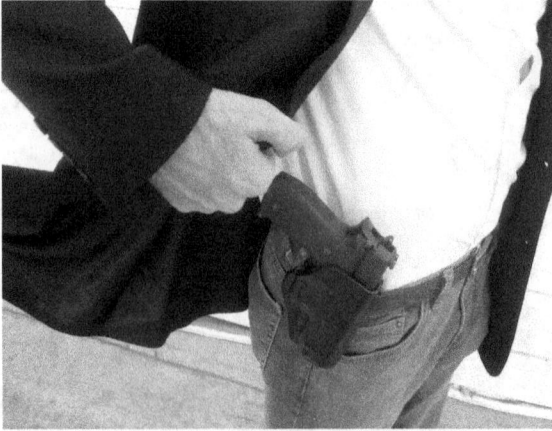

Keep the arm moving rearward until the jacket skirt is past the body.

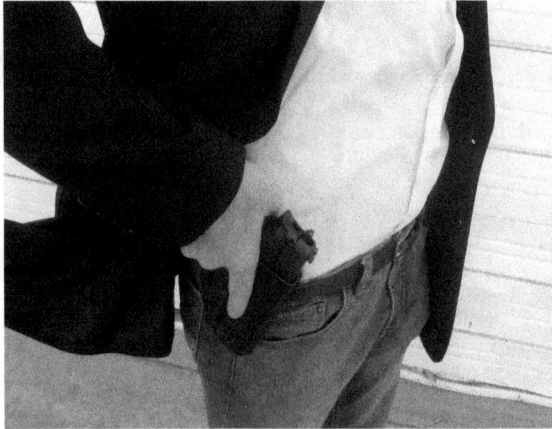

Secure your grip before the jacket returns to cover the holster.

A few things to know about the sweep and draw:

- The three fingers are raking the jacket, not grabbing it. If the jacket is grabbed and released at the end of the sweep, the practical reality will be that the jacket doesn't travel fast enough to offer a clean draw. The entire movement takes a split second, so there's no time to consciously grab and release—just rake.
- A three-finger rake is a violent, forceful movement, intended to throw the jacket to the rear, like a cape in the wind. Force and speed are necessary: force to keep the fingers against the

body, preventing the jacket from sliding away under the fingertips, and enough speed to throw the jacket off the middle of the back.

- During the movement the hand must pass close to the butt of the handgun. If the sweep is too high, the material will not be moved from the handgun. If the sweep is too low, the material will wind up between the hand and the grip. Imagine a line around your middle just above the grip of your handgun—that's the sweep line. In some cases the opening of a particular jacket may require higher contact with the shirt by the three fingers, nearer the bottom of the chest. In that case the sweep will make a slight downward arc. No matter where the sweep begins in terms of height, it must hit the mark just above the holstered pistol butt.

- A missed sweep is remedied by a perfect sweep. Never try to grab the jacket by the fingers and pluck it out of the way. If you fail the first time, scratch harder and higher on the second attempt. If you train for this technique, you will find it very easy to master and utterly reliable, but mistakes happen. Never abandon good technique for a panic-and-pluck attempt.

- The movement from the end of the sweep to the butt of the handgun is equally forceful. While the jacket is flying to the rear, the hand is grabbing the gun and executing a good Practics draw.

- If a magazine pouch is present on the support side (strongly recommended) and an additional magazine is needed, its access will require a mini-sweep, which is done by raking the jacket with the three fingers of the support hand and jerking the elbow slightly to the rear as the wrist is flipped inward. This short, quick motion will throw the jacket clear of the pouches and allow the hand an instant to gain control of them before the jacket swings back. As mentioned, strapless pouches will assist with accessibility for those with large bellies.

## Weak-Hand CCW Draw

Not being able to draw your concealed weapon with the weak hand means being unarmed in some fairly common circumstances.

Having a person grab your strong arm should not prevent you from being able to draw your weapon. The weak-hand concealed-carry draw is very similar to the weak-hand draw normally used in Practics, the differences being the path the hand travels to the gun and the entire technique being done under the jacket—there's no sweep with the weak-hand CCW draw. If the defender has the flexibility for a reverse-hand draw, then the draw is completed under the garment, and the handgun is brought out and onto the target in the normal fashion. In the event the defender lacks sufficient flexibility for a reverse-hand draw, one of the three transitions must be used. In either case the concealed weak-hand draw is very similar to the unconcealed weak-hand draw:

- The weak hand is opened with the fingers fully extended and the thumb along the side of the hand.
- The hand is placed to the weak side of the torso centerline.
- Pressing down slightly with the fingertips, the weak hand slides along the abdomen (under the open jacket) until reaching the holstered firearm.
- Retention straps are disengaged.
- The hand is reversed with the palm outward, grabbing the butt of the handgun and completing the draw; or the handgun is removed form under the jacket and transitioned to a proper grip using the platform, armpit, or cowboy transitions.

## Elemental Skills Training

The following training will provide the student with a solid platform on which to build Practics en motion shooting skills. Elemental skills must be second nature to the Practics defender. The more success the student has in developing these basic skills, the easier it will be to develop advanced Practics techniques.

**1. Foot-Line Drill**—This exercise requires an approximately 4' to 6' long, lightweight pole (e.g., PVC pipe or long broom handle). Hold the pole in your shooting hand and close your eyes. Point the shooting foot in any direction while striking the ground with the pole in front of and immediately in line with the foot. Open your eyes to check your accuracy. Repeat the exercise but always point the foot in a different direction. This drill will give you confidence in your ability to track the line of your foot and, more importantly, develop your ability to read foot placement without looking at your feet. The training partner will ensure that the student strikes the ground decisively and does not attempt to correct by dragging the tip of the pole across the ground.

Foot-line drill confirms that are hands and feet are naturally coordinated.

Skill-Installation Requirement: 20 reps · five sets

Maintenance Requirement: Practics live-fire training will render this drill unnecessary unless the shooter lapses in training, in which case the above installation requirement should be repeated.

I'm sure it is no great surprise at this point that the student must repeat the above with the weak hand and off foot.

2. **Grip-and-Draw Drill**—This is a drawing drill but with two goals: first, to bring the weapon directly onto target in a straight, smooth sweep; second, to acquire a perfect grip—high and centered. A storage-safe weapon will be used, and no ammunition can be present. All safety requirements apply. The training partner will also act as a safety officer, commanding the training area. Facing a silhouette target in the Natural Stance, the student will use the shooting foot to orient the body to aim at the target. Moving at a relaxed pace, the student will properly grip the handgun, disengage all holster straps, and draw the handgun. The muzzle of the handgun will follow the line of the foot up the center of the silhouette. As the handgun moves onto the target, the student will transition to the sights. The challenge will be to stay aware of the foot and the target position and to keep the non-sighted portion of the draw on a straight track

toward the silhouette. The training partner must be watchful for deviations or wild swings as the shooter goes from the holster over the ground. Once the shooter has brought the handgun to the high chest of the silhouette, the movement will stop, and the training partner will examine the grip. Once the grip has been verified, the handgun will be re-holstered with only the shooting hand and without the shooter looking. Repetitions that are incorrectly done disqualify the entire set. The Practics Draw is not difficult but requires attentiveness during training.

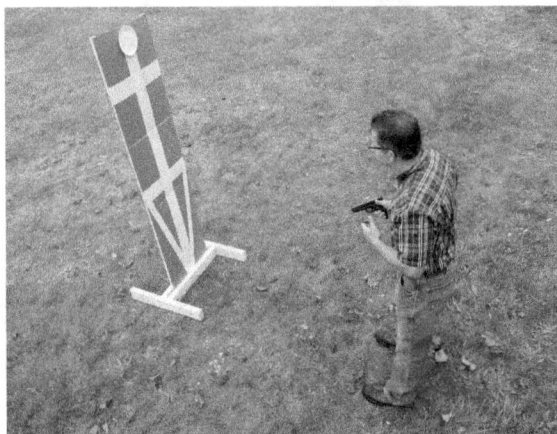

Practics draw on the Charging Man target.

Skill-Installation Requirement: 10 reps · 10 sets (Two-minute breaks may be taken between sets, as needed.)

Maintenance Requirement: five reps · one set weekly for the duration of your shooting career

Repeat the above using a waist-high table on which to rest the handgun. Put the table on the weak-hand side of the shooter, slightly forward of the trouser-seam line. Conduct the above training with the weak hand.

3. **Weak-Hand-to-Target Drills**—Here's an opportunity to practice and develop the skills needed to either draw from the holster with the weak hand or transition the grip after drawing with the weak hand. You will remember from the text that the Reverse-Grip Draw can only be done by those with sufficient flexibility to turn the weak hand completely palm outward during a cross-body draw. The three

transition techniques are for those shooters who cannot execute a Reverse-Grip Draw. This collection of drills is entirely dry fire: Weapons must be storage-safe, and no magazines or ammunition may be present. Training speed should be slow, working toward moderate. Goals include perfect alignment of the thumb and fingers with any holster snaps, an economy of movement during the release of any internal holster-retention devices, and a fumble-free transition. The training partner will watch for wasted or confused movements.

The Reverse-Grip-Draw Drill requires the student to draw the firearm and bring the muzzle to bear downrange using weak-side Linear Balance.

Armpit Transition must be done with precautions for the muzzle to point behind the student. The student will draw and transition with the Armpit Technique and bring the muzzle to bear downrange using weak-side Linear Balance.

Platform-Transition training requires a waist-high table in front of the student. The student draws and uses the table to transition to a shooting grip before bringing the muzzle to bear downrange using weak-side Linear Balance. The student will also execute the Platform Technique using a thigh while in the kneeling position.

Cowboy Toss will require a waist-high table large enough to catch the handgun and a large pillow for cushioning any drop. Draw the handgun and conduct a Cowboy Toss before bringing the handgun to bear downrange using weak-side Linear Balance. The toss comes from wrist movement, and no more force than necessary to right the handgun is needed, allowing the weak hand to re-grip it with a proper shooting grip. This is not a Roy Rogers trick. It's a small, quick movement with the firearm never more than an inch or two from the shooting hand.

Skill-Installation Requirement: Reverse Grip is only to be done by those who can do it safely. 10 reps · 10 sets; Armpit, Platform using a table, Platform using the thigh, and the Cowboy Toss require 10 reps · 10 sets each (Two-minute breaks may be taken between sets.)

Maintenance Requirement: 10 reps · 10 sets each, quarterly for the duration of your shooting career (Two-minute breaks may be taken between sets, as needed.)

Good News! This drill does not require ambidextrous training.

4. **Trigger Reset and Over-Travel Exercise**—Dry fire with a storage-safe weapon, paying particular attention to trigger reset and

over-travel. Over-travel is pressing the trigger farther than is needed to fire the weapon. The handgun will be dry fired while the shooter ensures that the trigger is (a) pressed no farther than is necessary to release the hammer and (b) allowed to go no farther forward than necessary to reset the trigger. The trigger reset can be felt and makes an audible "click." The shooter will know when sufficient press has been applied because the hammer will fall and the forward trigger motion may immediately begin. This drill needs to be done slowly and deliberately. The training partner will ensure the pace is controlled and trigger travel is constant and smooth. Pausing, milking, or varying speed is not permitted and disqualifies the entire set.

Skill-Installation Requirement: five reps · 20 sets (A 30-second break is permitted between sets.)

Maintenance Requirement: five reps · one set weekly for the duration of your shooting career

5. **Practics Universal Malfunction Clearance**—The Practics malfunction remedy is also the Practics reload. The built-in training advantage to this system is that each time the shooter conducts a reload, he is practicing a malfunction drill. This drill will need the active participation of the training partner and is one of the drills in which speed is deliberately increased. Use of several practice magazines is recommended for this training. All magazines must be empty, and no ammunition may be present. The student will stand on the firing line with a holstered, storage-safe weapon. The training partner will stand to the support side holding a small cardboard box. The student will draw the handgun and bring it to bear on a target before firing a dry-fire round. At the instant the hammer falls, the shooter will assume a malfunction has occurred and will execute the Practics remedy:

A. Move the support hand toward the pouches to retrieve a fresh magazine as the shooting-hand trigger finger indexes and the thumb ejects the stale magazine.
B. Slam the fresh magazine into the pistol with the support hand.
C. Pinch the rear of the slide (Modified-Slingshot method) and crisply yank the slide to the rear in a fluid movement while rotating the handgun more than 90° to the support side. Release the slide at the end of its travel without hesitation or assistance in moving forward. A clean break is mandatory to prevent another possible malfunction. Return the handgun to

its upright position. The muzzle must stay on target during this exercise.

D.  Sweep the safety (if your handgun has an external safety) and return the trigger finger to the trigger and press.

The training partner will hold the box just below waist height in front of the shooter. When magazines land in the box, the training partner will quickly grab one or two and hold them against the magazine pouches. (There will not be enough time to refill the pouches.) The magazines must be held downward and pointed toward the shooter, exactly as they would be in the pouches. This will provide the shooter with an endless stream of magazines, which will allow training to continue uninterrupted. Every trigger press will begin a new reload. Begin each set slowly and work up to your maximum speed. Slow down only when a mistake is made. A single error disqualifies the entire set.

Skill-Installation Requirement: 20 reps · five sets (Up to a five-minute break may be taken between sets.)

Maintenance Requirement: Monthly live-fire training involving at least 20 magazine changes is a sufficient minimum to maintain proficiency. Otherwise repeat the above quarterly.

Conduct the above training for the weak hand by starting with the pistol in the weak hand but require the magazines to come from the pouch side—don't switch them to accommodate the support hand. If you can't do it with the other hand, you're taking an unnecessary risk.

6. **Top-Rack Drill**—Shooters must be able to use the Top-Rack method for clearance and reloading in confined spaces or when experiencing injuries that preclude using the Practics Universal Malfunction Clearance. The training partner will hold the box and provide fresh magazines at the pouches, as done in the previous drill. The shooter will follow the previous pattern for speed. The Top-Rack clearance/reload has the same requirement to keep the muzzle pointed downrange. The pistol will have to be brought closer to the body in order for the support hand to reach the slide. The Top-Rack sequence is as follows:

A.  Move the support hand toward the pouches to retrieve a fresh magazine as the shooting-hand trigger finger indexes and the thumb ejects the stale magazine.

B.  Slam the fresh magazine into the pistol with the support hand.

C. Bend the shooting arm slightly, bringing the pistol closer to the body. Use the support hand to grab the slide from the top, thumb side toward the rear of the pistol, and vigorously pull the slide to the rear in a fluid movement while rotating the handgun *more* than 90° to the support side. The rotation movement may require the shooter to lift the shooting elbow. Release the slide at the end of its travel without hesitation or assistance in moving forward. A clean break is mandatory to prevent another possible malfunction. Return the handgun to its upright position. The muzzle must stay on target during this exercise.

D. Sweep the safety (if your handgun has an external safety) and return the trigger finger to the trigger and press.

<u>Skill-Installation Requirement</u>: 20 reps · five sets (Up to a three-minute break may be taken between sets.)

<u>Maintenance Requirement</u>: Monthly live-fire training involving at least 20 magazine changes is a sufficient minimum to maintain proficiency. Otherwise repeat the above quarterly.

Repeat the above training for the weak hand.

7. **Speed-Loader Drill**—A good revolver shooter can fire and reload more quickly than an average pistol shooter, but training makes the difference. Even between two good shooters, the revolver is not far behind the pistol. The difficulty with speed-loader training is that the loaders must be loaded with ammunition or at least inert training ammo. If you have access to several speed loaders, a good stock of ammo, and a second training partner to refill the dropped loaders, you're in business. If not, try the following homemade training device.

A two-square-foot piece of Styrofoam no thicker than 2" is required. Use a sharp knife to cut Styrofoam circles the size of a speed loader. Cut as many as possible because the rings typically won't last beyond a couple uses. Make six small holes around the edge of the circle that match the position of rounds in a speed loader. The holes need not be cut to the full diameter of a round; they'll squeeze in. Take six rounds and insert them bullet first into the Styrofoam circles. The rounds should be slightly tilted outward. These devices are your speed-loader loaders. They will greatly aid the training partner in refilling your speed loaders fast enough to prevent a break in your drill. The training partner will hold the foam-loader primers up, pressing the rounds inward with the fingers as needed while lowering the rounds into the speed loader. When the training partner locks the speed loader, the Styrofoam ring is pulled away and a practice speed loader is ready for training. The foam loaders will let you get by with what you have while not requiring you to slow down for the training partner. Assuming the student has two speed loaders, 18 foam loaders will be needed for one full set of 120 rounds or inert training rounds.

The drill requires the student to stand on the firing line (inert training rounds will allow greater location flexibility) with the training partner on the speed-loader pouch side. *This is a non-firing drill.* The training partner will place a cardboard box on the ground in front of the student. Loaded foam rings are placed on a table or mat beside the training partner.

Beginning with an empty revolver in hand, the student will conduct a reload as previously described, first using the centermost speed loader in the pouches. When the speed loader is discarded, the training partner will retrieve the loader from the box by pulling the box off to the side of the student. The training partner never steps in front of the student or crosses the firing line. The training partner refills the speed loader with a foam ring and presses it into the outside of the pouch (it is unlikely that he will have time to replace the loader into the pouch). The process continues until the foam loaders are exhausted. The student should begin slowly and increase speed during the set. Speed may not exceed the tempo at which a mistake occurs. In other words, any error disqualifies the entire set. The training partner will be occupied with loading the speed loader but will be able to verify whether the shooter fumbles for the speed loaders. The student will be responsible to determine whether the rounds were properly loaded into the revolver. Both student and training partner must pay attention to ensure that the speed loaders are taken in order: center pouch and then outside pouch.

Skill-Installation Requirement: 20 reps · five sets (Resupply the foam ammo rings as quickly as possible for the next set.)

Maintenance Requirement: Monthly live-fire training involving at least 20 speed-loader feeds is a sufficient minimum to maintain proficiency. Otherwise repeat the above quarterly.

Use the weak hand as the shooting hand and keep the pouches in their normal position on the belt to execute a complete weak-hand training of the above drill.

**8. Old Marine Corps Speed-Loader Drill**—This non-firing

drill is a simple repetition of the technique as described in the text. The student will stand on a firing line with an empty revolver in the support hand (cylinder open) and a pocket full of ammunition. The student will quickly grab an estimated six rounds from the pocket and execute the Old Marine Corps Speed Load. The training partner will stand as a safety officer but will also ensure the student does not waste time counting rounds in the pocket. The student must develop a *feel* for six rounds, not count them. After the cylinder has been loaded, empty the rounds and replace them in the pocket. Repeat.

The more violent the shaking motion and the more space the hand allows the rounds to move about, the more successful the results of this technique will be. Students with certain calibers will not be able to do this technique as well. For instance, a small hand and six .45 Colt cartridges are not likely to produce the desired results. Generally, mid-size hands with .38 specials will have no problem mastering this technique. Many shooters will find .357 magnum cartridges quite manageable.

Skill-Installation Requirement: 20 reps · five sets (Two-minute breaks between sets is permissible.)

Maintenance Requirement: 10 reps · five sets twice a year for five years

Repeat the above with the weak hand, but you may also use the weak-side pocket.

9. **Pivot Exercise**—The student will hold a toy gun or other object that reasonably simulates a firearm. Using the 12-hour clock for the student, the training partner will quickly walk to a destination between nine o'clock and three o'clock, stop, and give a command to pivot. (The clock shifts with each pivot, so the student is always beginning at 12 o'clock.) The student will pivot to an aiming position on the training partner. While pivoting, the student must index but keep the weapon pointed at a high-ready position.

The training partner will determine whether the student has pivoted to the proper angle (the muzzle of the toy gun should point directly at the training partner) and whether the student is squarely facing the training partner at the end of the pivot. After each pivot the training partner will move to a new location. The pace is brisk, but it is not a sweat-and-pant exercise. The purpose is to train the student in smoothly and accurately pivoting toward a target.

Skill-Installation Requirement: 10 reps · 10 sets (Take a five-minute break between sets.)

Maintenance Requirement: 10 reps · one set monthly for six months

10. **Reversal**—The student will hold a toy gun or other similar object as if it were a handgun. While the student is facing forward, the training partner will select a position on the back plane between three o'clock and nine o'clock. On a command that identifies the training partner's location ("seven o'clock"), the student will reverse direction to that location. This drill is difficult, but it will teach students how to aim a reversal and how to adjust during a reversal movement. Remember to index and keep the toy gun at high ready. The training partner will determine whether the student is accurate, quick, and stable throughout the movement.

Skill-Installation Requirement: 10 reps · 10 sets (Take a five-minute break between sets.)

Maintenance Requirement: 10 reps · one set monthly for six months

11. **Shooter-Shuffle Exercise**—No firearms or gun simulators are necessary for this exercise. The purpose of this drill is to teach the student how to high step and maneuver body weight. A smooth, flat, open space is needed for a training area; pick an area with no trip hazards. Safe obstacles can be had with a bag of balloons from the local dollar store or 8" wads of crumpled newspaper. The training partner will scatter the objects around the training area, placing enough objects for the student to encounter one obstacle every two or three steps. The student will stand blindfolded in the center of the training area. The training partner will give the commands "shuffle forward," "shuffle rearward," "shuffle left," or "shuffle right." The training partner is responsible to determine whether the student properly shifted weight prior to taking a new step. The student's steps should be high enough not to bump the obstacles. When dropping a foot on an obstacle, the student must sense the obstacle and step back, awaiting a new command. The training pace is slow.

Skill-Installation Requirement: 10 minutes · two sets

Maintenance Requirement: Repeat the above requirement quarterly.

12. **Six-and-Twelve Dry Fire**—This drill requires a storage-safe weapon and the absolute absence of any ammunition. Treat this drill as you would any dry-fire exercise. Make two dry-fire targets by

using a marker to draw one cross on each of two plain sheets of paper. Place the target on the ground, ensuring it is taut and secure. The ground target, or the Six position, must be positioned between the student's feet during the drill. For the Twelve position, place another target above the student on a low ceiling (safety requires that there be no living space above the training area) and make certain that it is taut and secure. Review the Six and Twelve positions before attempting this drill.

The student will begin with the storage-safe weapon drawn and held at a low-ready position. It is the training partner's primary responsibility to ensure that proper indexing and muzzle control are maintained throughout the exercise. On the training partner's "start" command, the student will assume the six o'clock position and execute five perfect dry-fire trigger presses at the ground target. If the student is unable to obtain perfect dry-fire shots, he will conduct normal standing dry fire before reattempting this drill. After the ground-target trigger presses have been completed, the student will assume the 12 o'clock position and execute five perfect dry-fire trigger presses. Again, they must be perfect, and normal dry fire should be used if the student is unable to successfully dry fire from the 12 o'clock position.

Skill-Installation Requirement: 5 dry fires · 10 sets of each position

Maintenance Requirement: 5 dry fires · five sets (monthly). Due to the limited opportunity for students to live fire from these positions, dry-fire maintenance is critical to skill retention.

13. **Quadrant Live-Fire Drill**—The purpose of this live-fire drill is to train the student to master the shooting hemisphere in the Sphere of Responsibility (which, I confess, sounds like something from a Monty Python movie) through Linear-Balance Shooting adjusted by pivots.

The best method for learning quadrant firing is to have a tri-fold target platform: a target background with a flat center and right and left wings set to about a 40° angle, wrapping toward the shooter, and on which targets may be affixed. Manage the largest target area you can safely use. If necessary, a larger, flat target backing can be used if your range prohibits three-dimensional target backs. One method of compensating for a large, flat target area is to have the shooter closer to the target, which will force pivots and generally meet the training goals of this exercise.

The quadrants together represent half a sphere that covers the space in front of and to the sides of the shooter. The more three-dimensional you can make the target backing, the better the training. Bear in mind you will be firing at inclining and declining angles, so know your backstop. The target must be divided into four sections: low left, high left, low right, and high right. Use your belly-button height as a divider between low and high. Divide the target in the center to distinguish between left and right. In other words, you're going to draw a giant cross to divide up the available target backing area. Distance between the shooter and the target area will vary depending on the size of the target area, but it will fall somewhere between three and seven yards. Inexpensive target-backing surface can be made from any cloth or paper. Tape sheets of old newspaper together or use some old bedsheets that are headed for the trash bin. The frames can be made of four long, light wood posts (nothing that can deflect bullets). Thin gardener's stakes will work great. You can avoid horizontal braces if there's no wind and the target backing is sufficiently tight against the vertical poles. The entire tri-fold can be made out of three sheets of plywood but is quite a bit more expensive and limits you to an 8' height, requiring the shooter to be closer to the targets to experience sufficient angles of fire. Make a dozen 6" disks out of cardboard. Paint the disks in three different colors. Use a felt-tip marker to draw a cross on each disk. The training partner will tape or pin three disks to each quadrant and will position the disks without pattern and with the intention of forcing the student to shoot at targets throughout each quadrant.

The training partner will be positioned behind the student shooter and will act as a safety officer, ensuring fire never exceeds the target area and safe handling is observed at all times. Using commands such as "high-left green" or "low-right red," the training partner will task the shooter with a target. Varied commands will continue at a brisk pace. Students can be challenged with more dramatic pivots by lessening the distance to the targets. However, the priority of this drill is perfect execution of technique, not speed. The training partner will keep the shooter moving but will not push the shooter beyond good Linear-Balance technique. Twenty rounds complete one exercise.

On the training partner's command, the shooter will pivot toward the target. The shooting foot sets the line to the center of the target and more than half the body weight must be shifted onto the shooting foot for unsighted fire and relaxed back to 50/50 for sighted fire. The shifting movement is subtle and will become second nature to the well-practiced student. Refresh your knowledge of Linear-Balance Shooting before beginning this drill. All low-quadrant shots are to be unsighted, and all high-quadrant shots are to be sighted. This drill will assist you with point shooting, marksmanship, and transitioning between the two.

The Quadrant

Defenders must be able to control the entire Sphere of Responsibility without having to setup elaborate positions. Train for fluidity.

Skill-Installation Requirement: 20 rounds · two exercises (all shots sighted), 20 rounds · two exercises (high quadrants sighted, low quadrants unsighted), 20 rounds · two exercises (all shots unsighted)

Maintenance Requirement: Conduct the above requirement quarterly for two years.

Repeat the above training with the weak hand.

14. **Chasing-the-Line Live-Fire Drill**—This core element of Practics training is a great range drill, though it will require an outdoor range that will allow firing at targets on the ground. As you develop en motion firing skill, this training will become increasingly relevant. The preparation for this drill is simple but will require a large roll of 4" wide tape (i.e., caution tape, duct tape). Set up a silhouette target on a non-deflective target stand in front of a five- to seven-yard firing position. This distance can be increased as the student becomes more proficient. Run the tape in a straight line from two yards in front of the position of the shooting foot, along the ground to the base of the target, and up the target to the top of the silhouette's chest. The effect will be a long horizontal trail of tape rising at a 90° angle up the

silhouette—a direct path from shooter to target. Make certain that nothing is present on the ground or just below the surface that could cause ricocheting.

The scenario that this drill represents is a charging attacker that requires point shooting in self-defense. In other words, there is no time to raise the handgun to eye level. However, our training target doesn't actually move, and that requires us to train on the path of the bullet rather than on the static target. Such emphasis has the training benefit of teaching an unsighted but accurate path of fire that can be used at much greater distances than skill acquired during flat-target shooting. Once the Chasing-the-Line skill is achieved, the shooter will be able to point shoot out to mid-range distances. The line of tape serves as a continuous aiming point for the shooter, representing low to high fire. Unlike typical high-to-low "shoot to completion" drills, Chasing-the-Line teaches firing from the draw upward because that is how we encounter surprise attacks, before the handgun is drawn. Nearest the student shooter, hits to the tape will translate into lower leg shots on the attacker. As the tape moves away from the shooter, the muzzle must rise to follow, as if the shooter is raising the muzzle toward the attacker's torso. Don't worry about the silhouette. In fact, the only reason we use a silhouette at all is to prevent having to use a much longer line of tape. Of foremost interest to the Practics shooter is the accurate upward movement of the muzzle. This drill will teach you to draw and accurately fire unsighted shots from the knees to the chest on a close-range, high-speed attacker. Speed will come with safe, deliberate training. The firing pace is steady, not rushed, about a round per second. Your success will depend entirely on your self-discipline and dedication to proper technique. Never let the pace outrun safety or proper technique. It is essential that the student practice trigger-reset and over-travel control. Everything from holster to en motion firing is trained and tested during Chasing-the-Line.

On command from the training partner, who is acting as safety officer, the shooter will draw and enter a strict and proper Linear-Balance stance. As the shooter raises the handgun from the holster, he will begin firing at the ground end of the line of tape (no closer than two yards away), about one round every 3', closing to one round every foot on the silhouette. Firing stops after the tape ending at the silhouette's chest has been shot. The shooter must not look at the handgun during firing. Visual focus is on the target. Students will be aware of the line in peripheral vision, but sight must never be the means of aiming. Reliance on vision will prevent the student from using true Linear-Balance technique, making longer-distance point shooting impossible. Linear Balance is your unsighted method for accuracy—use it. A successful execution of this drill will have hits at the proper intervals and no farther than 2" from either side of the tape. As skill increases, the shooter may fire more shots at shorter intervals.

Skill-Installation Requirement: 20 successful runs through the above drill

Maintenance Requirement: at least monthly for as long as you keep a defensive handgun

The above drill is only concluded when the shooter has successfully completed it with the weak hand.

Elemental skills are the platform for en motion and special-circumstance firing, but, more than that, foundational defense skills are the bread and butter of your personal defense. You are always right to build and maintain your fundamental defensive-handgun skills. Basics are not amateurish; they're essential.

Chasing the Line: The white tape replicates a "low to high" line of fire.

15. **CCW-Draw Drill**—This is another drawing drill that requires a storage-safe weapon. The draw is executed the same as the normal Practics draw with the exception of the garment sweep. Body orientation and completion at the sighted position is exactly the same as the unconcealed draw. Due to the obstruction of the garment, the execution of this drill must be done quicker than the standard draw

training. Remember, no ammunition can be present, and all safety requirements apply. The training partner acts as safety officer. Any draw must start with a proper grip, but it is particularly important that the student ensure perfect grip because, as the garment swings back, a fumbled grip may require a second sweep. A cover garment is required for this training and should reflect the type of outer garment that the defender is actually likely to use. If you live in Minnesota, training with only a thin windbreaker is not realistic. The garment must not be buttoned but should be secured if the Velcro modification has been done. On the command to draw the student will do the following:

Begin with the hands hanging at the sides in a normal manner. Hook the jacket with the first three fingers of the shooting hand and make a forceful rearward motion along the body, ending at the rear of the torso with the thumb touching the body and the three fingers pointing toward the rear. At the instant the hand has reached the end point of the rearward motion, it immediately moves to the grip and begins the draw. Speed, force of movement, and an abrupt change of direction will put the garment to flight behind the student. Tentative movements will make this technique impossible to execute. The goal is an action much like throwing a bucket of water—the bucket stops and the water keeps going.

Skill-Installation Requirement: 10 reps · 10 sets (Two-minute breaks may be taken between sets, as needed.)

Maintenance Requirement: five reps · one set weekly for the duration of your shooting career

16. **Magazine-Pouch Sweep**—Here's a supplemental drill for those who carry magazine pouches or speed loaders with their concealed handguns. Again, we'll use a storage-safe weapon and ensure the absence of ammunition from the immediate training area. The student will hold the handgun at high ready in the strong hand. On the start command the weak hand will hook and sweep the garment from the magazine pouches. The pouch sweep does not require the breadth of sweep used for the holster. The movement is largely a function of the wrist. The garment is flipped back, and the hand moves to the pouch. Flip the retention strap up with the middle finger or index finger (or both), bring the hand under the strap, and grab the magazine. Conduct a normal reload. Once the magazine has been inserted, continue with a second sweep to collect the outside magazine. It is

important for the student to be able to access both pouches and to be assured that the sweep is sufficient to clear the garment for access to the outside pouch. Therefore, the drill requires two magazine reloads for each execution.

Skill-Installation Requirement: 10 reps · 10 sets (Two-minute breaks may be taken between sets, as needed.)

Maintenance Requirement: five reps · one set weekly for the duration of your shooting career

17. **Weak-Hand CCW-Draw Drill**—This drill requires a storage-safe weapon and the absence of ammunition. The weak-hand CCW draw is a duplication of the regular weak-hand draw except that the CCW technique requires the weak hand to slide under the garment by following the surface of the body to the holster. The CCW draw is done under the garment in exactly the same way as the normal weak-hand draw is done without the cover garment. The weak hand requires some inward pressure to ensure that the fingers will not become entangled in the hanging garment. The defender can increase access by leaning slightly forward and causing the garment to drop away from the body. Nonetheless, leaning forward may not always be possible, making good finger contact with the torso a necessity. This exercise will end when the handgun is properly gripped in the weak hand and pointed downrange. The student may use a reverse grip or a transition technique.

Skill-Installation Requirement: 10 reps · 10 sets (Two-minute breaks may be taken between sets, as needed.)

Maintenance Requirement: five reps · one set weekly for the duration of your shooting career

# PRACTICS 102: Motion and Fire

# Chapter Six: En Motion and Movement

*In skating over thin ice our safety is in our speed.*

Ralph Waldo Emerson

*The greater the difficulty, the more the glory in surmounting it.*

Epicurus

*Quick as lightning Wild Bill pulled his revolver. The stranger fell dead, shot through the brain.*

Buffalo Bill

Fights involve motion. One of the most disappointing things about boxing is the other fellow never seems to want to stand still for it. Most punches and kicks miss their intended targets. It is the same for many deadly force incidents. Bullets don't require swinging or throwing, but, like fist-fighters, many armed close-range combatants move quickly to avoid an opponent's fire. Close-range deadly force incidents in which both sides are armed tend to involve a bit of footwork. Men fighting over a gun are likely to cover the distance of a few steps, and enough recorded evidence cautions against expectations of a perfectly static gunfight.

The truth is handguns are only used about half the time in armed attacks. A few chapters ago we examined the use of deadly force. One of the challenges that defenders face is making deadly force decisions when attackers use weapons other than firearms. Practics students know the weapon is not the factor in determining the need for deadly force, but the type of weapon is significant when evaluating threats. If an attacker points a firearm at you, the odds are you'll have little doubt of how to respond to that particular threat. The greater difficulty occurs when it's a fire poker or flowerpot. A handgun at five yards or 100 yards prompts the exact same urgency. That's not true with a non-missile-firing weapon. Weapons other than firearms make time and space much more relevant to the defender.

One of the first rude awakenings for a young peace officer is the realization that not everybody cares if you point a gun at them. I was told more times than I can recall, "Go ahead, shoot me," or "You can't shoot me; I don't have a gun." No one knows as well as experienced criminals that American cops aren't likely to commit murder. On the other hand, hoodlums aren't so sure about private citizens. Nonetheless, armed defenders should expect to be challenged by unarmed or non-firearm-carrying attackers. A defender has to have a plan when the presentation of a firearm fails to gain cooperation. The presence of your firearm may not gain compliance, but it may allow you to hold your ground or safely retreat. Remember the Practics Gold Standard and have an exit strategy.

While considering how movement affects close-range fighting, let's take a moment to see what weapons a defender is likely to encounter.

Following is a list of DOJ/FBI national murder statistics by weapon for 2011 (from their Web site):

- 12,664 total murders
- 8,583 firearms
- 6,220 handguns
- 1,694 cutting implements
- 1,684 unknown guns
- 726 hands and feet
- 496 blunt objects
- 356 shotguns
- 323 rifles
- 75 fires
- 12 explosives
- five poisons

What do the above facts tell us? About half of all murders are committed with handguns. The other half is not. Statistically speaking, you can forget about rifles and shotguns. Murderous attacks are far more likely to come in the form of punches, kicks, blunt objects, and bladed weapons than they are from rifles or shotguns. You must be prepared for a long-range attack but are much more likely to encounter a close-range assault. Bear in mind the above stats focus on murder only. Most violent attacks don't leave the victim dead, making the overall number of potential deadly force cases significantly greater than the number of actual deaths by criminal acts. Favored weapons, such as bladed or blunt objects, require substantial physical movement. It is a fair assumption that most deadly force attacks will be close and quick moving. The defender must be prepared to shoot as fast as deadly force targets can be recognized.

## Distance for Danger

The broadly accepted law enforcement minimum standard for the distance at which an officer can draw and shoot a knife-wielding attacker before being stabbed is 21'. That standard is, in my opinion, dangerously off the mark. Trying to draw and fire as a man runs 21' toward you is impossible for most shooters. Bear in mind that a stab or slash can occur at arm's length, and the 21' becomes 19'. Beyond the problem of distance is momentum. The knife-wielding attacker doesn't lose mass or inertia the instant he is shot. Some may drop immediately, but not all. The 21' rule is in reality a 5' rule—don't count on it.

You can test your ability to draw and fire at charging targets with this great drill, which will let you know your draw-and-fire limits.

**Charging-Attacker Live-Fire Exercise**
You will need an outdoor range with an agreeable range master. The shooter stands on the firing line with a holstered weapon. A fit, unarmed person (the runner) stands back to back with the shooter. On a whistle from a third party (training partner), the runner sprints up-range (away from the shooter and target) as the shooter quickly draws and fires one round. When the runner hears the report of the round fired, he stops and stands in place. The shooter makes safe and re-holsters his weapon. The distance between the runner and the shooter is the distance that the runner covered before the shooter was able to fire a single round. In other words, that distance is how far an attacker could have run toward a defender in the time the defender took to fire.

To make this exercise more realistic, require the shooter to score a debilitating hit on a silhouette target before stopping the runner. The training partner blows the whistle a second time to signal the runner to stop.

Do the above drill often, and you will learn several things. Most importantly, fumbles and missteps happen. Bear in mind that in the exercise the shooter is expecting the attack. No time is spent on even a split-second of evaluation or surprise. Certainly, training can get the blood pumping, but that is hardly the same as the fear felt during a physical attack. My point is that the above exercise gives you an idea of what your *best* response might be, rather than a realistic measure of your actual response. During a training I presented for a sheriff's department, we performed the Charging-Attacker exercise using one of the department's lieutenants as the shooter. The lieutenant carried a revolver in a breakfront holster. When the whistle blew, the runner sprinted away, and the lieutenant grabbed for his gun. His grip was slightly misplaced, which prevented his wrist from pulling the revolver straight forward and out of the holster. The lieutenant had to slide his hand farther along the grip to complete his draw. The fumble confused him and made the entire attempt clumsy and awkward, but he got the weapon out and fired a shot. From whistle-blow to gunshot, the runner covered just over 50 yards. To be fair, that example was extraordinary, but runs *over* 25 yards are not so uncommon. Twenty-one feet is not enough to draw and fire against a charging, deadly weapon-wielding attacker.

When do you draw your handgun?

The instant you clearly spot approaching and unavoidable danger.

## Primary Defensive Target (PDT)

Before we can go further in discussing how to aim, we must consider what we're trying to hit. There are certainly times when defenders will be aiming for whatever portion of the attacker is exposed: hand, foot, leg, or buttocks. Those targets are targets of circumstance, forced on the defender by location, obstacles, or juxtaposition of bodies. Our primary target, however, doesn't change. All things being equal, the defender's target is the upper chest of the attacker. The bullseye of defensive shooting is the area between the shoulders intersecting with the vertical line running down the center of the face and neck. The nervous, circulatory, and respiratory systems and the bones necessary for upper-body mobility are all impacted by hits to this area. While many law enforcement agencies still train rank-and-file for center-mass or torso hits (which tends to translate into aiming for the top of the abdomen), SWAT began training to hit the "upside-down T" in the 1990s. The higher point of aim creates a greater potential for misses over the shoulders and slightly less potential for a miss to either side due to greater target width, but PDT hits are the best we can do aside from direct head shots. The head is too small and too mobile to serve as a primary target. A shot striking the PDT is much more likely to immediately stop a threat than is a shot to the abdomen, mid-torso, or a glancing shot to the head.

## En Motion Vs. Movement

The simple difference between Practics En Motion Firing and what is currently being taught is timing. Today's shooting students are moving their "point" from target to target and running from one barricade to another, but it's typically stop-motion firing. That is, the shooter is always firing at the end of the motion. I certainly have no complaint with that. Firing from a stop or rest position is very often necessary and often preferable. However, high-speed/short-time encounters may not wait for the completion of a movement, and in such cases the defender had better be able to fire while moving his shooting arm. Likewise, firing while walking is a valuable skill, but that is movement firing—not firing the handgun within motion.

Multiple targets, moving targets, and adjusted fire (moving the aim as rounds strike the target) all require the ability of the shooter to shoot under motion. Many shooters consider themselves to have mastered firing en motion, while in reality most shooters are only capable of fast target shooting: point here and fire, point there and fire, and so on. Real speed means never stopping the movement until the shooter has reached the primary target, which, as discussed, is typically the upper chest. Practics En Motion Firing includes shots en route to the primary target; this strategy supplements PDT firing. We want to fire en route to our target destination without stopping: Shoot at the feet, thighs, or abdomen while moving toward the primary target. Multiple targets also present a deadly challenge to the shooter's speed. Any delay or halt in motion for the sake of firing endangers the defender by permitting the non-engaged targets time to attack.

En motion firing doesn't slow down but uses the delivery motion for additional fire.

**Movement**—The shooter runs, jumps, shuffles, walks, etc.

**En Motion**—The firearm discharges while being moved in an aiming arc.

## The Mechanics of En Motion Firing

1. **Fluid, Uninterrupted Motion**—Whether the gun is in the holster or in the hand, whether the muzzle needs to move 6" or 3', movement must be in an even arc, from start to target.
2. **Mastery of Trigger Reset and Trigger Over-Travel**—We see again that fundamental marksmanship skills are eminently practical. Proper trigger control can cut your multiple-shot time by better than half. In other words, you can fire twice as many shots in the same amount of time, but it starts with dry-fire training.
3. **Overpassing**—pressing the trigger as the muzzles travels over circumstantial targets en route to the PDT. The cardinal rule of en motion shooting is to not stop and to never slow down until you've reached your final target. If you slow the arc of movement to fire an extra round, you are, in a sense, changing your primary target. You were headed for the top of the chest but stopped at the legs. Slows and stops are not compromises of adaption; they are sabotage. Speed of delivery is what we hope will prevent injury to the defender. There can be no

slowing or stopping.

A small percentage of defenders will not be able to fire a single en motion round. While their weapons travel to the primary target, these defenders will not possess the muscle reflex speed to fire before arriving at the target. On the other hand, a very tiny percentage of shooters will be able to fire five en motion shots while arcing from foot to chest. The rest of us will be somewhere in the middle, with most of us able to fire one or two en motion shots while headed to a primary target. That's two or three times more shots than are currently being fired.

4. **Visual Target Fixation**—Unlike marksmanship, where fanatical focus must be on the front sight tip, en motion firing requires the shooter to focus on the target at the instant of discharge. Close-range en motion firing is too fast for even hasty-sight picture. If the shooter is using the sights—which would be proper under the right circumstances—he is most likely not shooting en motion.

**En Motion Skills Test**

In the training portion of this chapter you will find exercises that will help you develop the skills needed for en motion firing. Following is a test, which you can use throughout your shooting career, to test your en motion firing ability and skill level. Remember to never slow down for en motion firing.

A. The shooter stands at about the three-yard line in front of a full-size knees-to-head silhouette.

B. The training partner will give the command to fire and begin a stopwatch. The shooter will draw and, using Linear Balance, point shoot one round into the upper chest of the silhouette as quickly as possible.

C. The training partner will note the time it took for the round to be fired.

D. The exercise is repeated, but the shooter will fire one round en motion in addition to the final shot into the upper chest.

E. The training partner will note the time. If the shooter was able to fire an en motion round and a primary target (PDT) round (step D) in the same amount of time that it took for him to fire the single primary round (step B), the shooter has 1:1 en motion ability.

F. The drill continues with the shooter trying two en motion shots. If the shooter is successful, he has 2:1 en motion ability. The drill stops when the shooter cannot fire any more en motion rounds without slowing the upward arc toward the primary target.

Your results will change with training and practice. Don't worry if you can't master en motion firing. En motion shots are extra—your primary goal never changes.

## Practics Punch Firing

Combat-shooting advocates have long complained that marksmanship fails under duress. They say that sighting, grip, trigger control, breathing, and stance go out the window when fear and adrenaline walk in the door, and they have plenty of cases to prove their point. Marksmanship advocates, on the other hand, can draw upon countless encounters where skills were diminished but not eliminated by situational duress. In fact, defenders who were in fear for their lives have made many difficult shots. The potential success of the two schools of shooting depends entirely on the distance and speed of attack. At a few yards, marksmanship tends to work well because there's time for the handgun to be brought to eye level and for the body to follow subconscious habits developed by training. At a few feet, it's point and shoot as quickly as possible. Sadly, those closer ranges are where too many of our trained peace officers are falling. While I know that marksmanship training is essential for anyone who carries a gun for self-defense, it is undeniably true that very fast, very close-range encounters cannot be satisfied by marksmanship skill. For the handgun to become the modern sword, its use must be instinctual and its ability to wound deliverable within motion. Before the point-shooting crowd cheers, I must say that what they have been doing over the last four decades has been neither instinctual nor motion delivered. Nothing has so failed defensive shooters like the crouch-grimace-and-jerk training of the last 40 years. If it worked, we'd certainly know it by now. The failure of both pure marksmanship and traditional point shooting tells us that a more accurate and faster means of delivering fire is necessary.

We've already discussed the inherent problems with triangulation firing, but what about real, honest, spontaneous one-handed point shooting? An officer confronted by a deadly force threat as he steps out of a store or enters a gas station is not atypical in law enforcement. Such encounters preclude proper stance or target orientation. Another common case for cops is to have a deadly force threat from one side and the suspect's screaming mother grabbing the cop's support arm from the other side. These close-distance threats, which are the most deadly for police and private defenders, can't be countered by stance-based techniques, because there is not sufficient time or freedom of movement to pose the body. Do we just swing our arms around and shoot? Apparently we've been doing that for a long time, and it has gotten us killed. Earlier in the book I explained that the biggest problem in marksmanship is overgrip, which torques shots low and to the inside. An old FBI flashlight technique taught agents to hold the flashlight out to the left as the agent lunged to the right and was intended to trick bad guys into shooting at the light instead of the agent. It worked. Bad guys pointed at the flashlight beams as they over gripped their handguns and shot the agents. The technique was abandoned. Pointing our hands toward a target is natural, but our use of a handgun by that method has proven to be awkward. Physiology requires almost all one-handed shooting to bend the wrist in some way. If we have to deliberately cant the wrist for accuracy's sake, then we can't instinctually point with the shooting arm. Reason it out for yourself.

Practics has an answer to the problem of no-stance, one-handed point shooting, which can be mastered by almost any shooter and is naturally and remarkably accurate. We just rotate the forearm 90° and fire with the hand and arm in a punching position. Punch firing is accurate for two reasons:

- Overgrip is managed. When the forearm is rotated and the hand subsequently turned to the side, the wrist no longer naturally turns down and inside due to overgrip. Over gripping when the hand and forearm are rotated 90° causes a straight downward turn. Shots will go low, but they won't wander off to the support side. A punch shot to the chest area may hit the lower abdomen, but it won't miss the torso altogether.
- Wrist is held naturally with a slight cant to the outside, which "straightens" the aiming path from eyes to target. To see this phenomenon, hold your arm out in front of you as if you're throwing an overhand punch. You will notice that your fist is slightly and naturally canted towards the outside. When holding a handgun, this slight outward cant of the fist ensures the muzzle is pointed straight at the target in line with the shooter's sight, provided the punch is aimed toward the target. Bending the wrist when aiming the fist is unnecessary. Point with a punch fist, and you're on target.

Practics Punch Firing is a remarkably easy-to-acquire skill that almost anyone can use quickly and accurately. It is NOT Hollywood, street-corner-hoodlum-wave-the-gun-sideways-with-a-bent-wrist foolishness. Punch Firing is simply using the instinctual human ability to accurately point the fist under duress as a means of aiming a handgun.

Punchfire

## Groucho Walk

The late comic Grouch Marx was not known as a special-operations innovator, and that's too bad because his contribution to SWAT team movements has been of singular importance. Groucho taught us how to move, or at least how to walk with minimal disruption to the head, shoulders, and arms. The next time you see a film of Special Ops or SWAT members moving in a column, pay attention to their singular gait; it was first performed by the old vaudeville comic. Marx performed this wonder of movement in films including *Duck Soup*, *A Night at the Opera,* and the always tactically important *Horse Feathers*. The essence of the walk is to lower the body by bending both knees, keeping the knees bent while extending the gait and stepping with the feet landing flat. Whereas the late Mr. Marx performed his tactical walk with one hand behind his back and the other clutching a cigar, defenders carry the firearm in the sighting or high-ready position. The Groucho walk can be done very quickly, but those with weak knees or atrophied thigh muscles may not be able to fully perform the movement. Any degree of lowering the body on bent or relaxed knees and stepping flat-footed will help the moving defender use the sights while walking.

Groucho Walk cushions the upper body, allowing easy sighting.

## Practics Running Fire

Groucho walking is good for slow movement but does nothing for the poor soul being chased by a big guy with a fire poker. Sometimes defenders must fire when running. I was never trained to fire while running. The thinking was, if you have to go faster than you can Groucho walk, run to cover or stop and fire. At any rate, there has been something of a hole in quick-movement training.

The Practics solution is Running Fire. The shooter runs as fast as the shooter wants to run with no regard to keeping the shoulder carriage steady. Just run. However, a person cannot run very well and fire with two hands. The body needs the arms for balance. The answer is to punch fire. Punch fire will allow the defender to run unhindered while firing to the sides or front. What makes Running Fire a technique is the coordination of footfall and trigger press. (Again, fundamental marksmanship skills are also point-shooting techniques.) The defender points at the target while running but presses the trigger only when the forward stepping foot hits the ground. Trigger press can be done with every step, but the majority of shooters will want to restrict themselves to every other step. A right-handed shooter may find it preferable to coordinate fire based on the left foot striking the ground. Opposite foot and hand are recommended for beginners, but this is a matter of individual preference. Nobody is going to win a bullseye competition with running fire, but at close range this technique is sufficiently accurate for anything bigger than a small dog.

186

Three tricks will assist you with Running Fire:

- Aim high before the step. You must fire the instant the foot hits. This is point shooting; practical accuracy with speed is everything. As the foot strikes the earth, the extended shooting arm will dip a few inches. You may easily compensate for this phenomenon by aiming for the head or neck in order to hit the chest. The choice of head or neck depends on the distance between attacker and defender. At very close range, the dip won't make any appreciable difference. During training, aim a bit high.

- Look where you're running. If you look off to the side, your speed will slow, exposing you to greater danger, and your balance will be greatly diminished. So split the difference. If you're running toward 12 o'clock and your attacker is at three o'clock, turn your head to about one o'clock. You'll have good forward vision and sufficient peripheral vision to accurately punch fire at the attacker.

- When the defender is running directly toward the attacker, the defender will experience the shooting arm moving laterally to the outside on the fall of the shooting foot. Compensate by (a) firing on the fall of the support foot or (b) bringing the aim to the far side of the target. For instance, if a defender has a handgun in the right hand and is running toward an attacker, he can adjust for the lateral error caused by the strike of the right foot by aiming to the left side of the target as opposed to the center of the target. I included two compensating measures because people move differently and one may not work for every defender. Each student must experiment before accepting either technique.

Practics Running Fire requires training and practice that are well within the capability of most students.

Running fire requires an oblique visual focus between target and direction of travel.

This skill is about coordinating the stride with the rise and fall of the arm.

## Terminal Firing and Supplemental Targets

Movement doesn't necessarily stop when an attacker has been successfully hit. According to the Center for Disease Control, over

60% of all gunshot victims survive. In other words, a defender's first hit may not stop the threat. Firing must continue until the threat ceases to exist—not the attacker, the threat. *When deadly force is justified, deadly force continues until the threat is removed.* Defenders need to be mindful of the Gold Standard when considering the circumstances that turn "threat" into "non-threat." Your responsibility doesn't end with the decision to shoot. Changing circumstances require constant evaluation. If the threat is still threatening, fire continues. There is no round count or force measurement beyond what is necessary. Even here, when discussing technique, we go back to the Practics Gold Standard.

We know failure is part and parcel of defense. Not all shots or string of shots will stop a threat. The defender must react to changing circumstance and needs, such as a failure of rounds to stop a threat or target movement. Examples of movement during terminal firing include an armed suspect stumbling backward as he fires his handgun, or a running attacker who speeds up when shot, or a close-range knife attacker who grabs the defender's waist and attempts to move behind him. These examples may each require additional firing. In some cases the point of aim will have to be adjusted. For instance, if shots to the upper chest do not stop a close-range charge, a change is needed. The attacker may be wearing body armor, under the influence of drugs, or insane. Whatever the reason that insulates an attacker from the effects of being shot, the shooter must adjust fire. Let's consider two supplemental targets when hits to the PDT or to circumstantial targets (portions of the attacker that are exposed to defensive shooting) fail.

**Head**—The head and neck are difficult targets to hit even at normal pistol distances because the head tends to move during a fight. During a charge the head and neck move much less. People don't flop their heads from side to side when they run, but the head is often lowered, presenting a smaller target. Hits to the head require accuracy. The head, like the leg or arm, can be harmlessly scraped by fire and have no immediately debilitating effect on the attacker. Shots along the eye line or bridge of the nose, however, are likely to be effective. Law enforcement countersnipers train for the top of the mouth because the medulla oblongata sits at the top of the spinal column and is roughly parallel to the roof of the mouth or bottom of the nose depending on the cant of the head. A hit to the medulla oblongata will shut down all movement and prevent sympathetic muscle reactions that could jerk a trigger. I realize some readers may think I'm splitting hairs by discussing targets within the head, but a remarkable number of people who have been shot in the head were able to continue functioning. Plenty of bullets have skipped around skulls despite the rounds having sufficient energy to smash flat bone. Headshots may be the best and final option of a defender and are worthy of dedicated training.

**Pelvis**— Hits to the pelvic girdle are exceptionally likely to stop a threat. It is hard to stand on a leg partially detached from your skeleton. The firearm-equipped attacker may resume the attack from the ground, but bullet strikes to the pelvis will most likely drop the attacker. This is not a "less-lethal" target. Arterial bleeding is a strong possibility since arteries run along major bones. While pelvic damage is unlikely to disrupt the nervous system, it is likely to stop or confuse fine motor skills. The pelvis can be located by imagining a horizontal line between the hips. The pelvic targets are the areas to the inside of both of the attacker's hips. Not the waist or beltline—the hips. Hits to either end of the pelvis will likely stop most charging attackers.

## Warning Shots

Today most progressive law enforcement agencies strictly prohibit the use of warning shots due to liability concerns. A round fired up must come down somewhere. In the past, most warning shots were fired under duress into open air without much regard for where they would strike. Sometimes they were fired prematurely or inappropriately when the deadly force threshold was not apparently imminent. Warning shots require moving the weapon off the threat and recovering from a fired shot before resuming threat-sighting, which may be a deadly detour for the defender. I have fired warning shots, and the results were mixed, more favorable than not. Counterintuitively, in my anecdotal and limited experience with warning shots, such firing was good at turning a violent mob, but not so good at turning a close-range individual threat. Here's the Practics rule concerning warning shots: Warning shots are never fired unless the defender believes that a warning shot would likely prevent the immediate need for the use of deadly force and that the warning shot can be fired in accordance with the Four Rules of Safety. If you're standing in your driveway beside a 10-cubic-yard pile of pea gravel with your pistol in your hand and a man with a knife is threatening you from 15 yards away with "I'm going to stab you right now because that's not even a real gun," perhaps a shot into the gravel pile might be appropriate to prevent a possible death. Understand that discharging your weapon in a populated area without the clear need to immediately prevent a death, serious injury, or grave bodily harm is probably going to get you arrested. Rightfully so. A Practics warning shot is *not* a threat. It's *not* to prove the seriousness of the defender. A Practics warning shot is an audible and visual signal that communicates deadly force is within the defender's ability and is imminent unless the attacker immediately ceases the attack, which if continued would merit a deadly force response. I *do not* generally recommend warning shots and strongly advise against them as standard practice, but if the only alternative is deadly force and time and circumstances allow a terminally safe warning shot, the defender alone must make that decision based on conscience and immediate circumstances.

## Moving Targets

Sometimes the defender has to move, and sometimes the defender has to contend with the attacker refusing to stay put. Moving targets are more of a challenge at greater yardage, but even close-range encounters have shown that defenders have difficulty striking moving targets. Marksmanship will answer for greater distances, but for less than 25 yards the answer is a simple one—aim for the leading edge. Closer ranges (10 yards or less) require the shooter aim only for the leading *half* of the target. The reader is likely to think I've offered so little as to offer nothing at all, but this skill is not quite as easy as it is simple. Training is critical. Three problems confound most shooters with moving targets:

1. **Hesitation**—The handgun must follow the target but not stop at the leading edge. Fire must be en motion, or a miss will occur. When the defender hesitates and the attacker keeps moving, the shot will miss.
2. **Trigger Control**—If you have not gathered all the slack out of the trigger before tracking the target, you risk a late shot. Trigger control always matters.
3. **Intimidation**—Do not think about the leading edge as a line or narrow target. Just shoot at it. All the defender needs to do is adjust for target movement by aiming for the leading edge of the target and firing when the muzzle passes the target. At most distances for which the handgun is used for self-defense, any aiming point will suffice. It is when the target is moving fast in a perpendicular direction to the shooter that the leading-edge aiming point becomes necessary and, fortunately, easy. The defender knows the target, where the target is, and where the target is going. The bullet will cover most likely distances before the attacker moves an inch. Resist "leading" the target by aiming at open space, and the odds are your aim will be good enough. Don't estimate, guess, measure, or wonder. Just find the leading edge and press.

## Practics Falling Fire

The reader will hopefully never need anything in this book. In fact, it's statistically unlikely that you'll ever be attacked, but that's small comfort to those who find themselves under attack. Some

Practics skills, like Linear-Balance firing and punch firing, are likely to be used by a Practics practitioner during most attack circumstances. On the other hand, Falling Fire is unlikely to ever be used during an attack. So why include it? Largely because every cop I know has fallen down during a chase or fight. People do fall down. When moving with a handgun under the watch of an attacker, the defender won't be looking at the ground. In a fistfight, falling down means the other guy winds up on top. During an armed assault the results could be even more dangerous. Hitting the ground has caused defenders to lose their weapons or injure themselves. It's not uncommon for a fallen person to take a few seconds for a physical recovery. On top of all that, if you fall on concrete, you may numb a joint or even break a bone. Falling deserves some preparation. Practics Falling Fire is a method of firing at a forward target as the defender falls, while also protecting the knees, elbows, and head. We don't want to be on the ground in most cases—the other guy's overgrip is going to send rounds low, not high. We only seek the ground when the ground is the only safe place in reach, such as behind a short concrete wall in an otherwise open area. Falling Fire is not a strategy; it's just making the best of a bad situation.

Terminal position of Falling Fire.

193

Many slow-speed falls cause the runner to pitch the upper body downward, which would prevent Falling Fire. However, high-speed falls drop the runner like a tree, falling at an angle from foot to head. In order to convert a slow-speed fall into Falling Fire, the defender need only bring both feet together and thrust the legs to full extension. Whether the fall is intentional or forced upon the runner, the elements of Falling Fire are the same.

A. Both hands go to the handgun, and the arms are extended over/passed the head.
B. The body is twisted to turn the support side nearest the ground, and knees and elbows are turned to the side to avoid impact. The head is shielded from direct ground impact by the shoulder with the two-handed, extended-arm position.
C. Eyes are focused on the target beyond the firearm. Due to the amount of movement involved, extreme limits on time, and likely element of surprise, point shooting must be used. Falling Fire is a very loose form of Linear-Balance Shooting.
D. Shots are fired en motion from top to bottom as the falling shooter's line of fire passes over the attacker's body.

Falling Fire must include a recovery-and-defense movement—the shooter can't stay lying on his side. Practics has two Falling-Fire recoveries:

Rollover Recovery allows the shooter to give quick sighted fire from the ground. When the shooter has landed on the support side, he rolls onto his back, bends his knees, and places his feet flat on the ground while using a two-handed grip to extend both arms and fire sighted rounds upward toward the attacker. The Rollover can easily transition into the Kneel-Up Recovery.

You've made a defense while falling now you can accurately defend from the ground.

This is just marksmanship on your back.

Kneel-Up Recovery gets the shooter into a firing position while enabling him to stand. After landing on the support side, the shooter rolls partially forward and pushes up with the support elbow as the shooting foot is placed flat on the ground and the handgun is held on target. The support leg goes knee down and serves as a fulcrum to bring the body off the ground as the support hand pushes off the ground. Done at once, the shooter will come to a kneeling position ready for punch firing. From this position the shooter may easily stand and finish the recovery.

## En Motion and Movement Training

The skills that are the focus of this chapter are fairly easy to explain. None of this is rocket science. Like any other worthwhile physical pursuit, the knowledge is in the doing. Diligent use of these drills is the best way to acquire the above critical abilities.

1. **Upside-Down "T" Drill (Live Fire)**—The primary defensive target (PDT) is the center of the attacker's upper chest, which forms an intersection between the vertical centerline of the head and neck and the horizontal line of the upper chest. This drill will assist the student in training to fire a little higher than center mass. All Practics shooting drills that are not specifically for marksmanship training should have the PDT as the target.

Prepare for this drill by taking a full-size silhouette target and, using a white marker or paint, draw a straight, horizontal line across the silhouette at about the nipple line. The PDT is the area above the white line and at the imaginary line running down the center of the target. The training partner will serve as a safety officer and timekeeper (requiring a stopwatch). Target range will vary from five yards to 15 yards, beginning at five yards and working back. On command the shooter will draw from the holster and fire 10 *sighted* rounds at the PDT. When the handgun is made safe and holstered and the line is secure, the shooter will move to seven yards and repeat the drill before moving to 10, 12, and 15 yards. If your local range doesn't offer the above distances, use what you have available and divide the 50 rounds equally among your shooting positions. Hits to the neck, head, below the line, or over either shoulder are misses.

Repeat the above multi-distance drill with a 12-second time limit for each stage (including a full and proper holstered draw). Twelve seconds may not be a relaxed pace, but neither is it overly demanding. Revolver shooters may add two seconds, for a total of 14 seconds. If you have difficulty with this drill, seek fundamental marksmanship training. The above requirement should be comfortably within your ability after a little practice. Armed defenders need to be capable of completing this drill without a single miss. In the marksmanship reminder section I used an example of an attacker in a shopping mall parking lot. This drill demonstrates a reasonable response to that threat.

The training partner will score the target after each leg—hits and misses. Touching the holstered weapon prior to the command to draw and fire is a disqualification. Keep your hands off the weapon before the command signal. A miss requires the shooter to repeat the entire exercise. You must be able to hit the PDT 50 times without a miss at these very common distances. Needing further marksmanship training and practice carries no shame, but changing the test to satisfy substandard ability has no excuse.

Skill-Installation Requirement: three times the above multi-range, two-phase 100-round drill

Maintenance Requirement: Maintenance for this skill will be better served through other drills that include terminal firing and supplemental targets. Your routine marksmanship training will suffice to maintain accuracy.

The above drill must be fully completed using the weak hand.

2. **Punch-Fire Drill (Live Fire)**—This is a fun drill, and the shooter will quickly gain a new skill with just a little effort. Up to this point the reader should have acquired good holster, trigger, and aiming skills. Additionally, we know our PDT and supplemental targets. Now we'll add punch firing. This drill teaches punch firing at angles without the benefit of an adjusted stance.

Prepare the range by placing three full-size silhouette targets side by side, about two yards apart. The middle target should be directly in front of the shooter. Raise the silhouettes so that the tops of the "heads" are approximately 5' tall, simulating a realistic height for a charging male adult. The training partner will act as a safety officer and timekeeper (requiring a stopwatch).

The drill begins with the shooter on the firing line facing the middle target. On the command to fire, the shooter will draw the handgun from a fully secured holster and punch fire two rounds onto each target. The shooter will begin with the shooting-side target before moving to the middle and support-side targets. PDTs are the hit goals for each silhouette. Three passes in the above manner will be done at a relaxed pace. Afterward the shooter will reverse the order and begin with the support-side target while still using the strong-side hand. After a total of six passes, three in each direction, the shooter may move to the timed phase.

Shooting-arm movement should be a smooth, even arc, rising gently in the center. Think about that. We don't point at three targets; we make one smooth pass. The forearm is rotated and the fist is holding the gun. Don't hold your breath; control your breathing. Remember your trigger discipline. All previous training should be paying dividends here.

The timed phase is conducted exactly as above with the exception of a seven-second time limit, beginning with a clean draw and ending with the sixth shot. Seven seconds is quite a bit of time, provided the shooter doesn't hesitate. This is the first time you will be able to try some horizontal en motion firing. We'll do some specific en motion training a little further on, but you ought to begin trying to fire during the movement of your horizontal arc. After you've completed all Practics training in this book, you can experiment with this drill by moving the targets to different positions, altering their spacing, and adding targets. This is an easy drill to set up, and it produces quick results. The timed phase also has a total of six passes.

The training partner will score the targets by counting all hits to the body. Hits to the head or arms are misses. Mid-abdomen hits are acceptable. Torso hits at the beltline are misses. Our goal is always the PDT, but we're happy with solid torso hits on quick, unsighted fire. As you become a better punch-fire shooter, you may restrict yourself to only the upper chest area and a four- or five-second time limit. We never want our pursuit of the PDT to cause us to shoot too high or to become unrealistic in our training program.

Punch at the target. A natural skill.

Punch firing on multiple targets includes a natural arcing swing.

Skill-Installation Requirement: five times the above multi-target, two-phase 72-round drill

Maintenance Requirement: quarterly for two years

Training in this section requires more ammunition and some discipline. Nonetheless, the weak hand must be trained in punch firing, making the above training mandatory for the *other* hand.

3. **En Motion Drill (Live Fire)**—Now you can fully test your Linear-Balance Shooting skills. This drill is a Practics staple, particularly for peace officers, and is a meat-and-potatoes exercise that you will want to use over the years to check your skill maintenance. Many of the skills taught in previous training are required in this exercise, but this drill is, above all, for the development of en motion firing.

Preparation for this drill requires a unique but easy-to-make target. You will need a paper surface about 6.5' long and about 36" wide. The blank side of two full-size target sheets can be taped together or pages of newspaper may be used. Cardboard works well. The figure that will be drawn or painted on the surface is the 6' tall Practics Charging-Man Target. The Charging Man or includes a 6" circle for a head and a 4" thick stripe that runs from the bottom of the head to the hip line (2' long) and serves to mark the centerline, or spine. Approximately 6" below the head an 18" wide horizontal stripe, representing the shoulders, will be drawn to evenly intersect with the spine. At the bottom of the spine a 4" thick horizontal line will be drawn to mark the hips (18" wide). Using the hip line as a base, two 4" thick lines will be drawn at acute angles to intersect 3' below the hips and in line with the spine—an upside-down triangle. The purposes in the design of the Charging Man are to teach shooters to stay close to the centerline of the body rather than the open area of a silhouette target, to offer clear PDT and alternative targets, and to simulate the wide-to-narrow space made by human legs when running. The PDT is the intersection of the centerline and shoulder line. Alternative targets are the head circle and the ends of the hip line. A cheap can of spray paint (orange, white, or red) or some paper plates, a stack of old newspapers or some cardboard, and a couple of rolls of tape, will quickly make all the Charging-Man Targets you can use during a training day. If you don't have to contend with much wind, cardboard will be sufficient to frame the targets.

The drill begins with the shooter standing on the firing line three to five yards from the target. Executed in six phases, this drill begins with an exaggerated slow fire. On the command from the training partner/safety officer, the shooter will draw from a fully secured holster and use the Linear-Balance method to aim the handgun as it is raised toward the PDT. When the handgun clears the holster and is pointed at the feet of the target, the shooter will begin firing. As the muzzle is raised toward the PDT, the shots will rise up through the triangle and onto the vertical centerline. Shots will continue to the PDT. Revolver shooters will shoot twice into the triangle, twice onto mid-centerline, and twice to the PDT. Repeat this phase five times, paying particular attention to en motion firing, trigger control, and good Linear-Balance technique.

Second phase is similar to the first phase but timed at five seconds. The training partner will serve as timekeeper. On the command to fire, the shooter will draw and begin shooting upward: one shot in the triangle, one along the centerline, two at the PDT, and one into an alternative target that the training partner will identify by *gently* touching the shooter on the back of the head or back of the hip during firing. This is not punch firing. Linear-Balance Shooting is based off the shooting foot. The arm-foot coordination will aim the handgun—don't wave your handgun around, hoping to hit something.

The draw is one-handed, but the support hand moves to join the shooting hand for a two-hand grip. Through previous drills you've already proven Linear Balance works, so trust what you know. Extra caution must be used during this drill due to the need for the training partner to touch the shooter. It should be clear that any spoken communication, once firing has begun, is assumed to be a safety command to halt firing and make safe the range. Repeat the second phase five times.

Third phase is similar to the second phase with the exception of a four-second time limit. Shooting from the holster and firing en motion all the way to the PDT is desirable, but not all shooters can achieve five rounds in four seconds. Begin by trying five rounds and work your way down to the amount of rounds that you can fire. The goal is the PDT. Some shooters will not be able to hit the PDT with one round from a secure holster within four seconds. Those shooters will have to strive for one hit in the torso. Shooters who are able to fire the full five rounds within the time limit must add rounds en motion. Repeat third phase five times.

Fourth phase has a three-second time limit and requires two shots: one at the triangle and one along the centerline. This phase demands speed if a safety/retention holster is being used. Repeat fourth phase five times.

Fifth phase is simply one shot in two seconds from a secure holster. Many retention-holster users will not likely be able to hit the two-second mark. Don't change the time limit. Do your best to meet it. The shot must strike along the centerline. Repeat fifth phase five times.

Sixth phase has a four-second time limit and requires the shooter to fire five rounds with at least one round in the triangle, one round in the PDT, and one round in an alternative target of the shooter's choosing. The other two rounds will be fired en motion anywhere in the sequence. Repeat this phase five times.

The time limits in the en motion drill may seem difficult, but if the reader has indulged me by testing to see how far a reasonably fit person can run in two seconds, I think you'll agree that no further time could be allowed in order for this training to have any correlation with reality.

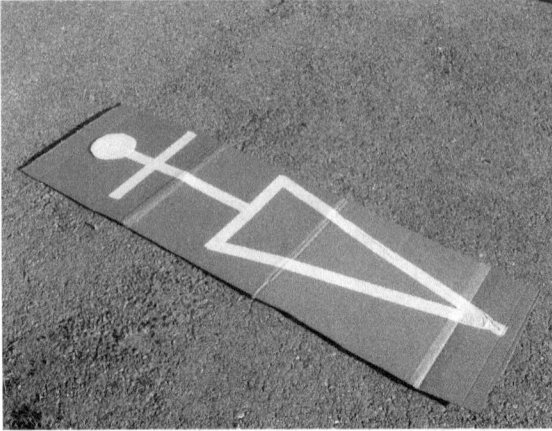

The Charging Man target.

Skill-Installation Requirement: six-phase drill (approximately 120 rounds) · two sets

Maintenance Requirement: semi-annually for three years

The above must be repeated with the weak hand. The handgun may be placed on a waist-height platform to the weak-hand side in lieu of the holster for pre-drill familiarization runs. However, students must conduct the training itself with a weak-hand draw from the strong-side holster. Three seconds may be added to each time limit to compensate for a weak-hand draw from the strong-side holster with the specific intention of the student manipulating the handgun at a relaxed pace under the supervision of the safety officer. Only the platform transition may be used during this live-fire drill.

4. **Groucho Drill**—Stand a string mop upside down in the center of a flat, open field or lawn. The stick end of the mop can be stuck in the earth with the mop's head standing at about 4' tall. A milk jug on a stick works just as well. Use a toy gun (with a front sight) in a two-hand grip and slowly Groucho walk around the mop in a large circle for at least two minutes. Sight the toy handgun on the mop's head. Reverse direction and continue circling for another two minutes. The training partner will watch to see if the shooter's head and shoulder carriage are properly dampened by the bent knees and gait to prevent vertical movement. Success or failure will be apparent to the shooter who tries to sight while walking. If the shooter was not able to maintain sighting or a smooth Groucho walk throughout the drill,

the effort is disqualified and must be done again.

Focus on the danger in this slow speed drill.

Skill-Installation Requirement: four-minute drill · five sets
Maintenance Requirement: monthly for three months

**5. Running-Fire Drill (Live Fire)**—Patience is required to master this technique. The movement is simple, but a willingness to train is mandatory. The student will have to be able to safely run, which is a matter of both fitness and environment.

Make certain that the range you use is flat and dry, has good traction, and is free from debris. No metal frames or poles are permitted within the firing area because this is a close-range drill and ricochets must be avoided. Place six full-size silhouette targets with the tops of the heads between 5'7" and 6' tall. The targets must be placed in line and evenly spaced at about 6" apart for the first run and extended to about 3' apart for the last run. Be flexible in target placement, accommodating the student's stride. The training partner will serve as a safety officer. This drill has three phases.

The shooter's starting position will be about 6' from the front of the targets and about 10' to the side of the line of targets. Stand with the shooting side closest to the targets with the line of targets viewable by the shooter (if right-handed, with the right side of the body closest to the targets; if left-handed, with the left side of the body closest to the targets). The handgun will already be in hand and pointing downrange in a punch-fire position. When the training partner gives the command, the shooter will trot in a straight line, taking slow, short

203

steps as he passes the targets. When the support-side foot hits the ground in front of a silhouette, the shooter will press the trigger and fire one shot. This is a slow, rhythmic drill, like dancing. Concentrate on the coordination between the shooting hand and the support foot. At the end of the line of targets, the shooter will make a safe weapon and holster before checking the targets. Verifying the targets is important, but keep it under two minutes. Muscles "forget" when there is too much of a break between sets. Repeat the above phase three times.

Second phase uses the first-phase range setup and is also a slow shuffle-step drill. The difference will be that two shots will be fired at each silhouette. When the support-side foot strikes the ground in front of a new target, one round is fired. When the second foot strikes the ground, the second round is fired. This phase will help in developing shooting-foot coordination and will also increase shooter speed. Remember your trigger control. If you can't control the trigger, you'll never make that second shot at a dead run. Verify the targets as above and repeat this phase three times.

Third phase requires the targets to be extended about 30" to 36" between targets. The shooter will begin as with the previous two phases. However, on the command to begin, the shooter will jog using a full-step at about half-speed. Two shots will be fired at each target, coordinating each step with the shooting hand. Repeat this phase 10 times.

Skill-Installation Requirement: all three phases (174 rounds total) · two sets

Maintenance Requirement: above requirement quarterly for three years

The above training is not successfully completed until also conducted for the weak hand.

6. **Moving-Target Drill (Live Fire)**—The theory is simple, but the accomplishment requires practice, and some range preparation is required. If you have access to moving targets, you're ready to go. Otherwise, you'll have to make your own, and the following is a cheap method of setting up a moving target. Secure two upright posts about seven yards apart on the target line. The tops of the posts must be about 5'5" to 6' above the ground. Secure a single piece of clothesline between the tops of the posts. The target will hang from this top line. Place a cardboard backing on a full-size silhouette target and use two

hooks (plastic shower curtain hooks work well) to puncture the cardboard and attach the target to the top line. Tap an eye hook, or a nail (bending the nail upward to form a hook), into the outer side of each post at the mid-line of the hanging, full-size silhouette target. Attach clotheslines to either side of the target backing and run each end through the eye hook, or bent nail, on the corresponding post. You'll need enough clothesline to allow the training partner to take the running ends and draw them together at a 45° angle directly behind the shooter. The ends must be tied together, forming a triangle with the training partner at the point and the target at the base. By pulling on either end, the training partner can make the target slide along the target line. The target should slide easily from side to side on the target line, which must remain taut. Ideally the shooter should be positioned at five to seven yards from the target line, inside the triangle. You'll need 35 to 40 yards of clothesline, which will cost about three bucks at a dollar store. If you've got hard earth, you'll need stakes and guidelines to hold your posts upright. The rope may jump the hooks during use—it doesn't matter as long as it works. None of our training aides have to be pretty, exact, or perfect, just effective.

The drill begins with the target off to one side and the shooter centered in front of the target line, five to seven yards away. When the training partner gives the command, the shooter will draw and fire at the target. The training partner will begin pulling the target toward the opposite side.

This drill consists of three phases: First phase is paced with the target moving one yard per second. The shooter will draw using Linear Balance, continuing to a sighted-fire position. All shots in this phase will be sighted fire. A minimum of 14 shots is required for the pistol and 12 for revolvers for a single directional pass of the target. At the end of the target movement, the shooter may reload and prepare for another pass. This phase requires 10 single-direction passes. Second phase requires the training partner to pull the target two yards per second for an approximately 3.5-second drill. The shooter will draw and fire using the Linear-Balance technique for unsighted fire. Six shots are required for a single-direction pass. Repeat 10 times. Third phase requires punch firing for four shots as fast as the trainer can manually pull the target rope, also for 10 passes.

The PDT is your target. Target speed may be increased in subsequent runs, but it does no good if the shooter is unable to score good hits and therefore learn from the experience. Repeat 10 times.

This is a cheap easy arrangement that many ranges will allow.

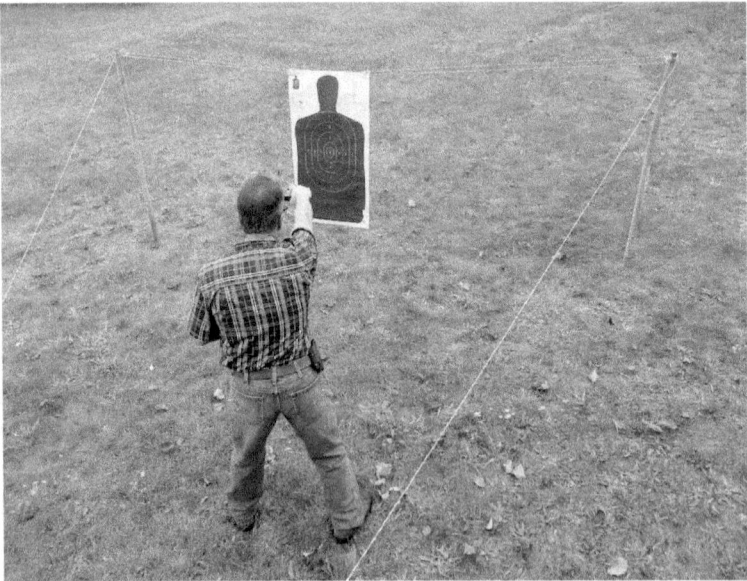

Begin training slow and at close distances.

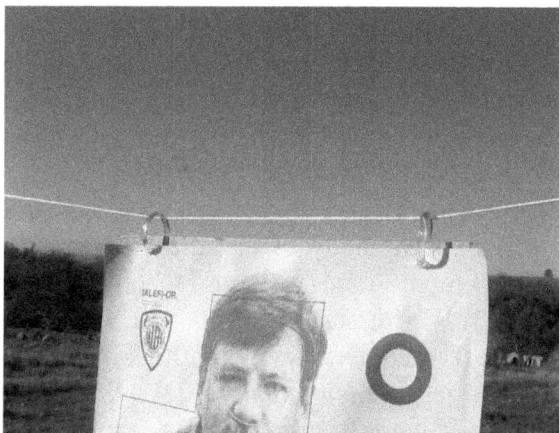

One dollar shower rings and some two bucks worth of clothesline.

Skill-Installation Requirement: first and second phases twice, third phase · five

Maintenance Requirement: phase three · five (using half-size targets), quarterly

Repeat the above training requirement for the weak hand. You may begin with gun in hand.

7. **Falling-Fire Drill (Dry Fire)**—This drill requires a storage-safe weapon and the absence of all ammunition from the area. A silhouette target is placed on a stand with the top of the head between 5'9" and 6' high.

Approximately five yards in front of the target will be the "drop zone" for the student. Falling-Fire training requires a safe, cushioned surface. A stack of two bed mattresses works well when placed lengthwise toward the target. A single mattress *may* work if it is of sufficient quality. Nonetheless, mattresses must be placed on grass or soft dirt. Placing a worn-out mattress on concrete and falling on top of it may wean the student from any desire for further training, so old bed mattresses on soft ground are mandatory. Knee and elbow pads should be worn. If you miss your mattress or it fails to sufficiently cushion your fall, pads may save your joints.

This drill is done in four stages. The student will determine how many drops are necessary at each stage based on dry-fire success. I have given you minimums for each stage, but only you can determine if your dry firing is successful.

Begin by kneeling at the base of the mattress. Face the target with your handgun in the shooting hand and extended in front of your body. This will simulate running with a one-handed grip toward the target. On command from the training partner, the student will slowly lean forward and fall. During the fall, the shooter will grip the handgun with both hands and extend the handgun straight outward. The student will twist the body so that the support side lands on the mattress. The twisting motion is awkward when kneeling and is all the more reason for soft ground. Kneeling will enable the shooter to master the basics for contending with the full drop. Conduct the kneeling drop 10 times *without attempting dry fire*. Focus on the twist and ensure your body lands in this sequence: support leg, support hip, support shoulder. The head must be protected between the shoulders and arms. If the head strikes the mattress with the shoulder, the student has failed.

Try a second set, but this time you may begin parallel to the target with the support side toward the target. As you fall from the kneeling position, attempt one dry-fire shot during each fall. Follow the centerline of the target from top to bottom. The handgun is held in a high-ready position. During the forward drop the student will bring the gun over the head and see the top of the handgun; the muzzle and line of vision are in line. When the shooter's eyes see the head of the target, the first dry-fire round is fired. Don't think about points of fire—there is no time. By the time the shooter commits to the head, he will be firing at the torso. This type of firing cannot be intellectualized while in progress. Get on center and fire your way down. The goal is one good dry-fire shot at the PDT. The training partner can watch for form, ensuring that the student's body is turned to protect the knees and elbows, but only the student will know whether the dry-fire shots are good. Repeat this support-side-facing kneeling drop *at least 10 times but as many times as needed* to get good PDT "hits."

The third set will be done from a forward-facing crouch. Bend the knees to lower the body to two-thirds of your normal standing height. As you fall forward, conduct the described turn to the support side and attempt one good PDT dry-fire hit. Execute *at least 10* crouching dry-fire drops.

The fourth set is done from a full-standing position with the student facing the target. On command the student will drop, twist the body toward the support side, extend the two-hand grip, and dry fire. Take your time with this stage. Try for one good PDT shot. Continue to dry fire as many trigger presses as possible. Stop when you are unable to go any further. For instance, if you can do three good dry-fire shots, try for four. After each fall, alternate between Rollover and Kneel-Up Recoveries. Dry fire two rounds from the recovery positions. The student must make *a minimum of 10* successful drops at this stage.

The defender knows he is going to fall.

He assumes a two-hand grip and twists his torso to protect himself from the impact.

He begins his transition after impact.

The shooting knee and the support elbow get it started.

Focus is on the target.

The defense can be kneeling or standing.

Skill-Installation Requirement: The above drill is sufficient.

Maintenance Requirement: Live-fire training will maintain this skill.

The weak hand needs equal training in this drill.

**8. Falling Fire (Live Fire)**—Most ranges will not allow Falling-Fire training. If you cannot complete this training, return to the dry-fire version and use an increasingly narrower target or move the target to positions not directly in line with the shooter. Falling Fire requires extreme caution. The training partner must act as a safety officer. Prior to live fire, the shooter must immediately execute one set of 10 repetitions of dry fire. Failure to conduct the dry fire perfectly will disqualify the shooter from attempting live fire. The target frame must be made of wood to avoid ricochets, and the shooter must wear safety glasses and hearing protection as with any live fire exercise.

This drill is done from a full standing position with the student facing the target. On command the student will drop forward and twist the body toward the support side, extend the two-hand grip, and fire. Remember you are firing en motion. Trigger control is essential. Begin with one good PDT shot. Continue by firing two rounds, then three rounds, and so on. Stop when you are unable to go any further. After each fall, conduct a proper Rollover and fire three sighted rounds at the PDT. Do not hurry the Rollover. Firing at an upside-down angle will likely alter the shooter's normal eye relief (distance from eye to sights), and Rollover groups will likely be slightly different than normal marksmanship groups. The only way to master Rollover shooting is to do it, and the shooter should conduct Rollover shooting as a marksmanship study apart from Falling Fire. Rollover live-fire training may be done separately on normal ground. The use of the mattress makes rollover training awkward and clumsy but so does deep snow, mud, debris, and water.

Increase your fall height according to the training plan.

This trainee is using a reinforced mattress. Safety is paramount.

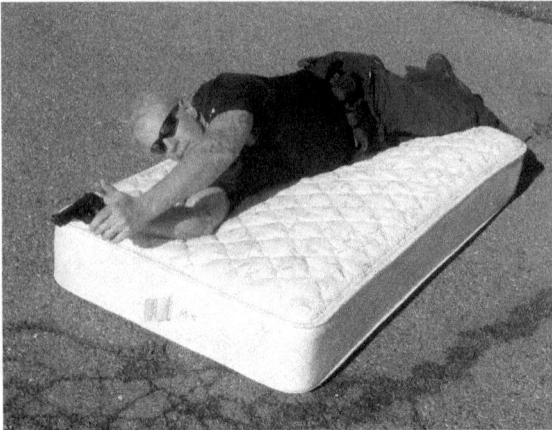

This skill will take a lot of practice. It is among the more difficult to master.

Skill-Installation Requirement: 50 consecutive hits allowing no more than five misses

Maintenance Requirement: quarterly for two years

Ambidextrous training is mandatory with this drill.

9. **Terminal-Firing Drill**—This drill requires the use of the Practics Charging-Man Target, as used during the en motion live-fire drill, with the clothesline and posts used during the Moving-Target drill. The target is set up by placing the two wooden posts at least 50" apart and affixing a taut clothesline between the tops. Post height should be 5'9" to 6'. The top of the Charging-Man Target backing will be tied to about 12 yards of clothesline placed over the taut target line between the posts. A small weight must be attached to the backside of the top of the target; an empty 50-round box filled with dirt and secured with the clothesline is enough. The foot of the target must be moved slightly forward of the head and secured to the ground by a weight or small stake, resulting in a slightly backward-leaning target. The running end of the clothesline goes above the shooter to the training partner. The training partner will need to be positioned higher than the shooter and can stand on a platform of plastic milk crates or in the bed of a pickup truck. Keeping the line taut, the training partner will keep the target upright. As the training partner slackens the line, the target will fall backward until reaching the ground, simulating a man staggering backward and dropping to a reduced height before falling to the ground.

The shooter will begin at three yards with the handgun drawn and in a low-ready, one-handed position. On the command to fire, the shooter will punch fire at the torso centerline as the training partner lowers the target. The shooter will continue firing until the target has fallen flat onto the ground. The training partner will control target drop, which will gradually get faster with each successful run. Success depends on hits being within 4" of the centerline of the torso. The goal is no less than four hits per two-second drop. This phase requires a minimum of 20 drops.

Second phase mirrors the first with two exceptions: a seven-yard distance and the use of Linear-Balance technique. The shooter will attempt to finish with sighted fire—point fire and then sighted fire, if and when possible. Again, the goal is four hits per two-second drop but start slower and finish with drops under two seconds. A minimum of 20 drops is required.

Don't stop firing until the falling man is down.

Skill-Installation Requirement: 100 consecutive hits allowing no more than five misses from both three-yard punch fire and seven-yard Linear-Balance fire

<u>Maintenance Requirement</u>: quarterly for the duration of your shooting career

You must conduct the above training for the weak hand.

If you have successfully completed all the training up to this point, you have greater technical point-shooting skill preparation than the vast majority of this nation's peace officers. Congratulations. All of us need disciplined training as shooters. Complex skills require individualized maintenance. When you find the recommended maintenance training to be less than challenging, adjust your training by changing distances, time limits, minimum round requirements, target size, target number, pre-drill physical exertion, no-shoot obstacles, and lighting levels. Many shooters will not be able to perform all the drills offered in Practics, but any skill acquired or improved is worthwhile. Learn what you can. If you have to adjust your terminal shooting—drop target speed to five seconds, for instance—do it. No one knows whether his training and experience will be sufficient for whatever challenge he may face, but we do know that no one ever suffered for improving his abilities.

# PRACTICS 103:
# Special Circumstances

# Chapter Seven: Ammunition Management

*Anticipate the difficult by managing the easy.*

Lao-Tzu

*Have no fear of perfection—you'll never reach it.*

Salvador Dali

Some time ago, I worked as a station commander with an international police task force in what had once been part of Yugoslavia. One day, local Serbs, wearied from ethnic Albanian attacks, got liquored up, kidnapped the half-wit who served as the UN mayor, and blocked a public roadway. During a confrontation with about 15 police officers, a large gathering of Serbs armed themselves with rocks and chunks of concrete, and offered the police a good medieval stoning. The officers fired several warning shots, and the whole thing descended into a gang fight and a foot race. At the after-action briefing I discovered that no officer who had fired more than one round knew how many rounds he had fired. Verification was only possible by checking magazines.

Nepalese and Zambian police officers probably weren't taught to count rounds, but I had no such excuse. In both the Marine Corps and in SWAT, I was taught to count discharged rounds. When training almost every day, I never lost count of my rounds, but without constant training my round counting was reduced to guesswork. Some shooters can accurately count rounds under duress without much preparation. I am not one of them. The overwhelming majority of police officers who fire multiple shots in the line of duty cannot give an accurate count of the number of rounds fired. Who cares? The truth is defenders are extremely unlikely to ever need a reload. Reloads are rare in deadly force confrontations with the exception of law enforcement feeding frenzies, which have more to do with group psychology than the need for more rounds. You have a better chance of being attacked by a shark than of needing more rounds than your handgun holds. So why do we need to count rounds? Because some people *do* get eaten by sharks, and some defenders do need additional ammunition. The firearm is not really a weapon. A bullet is a weapon. No rounds, no weapon. Multiple attackers, greater distances, better cover, and defender condition determine the amount of rounds necessary for self-defense. We don't know what will happen next. Round counting is like a fuel gauge on an airplane—either accurate or dangerous. Practics has a method for counting rounds under duress.

## Practics Four Counting

According to New York City Police Department statistics (NYPD SOP-9), officers averaged 2.86 shots per shooting between 1988 and 2001. In general, three-round averages are pretty reliable and seem to be consistent nationally, though data is scarce.

Let's start with the informed assumption that you're most likely to fire fewer than four rounds per incident. (Revolver shooters may fire fractionally fewer rounds than pistol shooters according to the above NYPD stats.) Of course, you already know how many rounds your handgun holds. Divide that number of rounds by four for a pistol but take the fractional advantage of the revolver and divide the number of rounds for your wheel-gun by three. For example, a 16-shot pistol holds four groups of ammunition, and a six-shot revolver holds two groups of ammunition. The method for using Four Counting (or Three Counting for revolvers) is treating every burst of fire as a discharge of four rounds.

Here's an example of Four Counting: A defender is surprised by an attacker in the kitchen and discharges rounds. Those fired rounds are counted as group one. The defender retreats to the children's bedroom, pursued by the attacker, where she discharges more rounds, designated as group two. At this point all the defender has to know is that she fired some amount of rounds on two occasions. She counts the fired rounds as two groups (eight rounds). She knows she has two groups remaining in the handgun (eight rounds). The odds are the defender's group count will keep her within the three-round national average and give her a clear understanding of when she needs to change magazines. It's that simple.

Magazine changes are done in safety, or at least that's the goal. In order for the defender to control the time and place of a magazine change, the magazine must be changed before the magazine is empty. When a handgun is allowed to run dry, a reload has to occur whether or not the defender is prepared. By being willing to change magazines early, the shooter has a greater chance of choosing the time and place of the change based on safety. In the above example of a home defender defending her children, she would begin to consider a magazine change upon moving to group three.

Is it more important to get all the rounds out of a magazine or to have a safe magazine change? The odds are against a defender exhausting a gun's ammo supply. The defender in our example is already a rare exception for having gotten to group three. Likely, she will not need to exceed group four, but if she does, the danger will be in when and where she attempts to change magazines. The danger during an exposed magazine change is significant.

What about revolver shooters? Should they look for a speed-loader change after three rounds, using Three Counting for ammo management? Absolutely, because making the decision to reload is making a decision to find a safe place to reload. That may not happen before another round is fired, but managing the tactical reload greatly reduces the possibility that the defender will be standing exposed before the attacker, holding an empty handgun. We're always planning to reload, reloading, or firing.

Practics does not waste anything. We want to retain the extra rounds and the partially empty magazines that are released during early magazine or cylinder changes. This raises a problem. People will act under duress the way they were trained to act. Training, intentional or otherwise, is effective. A little further on, we will discuss retrieving discarded ammo.

## Single Rounds and Group Combinations

Defenders who fire a single round may absolutely know that only one round was fired. The problem comes with multiple shots. Strictly Four Counting single shots would cause a 75% loss of magazine capacity. Single shots must be counted as one round. The principle behind counting single shots is *if* the shooter knows a single round has been fired, it counts as one round. When the shooter has any doubt as to the number of rounds fired, Four Counting (or Three Counting) applies. That is certainly easy enough, but what about when combinations occur? For instance, a defender fires one round at an

221

intruder who breaks into the garage and later fires multiple shots at the intruder inside the home. In such a case the shooter would have fired one shot and one group. None of this is rocket science, but it becomes more difficult if two or three single shots are fired along with a few groups. The best method for combining the count is to immediately marry any single round to a previous or future group. When a single round is fired immediately before a group, simply count the total as one group and forget about the single round. The statistical norms will carry the round. If a second single round is fired after a group, the count is one group and one round, pending another firing. Another single round, combined with the round already fired becomes a separate group. Likewise, if a group follows the single round, the single round is absorbed by the group and forgotten by the shooter. In the above example, the one group and one round would become two groups as soon as any other shot or shots were fired. This method is easier to do than it is to read. Just remember, you want to round up into groups as soon as your single shot becomes more than one round fired.

## Tactical Reload

A reload occurs when the handgun is without ammunition. If a revolver shooter fires all six rounds, it's time for a reload. When a magazine is emptied and the pistol's slide locks back, the shooter swaps magazines and releases the slide—a reload. When a shooter purposely chooses to change magazines prior to running out of ammunition for the sake of personal safety or to gain a defensive advantage, that magazine replacement is called a tactical reload. The advantage of a tactical reload is the shooter controls the time and place of the magazine change. Rather than waiting to exhaust the ammunition supply in the firearm, a shooter may swap magazines early while in a safe position and not under immediate attack. Additionally, no slide manipulation will be necessary. Tactical reloading is essential to defender safety.

The reader will recall that we always train to allow expended magazines to fall freely without shooter interference. Stuck magazines are pulled free and immediately released, minimizing the degree of shooter involvement with the discarded magazine. This emphasis on hands-off magazine removal poses a problem for tactical reloads. The cost of tactical reloads is a practical diminishing of magazine capacity.

In other words, if you change a 10-round magazine after firing only seven rounds, you have, for all practical purposes, a seven-round magazine. Therefore, retrieving partially full magazines is essential to defense longevity. Tactical reloading doesn't require additional handling of the magazine as far as a simple magazine swap is concerned. However, if we wish to salvage the partially full magazine in the most efficient manner possible, we can't let the expended magazine free-fall. Training to grab a dropping magazine is a serious matter. A defender who is confused by conflicting training may, under duress, cost himself valuable time fumbling with a spent magazine. Fortunately, training for Practics Tactical Reload is unlikely to cause any confusion. The defender that decides to execute a tactical reload does so consciously, not instinctively—and that's the difference. A tactical reload is a decision made by the shooter who is currently in control of his immediate environment and believes a tactical reload to be advantageous within his circumstances. Therefore, the likelihood of a trained defender improperly touching a falling magazine is extremely unlikely with Practics training.

## Practics Version of the Pistol Tactical Reload

1. Defender considers immediate circumstances advantageous for a tactical reload.
2. Support hand retrieves a fresh magazine from the pouch.
3. With the fresh magazine pointing upward, the support hand raises the fresh magazine just below and to the outside of the magazine well but slightly forward of a normal reload position.
4. Shooting hand ejects partially full magazine into the palm of the support hand, to the inside and rear of the fresh magazine. Partial magazine is held between palm and last two fingers.
5. The fresh magazine (still held by thumb and first two fingers) is brought slightly to the rear and slammed into the empty magazine well.
6. Support hand fully grabs the partially full magazine and inserts it downward with bullets outward into the rear-hip trouser pocket.

The above technique finishes with the partially full magazine ready to draw from the trouser pocket, avoiding confusion with fresh magazines in the pouches. Nothing is wasted, and the movement is natural and easy to learn.

## Revolver Tactical Reloads

In the 1990s, I oversaw the firearms program for a California sheriff's office. While deputies were allowed to carry their own handguns, our agency's issue weapon was the Smith and Wesson 686 revolver. Deputy Sheriff Rod Trumpf came up with the following method for conducting a revolver tactical reload. Trumpf used to comment on the vanity of well-known firearm instructors who slapped their names on slight variations of the most common firearm-operation movements. In the spirit of the fellowship and good cheer that imbues law enforcement, I threatened to publicly name Trumpf's tactical-reload technique after him if I ever had an opportunity. Years later, I wrote a book . . .

## The Trumpf Method

The Trumpf Method is a means of collecting unfired rounds without having to pick through empty brass. Revolver shooters have a unique opportunity. Firing expands brass, which allows for the Trumpf Method. When the revolver cylinder is opened and the weapon turned muzzle upward, non-expanded brass (fresh rounds) will drop free into the shooter's hand for placement in the rear hip or shirt pocket. The shooter then stabs the plunger and ejects the empty brass onto the ground before using a speed loader to reload the revolver. Loose, pocketed rounds are an ammo reserve in the event the speed loaders are exhausted. This method depends on cooperative brass and doesn't work every time for every round. What makes this method invaluable is that it prevents or lessens a shooter's need to pick through expended brass in order to save live rounds. Think back to the Old Marine Corps Speed-Loader Technique and consider how well that technique combines with the Trumpf Method for collecting and loading single rounds.

## Ammunition-Management Training

Managing your ammunition is not ever likely to concern you during a self-defense situation. On the other hand, "likely" doesn't really matter to the person who is the exception. Managing ammunition is too easily done to be excluded from defender training. The following drills will assist you in developing good ammo governance.

**Practics Ammunition-Management Drill (Live Fire)**—This drill represents the following scenario: The defender is intermittently covered during a ranging attack and able to conduct tactical reloads as needed. In order to manage the ammunition supply, the defender will Four Count rounds (Three Count for revolvers) and use the single-round/group-count combination method when required.

A common silhouette will be the target, and Linear-Balance Shooting will be used during this drill. The shooter begins on the five-yard line with the handgun in the high-ready position. Shots will be fired at the rate of one round per third of a second, or three rounds every second. It is the training partner's responsibility to give the "fire" command, which is communicated by the training partner quickly and lightly tapping the shooter one, two, or three times on the shoulder. The shooter will fire an amount of rounds corresponding to the number of taps given by the training partner. When the shooter determines that a tactical reload is necessary, he will immediately begin the tactical reload after completing a group of shots. Tactical reloads should take less than 3.5 seconds for revolver, take no more than 2.5 seconds for pistol, and be substantially quicker for each after training. However, the training partner will allow five seconds for reloads during the first two runs and then expect 3.5 or 2.5 seconds, respectively, on subsequent runs. Tactical reloads include putting the expelled rounds or partially full magazine into a pocket. Pistol shooters will use the Practics version of the tactical reload, and revolver shooters will use the Trumpf Method. The shooter alone is responsible for Four Counting/Three Counting, combination counting, and timely tactical reloads. When the shooter believes that the entire ammunition supply (pouches, speed loaders, cylinder, chamber) has been exhausted except for the last ammunition group, he will cease firing and raise his support hand.

The primary shooter objective during this drill is the successful counting of rounds using the Practics Four-Count/Three-Count Method—each firing occurrence counts as one group. However, single-round firings are counted as single rounds. The shooter must combine single and group counting as described earlier in the text. The shooter needs to know in advance how many groups of ammunition are at his disposal. Here are a couple of examples:

- three · 15-round magazines and one round in the chamber = 46 rounds @ 11 Four-Count groups
- two · six-round speed loaders and six rounds in the cylinder = 18 rounds @ six Three-Count groups

The secondary shooter objective is efficient tactical reloads when necessary. Additionally, this training will help the shooter develop habitual, straightforward round-counting skill.

Disqualifications will include firing the wrong amount of rounds, running the handgun dry, or failing to stop with the last group of rounds (three or four) in the handgun. Safety violations and poor technique are also disqualifiers. Revolver shooters will be very busy during this drill with tactical reloads. The frequency of reloads by pistol shooters will vary based on magazine capacity.

Training partners must randomly select one-, two-, or three-shot commands to add stress and prevent an easy count by the shooter. It is important for revolver shooters to have a greater mix of one- and two-shot commands. Otherwise, all the revolver shooter will learn is to reload continually after a group and not learn to properly count singles and groups. The training goal is to teach the shooter to count groups and combine groups and single rounds. While this drill is extremely busy for the six-gunners, it must be recognized that constant tactical reloads are not likely in real life but are a training reality for a handgun with only six shots. Training partners must remember that the shooter is trying to learn to count groups first and tactically reload second. This technique must be integrated into the student's normal tactical training behavior, making this baseline drill unnecessary after the skill is properly established. In other words, from now on, you always Four Count when doing any defense training.

Five runs are required to complete this drill.

Skill-Installation Requirement: five times the above drill (five runs with three magazines each or two speed loaders each)

Maintenance Requirement: three times the above drill (quarterly for the first year)

# Chapter Eight: Cover and Concealment

*We are not retreating—we are advancing in another direction.*

Douglas MacArthur

*Form follows function.*

Louis Sullivan

As you will recall from earlier in the book, most gunfights take place at very close range and consequently are over long before anyone can run for cover. On the other hand, police use patrol cars for limited cover during felony car stops every day, and home defenders do tend to prefer the concealment of doorways. Cover is always desirable, but training for its use to the exclusion of quick, close-range techniques is counter-productive. Let's take a look at cover and concealment from a Practics perspective.

*Cover* is the positioning of a person in such a manner as to place an impenetrable object of sufficient size to shield that person from anticipated paths of incoming fire. *Concealment* is the positioning of a person in such a way that denies the attacker's view of him. Therefore cover prevents rounds from striking a person, while concealment hides a person from view. Shooters can't fire through cover and can't see through concealment. Bullet-resistant glass could provide cover but never concealment. A pile of clothes may not stop penetration by a pellet gun but could deny an attacker the knowledge that a defender is within his reach.

Cover and concealment are usually brushed over as basic fare within armed self-defense instruction. The truth is that the ability to use cover or concealment well is extraordinarily valuable, but the likelihood of a defender using either is not that great due to the very close range of *most* defense shootings. However, many armed defenders have had cover available and failed to use it. One of the reasons why cover and concealment are taught as basic subjects is their general simplicity. Everyone agrees it's better to be behind a boulder than in front of it when someone is shooting at you. When being pursued, it's better to not be seen than to be seen.

The application of these simple truths is a bit more complex. Defenders can't hide behind anything without preparing for an immediate defense. If a defender sits behind a boulder and does nothing, an attacker may walk around the boulder and shoot the defender. Discovery during concealment, like the game of hide-and-seek, is most often a matter of *when* rather than *if*. Firing from cover or concealment requires body-positioning techniques that take advantage of any protection while still allowing an efficient defense.

Discussing very specific techniques for either cover or concealment is virtually pointless because every situation is unique; every object of concealment or cover is different. Instead, let's look at some principles and adaptable skills.

## Fundamentals of Concealment

- **Noise matters.** An attacker may walk right past a still defender under low-light conditions but will not fail to alert on a sniff, a shoe scrape, or heavy breathing. Stillness may make the open air an acceptable hiding place. Coughing can destroy the concealment of a hidden passageway. Noise discipline may trump environment when it comes to concealment.
- **The human being is first distinguished by shape.** When you drive down the street and see people within your peripheral vision, it is not the presence of color clothing that informs you of the presence of humans. In fact, color perception may initially be incorrect. What catches your attention is an object shaped like a human. Kids get scared at night by clothes thrown over coatracks because of the shape, not the color or features. That's why a human can't hide by throwing a sheet over himself; concealment requires obstructing the familiar human outline. Shooters use human silhouettes for training because silhouettes are sufficient for recognition. Concealing a person from sight requires a distortion of the human form.
- **Secondary recognition of a human being is most often done**

**by observing movement.** In the old days people walked beside horse-drawn carts and livestock, but today people do not walk *with* anything. Motor vehicles are too fast for us. People walking are usually the slowest, steadiest motion within our vision. A person in low light may be noticed striding past a herd of cows. If that person moves at the same disjointed, ambling pace as the herd, he is much less likely to be noticed. Also, human limb movements are relatively fast and long, whereas tree limbs and foliage tend to be active in wind but with very short, repetitive movements. All this we can recognize with our peripheral vision. By conducting a reload in slow motion or taking a few seconds to change a stance, the defender is much more likely to deceive the peripheral vision of an attacker.

## Fundamentals of Cover

- **The effectiveness of cover depends as much on what is being fired as the object being used for cover.** Defenders cannot make a ballistic study when being pursued by an armed attacker, but there are some guidelines to keep in mind. A decorative brick veneer may significantly diffuse most good handgun service rounds but do very little to a mid-caliber rifle round, depending on distance. There are some very powerful handguns with rifle-like ballistics, and plenty of rifles are chambered for the lightweight .22, but, generally speaking, a rifle quadruples your cover requirements. A few hundred yards will take the starch out of most high-powered handgun rounds but may fail to dampen the penetration capabilities of modern rifle calibers. A defender needs to look and listen to distinguish handguns from longarms when it is reasonable to do so.

- **Know your barricades.** A 10' pine tree and a 10' oak tree are significantly different in their abilities to stop rounds. A tree that has been soaking up hundreds of gallons of water will do better than a dying tree that can't drink. You don't have to be an arborist to know that hardwood trees *tend* to be better protection than non-hardwood trees of the same size. Big trees are better than small trees, and a tree without brush in the spring or summer is probably dying and possibly dry and brittle. Water is a great defense against bullets, which means mud is better than dirt. Modern housing materials should not be expected to stop rounds without distance and multiple layers, but hardwood, ceramic, and glass may deflect bullets. An interior wall (and most exterior walls) is concealment, not cover. A house or a few rooms may be cover, but may not be, depending on the attacker's caliber and ammunition choices. Glass has long been the bane of counter-snipers, primarily—though not exclusively—due to angle of impact. So much so that Remington developed an excellent law enforcement rifle bullet with good glass-penetration qualities. Glass is unpredictable and influenced by temperature. In the nineties, a San Diego-area officer found himself in front of a sliding-glass door with an armed suspect a few inches away on the other side of the glass. The sun had been extremely warm that day. The suspect fired directly at the officer, and the hot glass deflected the bullet almost straight upward, missing the officer but shattering the glass. Safety glass on automobiles is far more likely to deflect a round than the sheet metal of the car body is likely to deflect a bullet. A lot of buckshot has skipped harmlessly over the windshields of getaway cars in the past 60 years. Furniture is not cover, though your great grandma's solid-oak china hutch may do fine with some handgun rounds. Old furniture made of hardwood can stop some rounds, but most modern furniture, even "solid wood," is actually some form of laminate and pressboard. Examine your desk and bedroom set before you ever need to use them for cover. A final word about protective materials—angles matter. Cover is increased when the angle of impact is lessened. In other words, materials that may not "catch" bullets (glass, sheet metals, and finished woods) might possibly deflect them when the attacker's angle of fire is advantageous to the defender. Use what you have in the best manner reasonably possible.

- **Bullets don't always penetrate. They sometimes ricochet away or slide along an angled surface.** When considering cover, avoid placing yourself at the anticipated end of a deflected bullet path. For example, a low marble wall, when struck by a bullet at an angle, may force the bullet to slide along the surface of the length of the wall. In such a case the defender may do better to fire over the wall than to position himself at the end of the wall. Rather than leaning over the hood of a car, a shooter may do better to fire from underneath, due to the likelihood of windshield deflection. The engine is better protection than windows or doors, but the shooter must be aware of the likely angles of fire when choosing cover to be certain that the engine is actually between the attacker's line of fire and the defender. Even when the engine can be used, it may be advantageous to return fire from the front bumper area and avoid deflected fire from the windshield. Certainly, the "choosing" may boil down to being anywhere other than where you are at the moment of the attack, but that is not always going to be the case. When you have time to evaluate cover, pay attention to angle of impact.

- **Above all, cover only works when the defender is actually behind it.** Shooting *next to* cover is not the same as shooting *from* cover. The muzzle must clear the cover, and the eyes must be able to sight the weapon. The bad guy should see only a strip of forehead and a muzzle with a couple of eyes behind it; otherwise, the defender is not using cover. Occasionally, it is necessary to reveal a sliver of the shooting leg or hip. In instances where a traditional stance is desired, the shooter may move back from cover, still enjoying protection, but able to use common shooting and movement techniques. Cover only minimizes your target silhouette when you are returning fire. Cover doesn't cancel risk. The defender's use of cover determines the level of safety. Where no cover discipline exists, for all practical purposes, no cover exists.

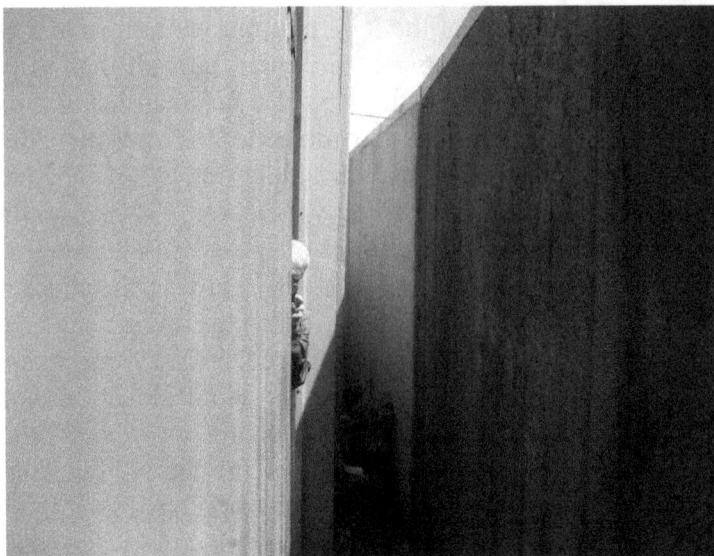

This defender is using cover as well as space and anatomy will allow.

**Handgun vs. Rifle**
Handgun: .357 Magnum 125 Grain
  5 yards: 1,300 feet per second / 470 foot-pounds of energy
Rifle: .30-06 125 Grain
  500 yards: 1,590 feet per second / 700 foot-pounds of energy

## Supplemental Firing Positions

When firing from a position other than your normal standing firing position, you will likely experience a change in eye relief. In other words, the sights being farther or nearer your eyes will alter your perspective, and your shot group will not be the same as when firing in your normal position. We see once again how marksmanship fundamentals are critical to mastering good defensive techniques. The only way to handle a change in eye relief is to train for it.

The size and nature of the cover or concealment and the juxtaposition of the attacker and defender will determine most cover-and-concealment firing positions. Above all, firing positions are determined by the shooter's need for protection. If bending at the waist and leaning against a manure spreader are necessary to deny the attacker a clear line of fire, then that is the proper shooting position. Here are a few basic supplemental positions that will allow you to adapt to most objects of cover or concealment. These positions cover a variety of heights. Consider these positions only as starting points, to be modified as needed.

1. **Modified Spetsnaz Prone**—Instead of trying to lie straight down, which requires you to bend your back like a cobra or assume a rifle-firing position that will more greatly alter your sighting, try this Practics version of a Russian special-operations technique. Lie on your side, facing your target. Pretend the whole world is turned on its side and you are simply leaning against a wall. Keep your head off the ground and in line with your sights. This is a great, natural firing position. You may position your legs forward and rearward as if running, but never let your knees pop up. You may flip the Modified Spetsnaz Prone to either side for shooting around barricades.

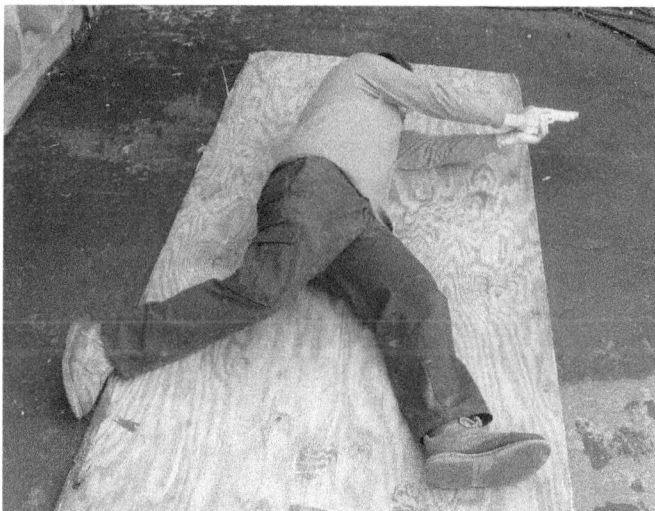

The Modified Spetnaz position allows ground level firing.

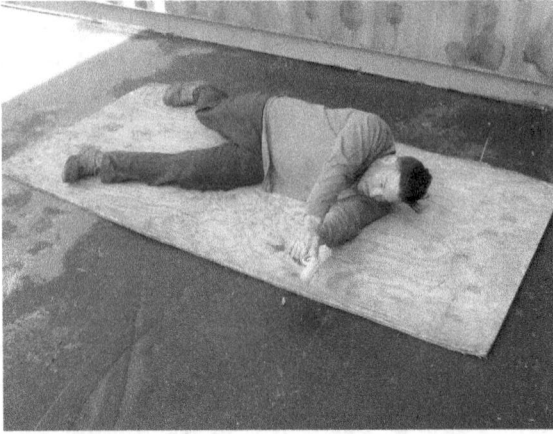

Keep your knees down.

2. **California Kneeling**—I hate the kneeling position. It hurts and is unstable, but we have it for a reason. If you have to kneel, try this method made popular with SoCal SWAT teams: Kneel with both knees, as if praying. Keep your upper body in the same position as when standing with the exception of transferring your body weight slightly behind the knees. You will find this position is actually comfortable and can be more accurate than standing.

The California Kneel is comfortable for most defenders and encourages extremely accurate fire.

This is practically a standing position in terms of posture.

3. **Cavalry Prone**—This position will give you the benefit of prone firing while offering a higher line of fire, though still lower than any kneeling position, like firing a carbine over the back of a dead horse. Due to the limited availability of dead horses, the Cavalry Prone requires the shooting arm to be braced by the support arm. The shooter's lower body rests in a traditional prone position with both feet pointed outward and against the ground for stability. The support leg may be bent at the knee. Similar to a traditional military rifle form, the support arm is placed with the elbow on the ground and the forearm raised with an open support hand, creating a platform for the shooting arm. The shooting arm is naturally extended and rests in the support hand just forward of the elbow. This position is particularly valuable when using high grass for

concealment.

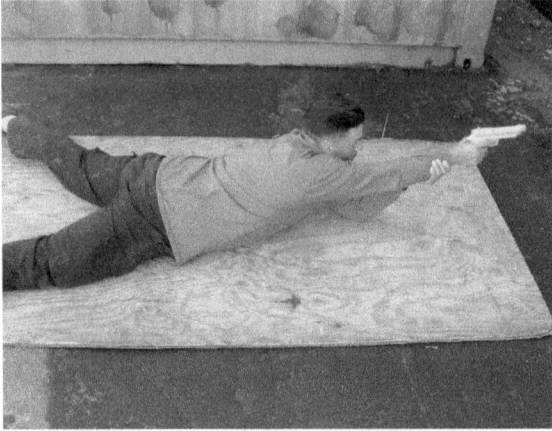

The Cavalry is very good for prone firing over moderately low obstructions.

Very similar to a traditional military rifle position.

4. **Parapet Sneak**—Here's a great transitional position between high prone and low kneeling. Another benefit of the Parapet Sneak is mobility; shooters may crawl from the Sneak. The shooter assumes a crawling position with the shooting leg forward and the support leg trailing. Resting the body back, over the shooting leg, the support leg is extended to the rear. The support arm is extended forward with the hand flat on the ground. Using a one-handed firing technique, the shooter

extends the shooting arm to aim. If the shooter has an object of cover to use as a rest, he may assume a two-handed position. Obviously this can be done from either leg, though the shooting leg will be more stable for most shooters.

The Parapet Sneak allows firing higher than the Cavalry can accommodate.

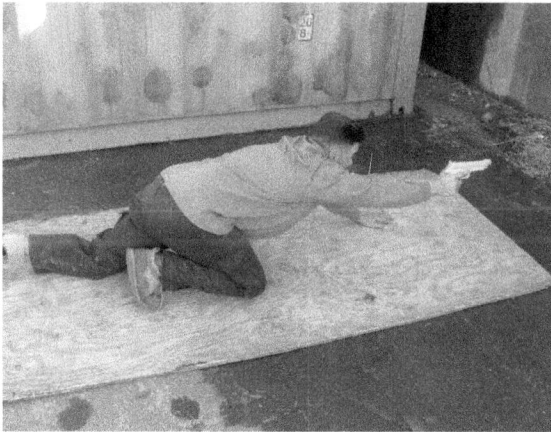

The defender can crawl in this position.

5. **Barricade Target**—This extraordinarily important technique is the starting position for most room and entrance clearances. Fortunately, the reader is already familiar with this position: Linear-Balance firing stance. The shooter brings the body slightly over the shooting foot, as in all Linear-Balance firing, extending only those few inches of the body past the barricade,

which is directly in line with the muzzle. Since Practics defenders train for ambidextrous mastery, you can use whichever hand your barricade requires. This is simple stuff with the only real addition being that the shooter will stand some reasonable distance behind the barricade, which will aid in viewing the attacker's position and reduce the perceived target size of the defender as a target. This position can also be executed by combining Linear Balance with the California Kneel.

6. **Practics Low Wedge**—This technique is intended for a low, cramped environment that forces the shooter away from the barricade but prevents sufficient distance to allow another kneeling technique, such as when forced to fire around a set of stairs or when firing between two parked cars. The shooter assumes a kneeling position, with the shooting leg kneeling and the support leg pointing toward the support side. The support arm is extended forward at a slight angle toward the shooting side, supporting and balancing the body. The shooting arm is extended for firing.

Practics Low Wedge.

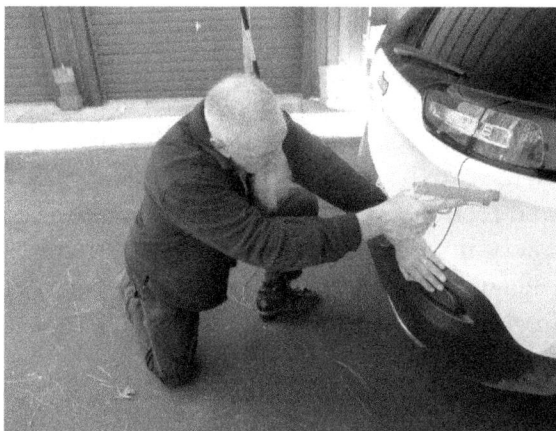

A practical use of the Low Wedge.

## Cloaked-Movement Techniques

Sometimes movement is required. In fact, movement is necessary to accomplish our security goals (which we'll discuss later). It does us little good to have good stationary cover-and-concealment firing positions if our movements do not take advantage of available C&C. I will not torture intelligent readers by teaching them how to crawl or squat, but some techniques can provide incredible protection if used properly.

**Sea-Turtle Crawl**—The goal here is to keep the entire body flat on the deck while crawling forward in a facedown position.

- Defender is flat on the floor from groin to chin.
- Knees are spread to either side at right angles from the body. Lower legs are parallel to the torso.
- Elbows are spread to either side at right angles from the body. Forearms point forward and are parallel to the torso.
- Head is tilted upward from the chin. The chin stays on the ground or no more than one inch above it. Head position is only tilted for the purpose of sight.
- Handgun is either holstered or held in the shooting hand, properly indexed and pointed straight ahead.

The Sea-Turtle-Crawl movement is a slide, pushing off the insides of the feet, the insides of the knees, and the insides of the elbows and forearms. During the exhale, the torso moves forward, followed by the limbs. If the slide is coordinated with breathing, the result will be a human moving along the ground with almost no further vertical exposure than the thickness of the individual's torso. It is essential that the head doesn't exceed the lift necessary when sight is needed. When the eyes are not required, the head can be turned toward an anticipated direction of attack with the cheek against the ground. It is also extremely important that the buttocks do not rise during the movement. Sea-Turtle Crawl can be done backward, allowing a change of direction.

Sea Turtle crawl.

**Heel Push**—This movement is for a defender lying on his back. The goal is to keep the entire body against the floor. Because this technique is propelled by a push from the heels, defenders without much leg strength may find this movement difficult when the heels cannot find sufficient purchase to push.

- Defender is flat on the ground from buttocks to the back of the head.
- Knees are spread at about a 45° angle, and the toes are pointed slightly outward.
- Weak-arm elbow is bent, and the arm is out to the side at about a 45° angle. The hand is flat against the ground.
- If the weapon is holstered, the shooting arm will duplicate weak-arm position and movement. When the handgun is in the shooting hand, the shooting forearm will be laid across the

chest sufficiently to keep the elbow off the ground but not far enough to cause the muzzle to point downward toward the weak arm. Ideally, the gun should rest at the center of the torso with the muzzle rising against the weak-side pectoral muscle.

- Head is tilted with the chin up and forehead down when forward sighting is required. Rearward sighting requires a slight lifting of the head to see over the chest. In all other cases, the head may rest with a cheek toward the ground to minimize height.

The Heel Push is a sliding movement done by pushing off the heels and, to a lesser extent, the hand(s). The defender pushes the torso forward and then resets the limbs for another push. Most defenders will not be able to keep the toes flat against the ground, but toes must be kept at the greatest angle possible to minimize exposure. Heel Push does not lend itself to reversing direction, though it may be possible in very soft dirt or sand.

The Heel Push: Keep your knees as low as possible.

## Slicing the Pie

Cover and concealment are more than locations. They're also tactics. We prefer to be covered or concealed during an attack, even during our own movements. In order to maintain the most cover and best concealment when moving, a defender moves with an awareness of his physical relationship to the object of cover or concealment. In other words, when the objective of movement is to pass through a

241

doorway, the defender uses the nearest edge of the doorway as a fulcrum from which an extended view of the adjoining room may be achieved while maintaining whatever cover the wall may provide. Certainly the attacker's position or suspected position is of the utmost importance, but the wall can be used to gain a view without actually entering the doorway. The technique used to obtain this covered or concealed view is called "Slicing the Pie." The name refers to the increasing angle of view revealed by the defender's movement; every step is a bigger slice of the pie.

Clearing doorways is among the most dangerous aspects of interior movement. We certainly don't want to clear doorways the way they do on television, standing outside and then hurling ourselves through while waving the muzzle around like a can of air freshener. The sanest way to clear a doorway is to see everything that can be seen in the adjoining room before making entry.

Here's how to Slice the Pie on a doorway or other constricted opening. Start off as close as possible to the wall on the nearest side of the doorway. Give yourself as much distance as is reasonably possible from the opening. Imagine the opening is the center of a clock and you are at either nine o'clock or three o'clock. Your intended path is to follow the semi-circle of the clock face to the other side of the doorway, which means that you will be the farthest back from the wall when passing the center of the opening. As you slowly Groucho Walk the semi-circle, you will keep your sights aligned on the doorway. From near your starting position you will be able to see if the attacker is hiding against the opposite wall on the far side of the doorway. You will slowly walk in an arc around the open door, pulling your sighting inward as you visually inspect the far side of the adjoining room. Slow and deliberate movement is mandatory. Don't out-walk your vision and ability to recognize danger. Slow means control. Attackers hidden further back along a doorway wall may not be seen. This techniques only reduces danger.

There are four advantages to this method. First, the bad guy usually assumes the entry attempt will be made from against the adjoining wall and will not focus on the interior of the adjoining room. Second, distance enables you to slowly scan the adjacent room with a greater angle of visibility. Third, you can use your normal firing position without having to compromise in order to fire around a doorway. In other words, you won't have to stick your head out or shoot single-handed. Fourth, the first portion of the defender seen by the attacker will be that limited portion of the defender's body that is directly in line with the muzzle. So if the defender is moving from nine o'clock counter-clockwise toward three o'clock, his muzzle and entire orientation will move from three o'clock (inside the adjoining room) back to nine o'clock. The attacker won't sight on the defender before the defender sights on the attacker. This level of control is what makes Slicing the Pie a literal lifesaver.

---

**Handgun vs. Rifle**

Pistol: 9mm Luger 115 grain JHP: 1,145 FPS @15'

Rifle: .223 Remington 55 grain: 3,215 FPS @15'

SAAMI Voluntary Industry Performance Standards

*Information from Sporting Arms and Ammunition Manufacturers' Institute, Inc.*

---

## Cover-And-Concealment Training

The positions offered in this section are intended to assist you in using your weapon without unnecessarily exposing yourself. Much of this training is actually a form of marksmanship training intended to make the student aware of personal deviations in bullet placement based on alterations in eye relief. The forms of the positions are of little concern (this isn't dance class), but the height and width exposure of the defender's person is most serious. Please be alert to where your head, shoulders, limbs, and buttocks are in relation to cover or concealment. Make your training partner work.

1. **Cover-and-Concealment Survey**—Conduct an inventory of available cover and concealment surrounding your home or place of business, or both, in the following manner. Inventory cover-and-concealment items within four seconds (based on the slowest member of your household or staff) of each building exit including accessible windows. Four seconds is a good general rule for determining whether you could seek cover or concealment, or if you would be forced to immediately turn and defend. Note which pieces of cover or concealment can be made serviceable by the preparation of the space immediately to the rear of the object. In other words, a big boulder is good cover and concealment but possibly not when surrounded by blackberry bushes or a pile of debris. Using each four-second piece of cover or concealment as a starting point, look for additional points of

protection that can be used to leapfrog away from the building. Try to locate cover or concealment flight paths of at least 75 yards in length. The length varies in rural locations, typically needing greater distances. The more cover-and-concealment paths you are able to plot, the better it will be when your movements are limited by the actions of an attacker(s).

Knowledge-Installation Requirement: one survey for each location of concern

Maintenance Requirement: Verify survey information seasonally or after a relocation.

2. **Modified Spetsnaz-Prone Drill (Live Fire)**—This is a marksmanship drill. Assume the modified Spetsnaz position on the 10-yard firing line. A soft surface is recommended. Your target will be a cross, drawn with a felt-tip pen on a blank sheet of paper. Slow fire five groups of five rounds. Note any differences in group position from your normal standing slow-fire striking point. The training partner will act as a safety officer and will ensure cover-and-concealment compliance by disqualifying any attempt in which the head, knees, or elbows are elevated above the topline of the body. When the shooter is in the Modified Spetsnaz Prone, the top shoulder should be the highest point of the body.

Skill-Installation Requirement: one time above drill (five groups of five rounds)

Maintenance Requirement: three times per year for five years

The above drill must be completed with the weak hand. The nature of cover and concealment is to minimize exposure through body location and position. Nowhere is weak-hand shooting more beneficial than when needed to maintain the best cover possible during firing.

3. **California-Kneeling Drill (Live Fire)**—This is another marksmanship drill from the 10-yard line with a cross target. Assume the California Kneeling and slow fire five groups of five rounds. Kneepads or a padded kneeling surface is recommended; however, do not over-elevate your position. Your point of impact should mirror your normal standing slow-fire striking point. If it does not, examine your position for Fundamentals of Marksmanship errors. The training partner will serve as a safety officer.

Skill-Installation Requirement: one time above drill (five groups of five rounds)

Maintenance Requirement: semi-annually for the first year
Drill must be conducted with the weak hand.

4. **Cavalry-Prone Drill (Live Fire)**—This is also a marksmanship drill from the 10-yard line with a cross target. Assume the Cavalry Prone and slow fire five groups of five rounds. A soft surface is recommended. Note any differences in your groups from those fired in your normal standing slow-fire position. The training partner will act as safety officer and ensure the body is kept below the muzzle and the head and that feet are pointed outward against the ground.

Skill-Installation Requirement: one time above drill (five groups of five rounds)

Maintenance Requirement: three times per year for five years
Ambidextrous training is required with the above drill.

5. **Parapet-Sneak Drill (Live Fire)**—Yet another good marksmanship drill to discover the effect of altered eye relief during positional shooting. This is a 10-yard drill, firing at a cross target five groups of five rounds. Your purpose, in addition to learning the Parapet Sneak, is to discover any alteration in your shot placement. The training partner again is a safety officer but also responsible for ensuring the body is kept down; this is not a high crawl.

Skill-Installation Requirement: one time above drill (five groups of five rounds)

Maintenance Requirement: semi-annually for the first year
Ambidextrous training is required.

6. **Practics Low-Wedge Drill (Live Fire)**—The last of the cover-and-concealment position drills is also slow fire from 10 yards at a cross target. Once again the training partner will double as safety officer and watch the position. The difference with this drill is that it requires something for the shooter to lean against. The rear of a patrol car will work for police officers. Shooters using a private range may seek permission to use an old file cabinet or other portable object heavy and stable enough to support the shooter. A rubber-footed stepladder may work well. There should not be a dramatic difference in group placement. This position is valuable for allowing good firing against the front of a stairwell or low barrier.

Skill-Installation Requirement: one time above drill (five groups of five rounds)

Maintenance Requirement: annually for the rest of your

shooting career

You know the above drill must be successfully executed with the other hand.

7. **Slicing-the-Pie Drill (Dry Fire)**—In this exercise both student and training partner may actively participate. You'll use two toy pistols. Make sure the toy guns are large enough for adult use and have some rudimentary sights (a front blade will suffice). This exercise requires two large room-size spaces divided by a wall with a doorway. The student begins with toy gun in hand and standing immediately in front of the wall on one side of the doorway. Distance between the student and the doorway should be about 20'. Unbeknownst to the student, the training partner will position himself somewhere on the other side of the wall. The training partner may choose to be against the wall on either side of the doorway or stand back somewhere in the room. The student will slowly begin Slicing the Pie. The training partner may choose to move during the exercise. Both participants will address their toy guns toward the doorway, seeking a clear "shot" at their opponents. When either party has sighted on his opponent, he will call out, ending that run of the drill. If the training partner beats the student, the student must consider that run a failure and retry, focusing on a slow, deliberate semi-circle of movement with proper body positioning. Two Practics students should spot each other at the same instant, which would be considered a successful run for both parties. The student will need the Groucho Walk to be effective during this exercise. This drill can be made more challenging through the addition of concealment objects and low lighting.

Skill-Installation Requirement: 10 successful consecutive runs of the above drill

Maintenance Requirement: 10 successful consecutive runs annually for five years

If you can't slice-the-pie with the other hand, half your home's doorways are indefensible. Do the above training with the weak hand.

8. **Sea-Turtle-Crawl Exercise**—Practicing this technique will allow the defender to know whether he has the strength and flexibility for it and to give a feel for proper execution of the movement. The training partner's job is to ensure that the body is kept as flat as possible. The defender will be tempted to raise the buttocks and back. The entire benefit of the movement is limited vertical

exposure. The training partner must be strict.

Skill-Installation Requirement: five-yard crawl holstered without error twice and five-yard crawl with handgun drawn (using toy gun) without error twice

Maintenance Requirement: above requirement annually

9. **Heel-Push Exercise**—Like the Sea Turtle, this slide technique is only of value because it allows a 6' tall defender to move along at about 16" high. The training partner must watch for raised knees and toes as well as a gun pointing at the weak arm.

Skill-Installation Requirement: five-yard crawl holstered without error twice and five-yard crawl with handgun drawn (using toy gun) without error twice

Maintenance Requirement: above requirement annually.

# Chapter Nine: Sub-contact Firing

*By failing to prepare, you are preparing to fail.*
Benjamin Franklin

*Everybody's got a plan until they get punched in the face.*
Mike Tyson

In 1934, Heavyweight Champion Max Baer fought 10–1 underdog James J. Braddock for the world title. Baer's handlers had selected Braddock as an easy payday for the champ. Baer was 26 years old; Braddock was 30. Baer was considered one of the most devastating heavyweights in the history of the sport. Braddock's record prior to the title fight was so bad that the fight would likely not be sanctioned today. However Braddock, aka the Cinderella Man, beat Baer, and the fight became one of the greatest upsets in boxing history.

Everything can fail. Anyone can lose. Statistics, percentages, and odds cease to mean anything when real life occurs. If you must defend yourself from another human being, there is an excellent chance that something will go wrong.

Practics considers the handgun to be a modern version of the sword or fighting knife, and as such the handgun must be effective at extremely close range. When people fight—really fight—they tend to wind up occupying the same space. When weapons or maneuvering techniques fail to keep the attacker away, the defender must be able to effectively fire the handgun quickly and within a few inches. Traditionally, firearm training has limited the use of handguns to arm's reach and beyond. Open-hand techniques were usually considered to be the best answer for attacks that had successfully breached the point-shooting plane. That view makes little sense. An encounter that merits deadly force doesn't require a lesser response when the handgun fails. It demands an even more aggressive and immediate firearm response due to the increased likelihood of defender injury and impending limits on defender consciousness or physical ability to mount a defense. When a handgun is present during a fight, someone is going to use it. Neglecting to use your firearm, when a firearm is required, is an invitation for your attacker to take your gun.

Close-range attacks are difficult to counter for two specific reasons: time and space. Time to retreat, seek protection, draw a weapon, give commands, or aim is greatly reduced when someone is choking the daylights out of the defender. The restriction of space needed to bring a weapon to bear is heightened when the defender has been pushed down and repeatedly punched. You can't point shoot if you can't point. Drawing and presenting a handgun in the traditional sense requires more space than a grappling match will allow. Since we're not willing to give up, we'll have to adjust the manner in which we present and use the handgun during close-range encounters.

Security is enhanced when the muzzle has some purchase on the clothing or flesh of the attacker. Sub-contact firing is discharging a firearm into a human being beneath the outline of the body. The defender uses the muzzle to press against the flesh of the attacker prior to or during discharge. The reasons for compressing the clothing and flesh of the attacker are security and accuracy. Accuracy must be achieved by touch; sub-contact firing is neither aimed fire nor point shooting.

To better understand sub-contact firing, let's consider how it may be used. A too common situation in law enforcement involves an officer knocked to a sitting or supine position with an attacker standing over the officer and continuing the attack with punches, kicks, or a blunt object. In many of these instances the officer will receive facial injuries, causing blood flow around the hairline, forehead, or brow. Thus the officer is injured, on the ground, under attack, and blind. Any form of aimed fire is impossible, and turning or elevating the body to face the attacker is unlikely while under a barrage of blows. In such a case, sub-contact firing is likely to be quick, accurate, and effective. For the sake of our example we'll say our right-handed officer is knocked to a sitting position with the attacker facing the officer and straddling his legs while throwing wild punches downward at his head. The officer's sub-contact firing response is as follows:

- Latch onto the attacker by wrapping the left arm around the attacker's left knee, placing the head to the outside of the attacker's left leg (this will provide a second of protection from blows). Pull the attacker's leg as tightly as possible against the upper chest and left shoulder.
- Draw the handgun with the right hand and thrust the handgun downward and forward onto the top of the attacker's left foot. The motion is a twist, like a punch.
- Close the eyes.
- The instant the muzzle is felt pressing against the attacker's foot, fire shots while continuing to press the muzzle into the attacker's foot.

Sub-contact firing can be boiled down into two elements:

**1. Secure the attacker.** Locking the attacker against your body guarantees that you will know where and how the attacker is positioned without having to see him. An attacker's instantaneous response to the presentation of a firearm is likely to be a withdrawal of the nearest body part. Securing the attacker ensures target access but also protects the defender by accounting for defender limbs in relation to the anticipated direction of fire. It is difficult to punch or kick oneself, and, likewise, it is difficult for an attacker to successfully strike a person who is clinging tightly against his body. When the defender uses his upper body to "lock up" the attacker, he also gains some protection against blows to the head.

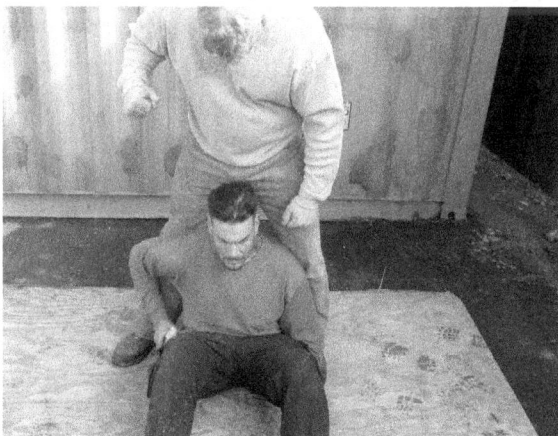

The defender is taking a beating.

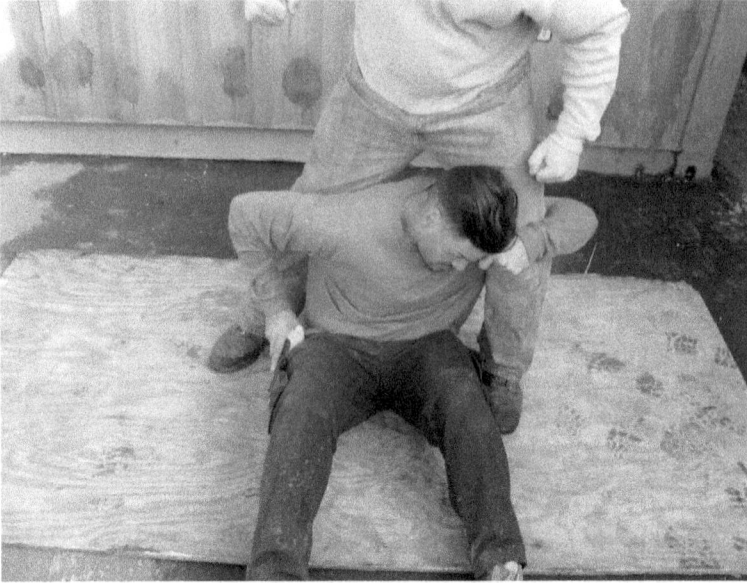

The defender secures the target and protects his own head by forcing the attacker to punch inward.

2. **Thrust the handgun into the target and fire.** Like the sword, the Practics handgun pierces en motion. By firing at the instant the muzzle strikes the secured portion of the attacker, the defender denies the attacker the opportunity to attempt to disarm the defender. Whether in the dark or blinded, recognizing the target with the muzzle ensures relatively safe and effective fire. Additionally, sub-contact firing is blisteringly quick because no aiming is required, only the split-second it takes to touch the attacker with the muzzle. It is worth noting that both point shooting and marksmanship require deliberate aiming to the extent of deciding where to point the muzzle, whereas sub-contact firing needs only contact, which can be done during absolute blindness or darkness.

Even blinded, the defender can find his target.

Naturally, the physical technique is a bit more complicated than "grab and shoot," but the process is logical and easy to learn. Once the student realizes the objectives of sub-contact firing, the technique can be applied broadly in a variety of circumstances.

Objectives:
- Prevent target movement.
- Protect defender's head and body.
- Deny attacker control of the handgun.
- Fire until the defender is free to gain a better shooting position, the PDT or other vital area may be engaged, or the threat has been stopped.

Preventing the target movement, as mentioned, is necessary to guarantee accurate fire but has some safety benefits as well. When the target is secured, the defender knows the location of his own body in relation to the intended path of the bullet. When thrashing about on the ground and firing into an unsecured portion of the attacker's body, the defender may inadvertently be firing into his own leg or hand by firing through the attacker. Locking the target greatly reduces the likelihood of such an error.

We don't want any portion of our bodies to be hurt, but sub-contact firing is about speed. All the defender wants to do is get shots accurately into the target. This offense is the best defense for a defender being repeatedly stabbed on the ground. So we will take a third of a second to protect the head (or throat) when the head is in immediate danger; it is reasonable to do so *because the head is needed to shoot.* There is no time to wrestle into a more desirable position, and, in fact, the defender may not be able to gain such an advantage. Sub-contact firing is done when the defender is a couple of seconds away from the end of his life. The attacker is welcome to chew on your neck for the two seconds it takes you to draw and fire rounds into his person. The head can be sufficiently protected against blows for two seconds by pressing it against the attacker or driving the chin into the chest and lifting the shoulders upward. This "turtle" technique can also buy a second or two when an attacker is attempting to choke or render unconscious the defender from behind. The objective is to protect only the head (and throat) and then only when necessary. Time is everything.

Bigger, stronger attackers can take your handgun away only if they can get their hands on it. When both parties are lying on the ground and the attacker is applying a rear-naked choke to the defender, it is paramount that the draw be quick and the handgun move below the waist. If the handgun moves above the waist, the attacker may use one hand to grab the gun or may abandon the choke in favor of taking possession of the gun. Of course, if there were time, a standing attacker could simply bend over to grab a drawn handgun, but the sitting defender needs less than two seconds to draw and put rounds in the target. You are making your projectile firing device into a short sword. Time is everything. Speed is the defense.

Again, everything in Practics (and, I will presume to say, within defensive shooting) is interrelated. Here we're talking about sub-contact firing and still must come back to the Practics Gold Standard. Firing begins with no intention of stopping and ceases the instant the threat has stopped. How many rounds? However many it takes. The threat may pause, which would allow a sitting defender to move into a Rollover or Kneel Up (remember Falling Fire) and aim at the PDT. I witnessed a man shot in the leg with a hot JHP round from about a 15" distance from the muzzle. The round certainly caught his attention, but it did not cause him to drop or lose control of himself. One of my colleagues shot an armed suspect in the side with a 9mm JHP. The impact only caused the hoodlum to run very fast. A couple of weeks later, he was arrested while hiding in his mother's home. Mom had cleaned and wrapped his wound, and he was in pretty good shape. People react differently to physical and emotional trauma.

Generally speaking, a bullet wound will buy a brief respite in the action and allow the defender an opportunity to gain a better position or make good an escape, but defenders should not expect a single round or even several rounds to end the threat. Firing stops when the threat stops.

Understanding the objectives of sub-contact firing will allow the reader to use the technique based on need rather than form. However, like most things, form is necessary to make physical the ideals of the training. Here are some simple rules that will guide you in developing Practics Sub-contact Firing Skills.

- The non-firing hand, arm, or leg is used to secure the target area. Always strive for 10" between the muzzle and the securing limb. For instance, a sitting defender with a standing, facing attacker may grab the right side of the attacker's belt and waistband while using the muzzle to compress the clothing and flesh at the junction of the attacker's left upper thigh and groin. Such a position is easily felt, and the defender—even without sight—can verify the relative safety of it.

Grab clothing or body fat to secure your target and prevent shooting yourself.

- The securing arm should be locked when straight. A locked arm—anybody's locked arm—is initially a bit harder to push away and, more importantly, serves as a directional yardstick, letting the defender know where the target is in relation to the

255

defender's body.

- When securing a target with the hand, the hand should always be a fist. If you grab a belt, do not allow the fingers to extend below the waistline. The less exposed you are, the less likely your rounds will strike you. If the defender's arm is wrapped around an attacker's abdomen and the muzzle is jammed down into the top of his hip, the hand should still be fisted. Grab some shirt and hold on tightly.
- Shut your eyes. This is not marksmanship. Shut your eyes to protect them from flying bone fragments and unburned powder and debris from your handgun. Practics Sub-contact Firing is as close as you'll get to a sure thing in shooting. Shut your eyes.
- Twist the gun like a punch. Screw it into the target, and it will go farther and affix more securely. Firing begins at contact but the screwing motion helps to prevent muzzle bounce, which could force the defender to relocate the target.
- Fire like a nail-gun operator. When the muzzle drills into the surface of clothing, fat, or muscle, firing instantly begins. As the muzzle hits the target, the finger moves onto the trigger, and all slack is taken from trigger travel. On the force of twisting contact, firing occurs.

## Dangers of Sub-Contact Firing

There is, however, a technical problem. Firing with the pistol inside a target of flesh or clothing can result in a slide that doesn't properly seat. The defender must be ready to Top Rack if failure occurs. Will failure occur? Count on it. Better yet, train for it. If we don't actually fire beneath the surface in order to avoid possible malfunctions, then we can't fire when blind, and we can't fire as quickly. Then we're back to where we started. Sub-contact firing requires a properly broken-in handgun and competent handgun maintenance.

The 10" rule is a goal that will not always be achievable. However, wrapping an arm around the back of a leg and firing through the front of the leg at the same level is deliberately shooting oneself. Even when the line of fire will miss the defender's body, strikes to bone are extremely likely to deflect bullets. Deflected rounds can travel several inches, more than a foot, inside the attacker's body before exiting and striking a defender. The 10" rule is no guarantee of defender safety, but the odds are good for missing the defender altogether or ensuring that a striking round has been greatly slowed before exiting the attacker.

I mentioned in the introduction that safety must share a proportionate risk with effectiveness of technique. Sub-contact firing is dangerous to both parties. I do not offer it lightly, nor do I recommend the reader acquire the skill without considering the potential risks. Things will strike you when firing into a solid object at kissing distance. If there is something else the defender can do to save his life, I encourage him to do it. Practics Sub-contact Firing is a last resort for a failing defender during what is potentially the last few moments of his life. It is not intended for a sporting day at the range.

## Practics Sub-Contact Firing Training

Training for this skill is difficult because firing is done closer than any public range will allow. The shooter is too close to the muzzle, and targets need to properly imitate the human body. Fortunately, we have some excellent dry-fire drills available. A full-size training handgun may be used instead of a storage-safe firearm without a magazine. Safety awareness must be flawless during sub-contact training.

1. **Pillow-Attack Drills**—These non-firing drills require an old, thin bed pillow; two pieces of wood poles (such as handles from shovels), 3' to 4' long; and a storage-safe weapon. No ammunition may be present. Duct tape the poles together, side to side, to prevent any movement. Wrap the pillow around the two pieces of wood as tightly as possible and completely bind the pillow with tape. The result will be a tightly padded cylinder with two "bones" running through the center and exposed on either side. Take a pair of old jeans from a portly friend and horizontally cut across the top portion of one leg in order to create a tube of fabric. Stuff the taped pillow inside the denim cylinder and tape the bottom and top of the denim to the wood poles tightly enough to hold the sleeve in place. The denim sleeve will simulate an attacker's clothing. The longer you can make the padded area of the attack pillow, the better, provided you leave at least 6" of exposed poles on either end for the training partner to grab. This completed object is your attack pillow.

The Pillow.

You know the objectives of sub-contact firing, and you also know that the actual positioning used depends on the attacker. The training partner will control the attack pillow for the student. The attack pillow can be used to simulate almost any part of the body, except for hands and feet. Whether lying down, kneeling, sitting, or standing, the attack pillow can be positioned to serve as a target for dry-fire training. The training partner may place one end of the poles against the ground and brace the top ends to simulate a leg, or he may hold both ends and present the pillow horizontally to simulate the hips and groin area. The student will discover that the pillow moves when struck unless secured. Bones can deflect a press. Clothing and flesh can be slippery. Use the pillow to simulate any relevant position imaginable. At the very least you must train for the following:

- Sitting with the standing attacker to the front
- Lying on your side with the pillow at your chest to simulate both parties on the ground
- Lying on your back to address the abdomen of a straddling attacker

258

Each of the above three positions requires 20 successful draws and sub-contact firings (dry fire). Student must have three good trigger presses without losing contact with the pillow. Muzzle slipping is a failure. Failing to twist into the pillow will disqualify the attempt.

**The training partner must never cross the line of the muzzle with his own body.** The pillow can be held from behind or to the side of the student. If necessary, two training partners will be used. Practicing slowly is perfectly all right, but the above requirements must be done at full speed and power. Your attack pillow should not have a long life span. Dry fire as you strike hard and twist in.

Sparring pillows should be abused. They're easy to make.

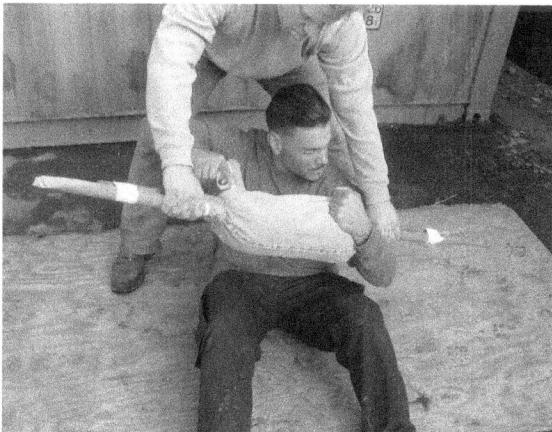

Pillow training device allows a safe simulation of limbs and body for sub-contact training.

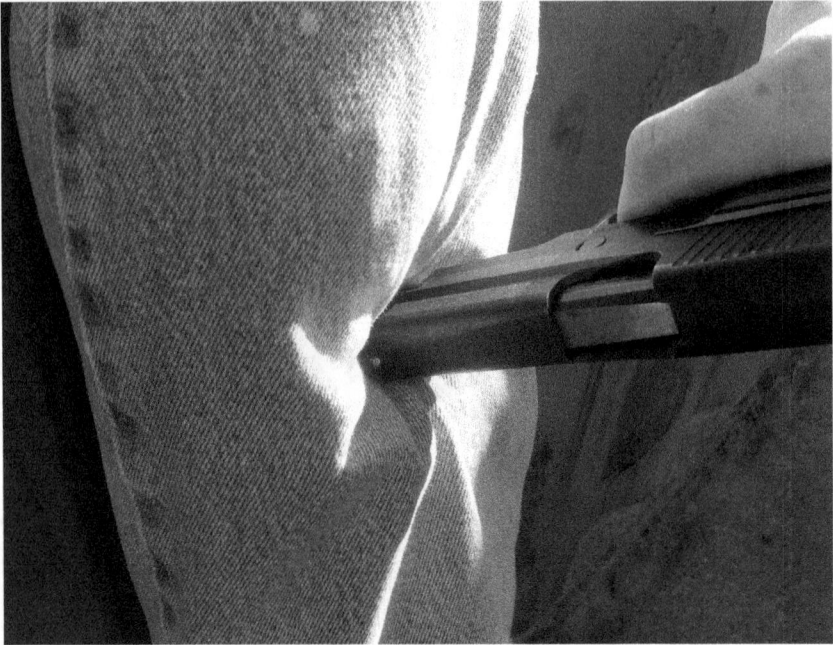

Sub-contact firing is shooting by touch. Plant your muzzle.

Skill-Installation Requirement: 20 reps of each of the three mandatory positions · five sets

Maintenance Requirement: above requirement bi-monthly for the duration of your shooting career. This is your version of a speed bag. Use it often.

What good is a last resort if the defender has to ask the attacker to wait until he can use his "good" hand? The above training must also be done with the weak hand drawing from the strong-side holster. By now you should be an ambidextrous shooter.

2. **Sparring**—This non-firing drill requires the use of a toy pistol the size of a real handgun. The student begins with the toy pistol in hand from a standing or sitting position while the training partner begins from a position of advantage, such as standing over the student. No takedowns are permitted. This is not a wrestling match. Decide in advance whether the drill will be standing, prone, or sitting. This exercise is intended to *simulate* fight positioning. Safety requires that both parties move at half speed. The student's learning goal is to

discover available points for sub-contact firing while protecting his throat or head. The training partner, moving at half speed, will swing gentle, open-handed slaps at the defender's head while trying to avoid the defender's gun. The defender has the responsibility to secure the attacker, twist in the gun, close his eyes, and fire his toy pistol. Remember to lock the arm securing the attacker and try for 10" between the muzzle's line of fire and any part of the defender's body. The training partner will disqualify any attempt in which the muzzle slips or the defender points the gun at himself (either directly or through the attacker's body). The student will simulate firing by saying "bang" until the training partner withdraws or pauses the attack, and the training partner will go no further than the fourth "bang." After cessation of the threat, a lying student will transition into a Rollover or Kneel-Up. Rollovers become Kneel-Ups, which then become standing positions. When the student is on his feet and has attained sufficient distance for sighted fire, he will give a proper command for the attacker to "Stop!" At that point the drill ends.

Skill-Installation Requirement: To the extent your health will allow, engage in a *half-speed*, free-flowing exercise of the above drill. Complete no fewer than five successful attempts. Take a break. Repeat five times.

Maintenance Requirement: the above requirement every two months for one year

Naturally, the entire above training must be immediately repeated with the other hand.

3. **Sub-contact Malfunction Drill**—This non-firing drill is about speed. The premise is that a defender has fired a sub-contact shot and suffered a malfunction. The defender must be able to work the slide using the Top-Rack method from any position. A storage-safe weapon is needed for this drill, no ammunition may be present during training, and the training partner will search the area for safety prior to training. No fight simulation or training attacker is permitted. The student will begin each position with the handgun in the shooting hand. On command from the training partner, the student will dry fire in a safe direction with one trigger press and assume a malfunction has occurred. An immediate Top-Rack remedy will be executed. A successful execution will keep the muzzle away from the defender and be completed in less than one second. The training partner will serve as timekeeper. Conduct Top-Rack remedies in each of the following

positions. All positions refer to the defender

Sitting Positions:
- (attacker in front) legs naturally open, handgun off to the shooting side
- (attacker to rear) legs naturally open, handgun in front of abdomen
- (attacker crawling, closing to defender's front) legs naturally open, handgun held overhead

Kneeling Positions:
- (shooting knee up) gun to shooting side
- (supporting knee up) gun to shooting side
- (shooting knee up) gun to support side
- (supporting knee up) gun to support side

Lying Positions:
- (on shooting side) gun at waist level
- (on support side) gun at waist level

The above positions are not intended to be positions of strict form or even actual defensive positions. The defender may very well wind up in such a position, but the intention is to provide changes in body balance and reach so that the student will be trained to successfully conduct a Top-Rack remedy in whatever position he finds himself.

Skill-Installation Requirement: all nine positions for 20 reps each

Maintenance Requirement: above requirement quarterly for two years

The above training must be repeated for the weak hand.

Practics Sub-contact Firing is extraordinarily simple but so is shooting a handgun. The difficulty is in doing it effectively. Please remember that the training suggested in this book is only my recommended minimum. Train like your life depends on it.

# Chapter Ten: Contact Fighting

*Victory is always possible for the person who refuses to stop fighting.*

Napoleon Hill

*Chance fights ever on the side of the prudent.*

Euripides

*I intend to live forever, or die trying.*

Groucho Marx

Most police officers of some experience have had their share of fistfights. A small percentage of those fights have involved an attempt by an opponent to possess or direct the officer's gun. Considering the distance between people during most gunfights (less than 6'), it is extremely likely that close-range deadly force encounters will include attempted gun grabs as well as punches and kicks. Sub-contact firing is typically the result of the defender being overwhelmed and forced to compensate for disastrous circumstances. Confrontations usually begin with the defender having some opportunity to attempt a standing defense of some distance. Everything that happens after the opportunity for a standing distance defense has passed is likely to be contact fighting—combatants within reach of each other.

Aside from the problem of protecting the gun during close-range confrontations, the greater problem is using the gun in defense. The handgun is never truly at rest in Practics. We are always drawing, presenting, firing, reloading, holstering, or protecting the weapon. If engaging the gun is not an immediate objective, then whatever you are doing is not Practics. The handgun *is* the defense, and the defender must constantly weigh the need to deploy the weapon against the Gold

Standard and the dangers of a possible gun takeaway.

**Drawing**—The firearm, once available, is—by threat or by use—the greatest magnification of individual power the law-abiding citizen wields.

**Holstering**—Using belt access as a platform for deploying the handgun enables the almost instant use of weaponry while allowing free use of both hands. The holster is essential to the successful use of the handgun in defensive situations.

**Protecting**—In cases where the attacker is attempting to disarm the defender of the holstered handgun, drawing may not be wise. The defender must protect the holstered weapon until drawing is possible or no longer necessary.

Always be thinking about your immediate handgun objective. It's the gun—always.

## Practics Holster Defense

Close encounters put the firearm at risk, whether in the hand or in the holster. Defending the holster is like defending the castle: If the attacker doesn't get tired and quit and the defender doesn't hurt the attacker, the gun will likely be lost.

In the nineties, one of my fellow officers was attacked during broad daylight in a convenience-store parking lot. The officer was knocked to the ground, and the suspect stood over him, yanking on the officer's safety/retention holster. For about two minutes the attacker yanked on the safety holster while the officer used both hands to force the pistol downward inside the holster. The attacker repeatedly lifted the officer off the ground by pulling on the gun. All of the officer's energy was spent reinforcing the holster. Eventually the attacker tired, losing arm strength, and released the holster and fled. The officer told me that he was convinced that the level III safety holster saved his life. At any rate, holding onto a holster with both hands may be necessary when nothing else is available, but it isn't a guaranteed winning strategy.

The first Practics objective during an attempted holster raid in which both parties are standing is to secure the gun. Even safety/retention holsters need help. The shooting hand must be placed on the butt of the weapon to force the gun down in the holster. Really grab hold of the gun—lock on it. Even if the scoundrel works the gun loose, you'll be the one with a shooter's grip.

Our secondary objectives are attacker minimization, balance, and gaining time. I realize that's saying a lot, but it's easier and more sensible than it sounds. For the attacker to muscle the gun out of the holster, he needs about a foot of space. Try it. Lifting a weight that is pressed against the lifter's body all but eliminates the use of the back muscles. It becomes a reduced arm-and-limited-shoulder effort. So, we take the support arm and throw it around the attacker, pulling him close with all the strength of the back, shoulder, and arm muscles. The defender needs to quickly close the distance between the parties with a fast step and continue moving forward faster than the attacker may back away. (The embrace may work with an attacker sitting or lying on the defender, depending on size and position of the parties.) Now attacker and defender are roughly chest-to-chest, and the defender is using his arm and shoulder to aid the holster in retaining the weapon. The attacker is trying an upward arm pull while being pressed against the defender and forced backward (attacker minimization). The threat is temporarily stalled. Throughout this objective, remember to keep a firm grip on the holstered gun with your shooting hand. Balance, the next part of the second objective, is critical because the defender will have to remove the support arm from around the attacker in order to finish his defense. During an attempted gun grab from the holster, the attacker and defender will often begin to move in a circular path, pivoting around the holstered handgun with ever increasing speed as the attacker attempts to leverage the handgun from the holster. If both parties continue spinning in a circular fashion around the holstered gun, the defender will find it difficult to bring the support arm to bear against the momentum of the movement. When the bodies are brought together, the defender will cease stumbling in a circle. The embrace temporarily steadies the defender and stabilizes both parties. Forcing the attacker rearward ends circling and reinforces defender balance. This is what buys the defender time for the next objective.

The third objective is to draw your knife with the support hand while keeping that shooting hand locked on the butt of the gun. Using an inward swinging motion, thumb forward, slam your blade into the attacker's back and twist. Repeat. At some point the attacker will momentarily release the holster. If the attacker pulls away between the embrace and the knife swing, the knife will likely land on the side or front of the attacker's torso. It makes no difference as long as the bad guy releases your gun. *Remember, your legs must keep forcing your chest against the attacker's chest. Keep pressing into the attacker.* While stabs to the face and throat will likely be more effective, few attackers will stand still for it, and such thrusts approach the target within the attacker's field of vision, encouraging a block or a knife grab. The most practical target for the average defender is the back of the attacker.

Finally, create distance and draw the handgun. If you're not in a crowd and don't fear other attackers and if you desire a two-hand hold (good for you), toss the knife behind you with a low, backward pitch of the hand and support the shooting hand with the support hand or leave the knife sticking in your attacker's back. In the event that you do not have a knife, swing your support-side elbow at the attacker's head. Swing like your life depends on it. Put every ounce of body weight behind the effort. When standing, the effort starts in the legs; when lying down, it starts at the waist. If the attacker is sitting on you, you won't be able to reach him with the elbow. In that case, as soon as the embrace is released, punch the attacker in the *front of the throat* with the *middle* knuckles of the entire fist (not the top or the base knuckles of the digits) of your support hand. Punching someone in the throat is more difficult than it appears in the movies because once the chin drops, the punch is blocked. If the fingers are folded at the middle knuckles and the thumb is laid alongside, the hand will likely fit under the chin and strike the throat. The punch must be done as the suspect is pulling away after the embrace because if the attacker is forewarned, he can easily avoid it. (I do not recommend eye gouging. Your idiot author learned the hard way by forcing a thumb into a madman's eye socket forcefully enough to push the eyeball back and hard enough to cause trauma but still unable to force compliance.) Criminals need to be conscious, and they need to breathe in order to attack you. Land a blow to the attacker's head or strike his throat. Focus on denying the attacker what he needs, and he'll let your gun go. Then create distance and draw your handgun.

Use your shooting hand to secure your handgun in the holster.

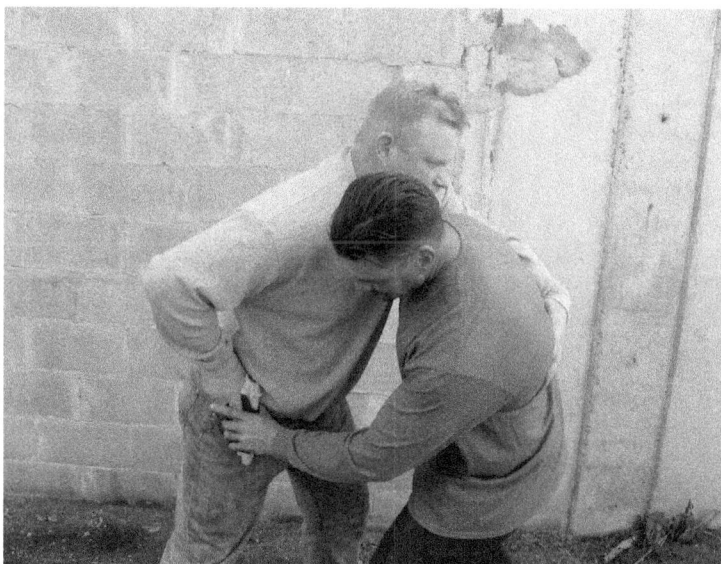

Use your support arm to close the distance between torsos.

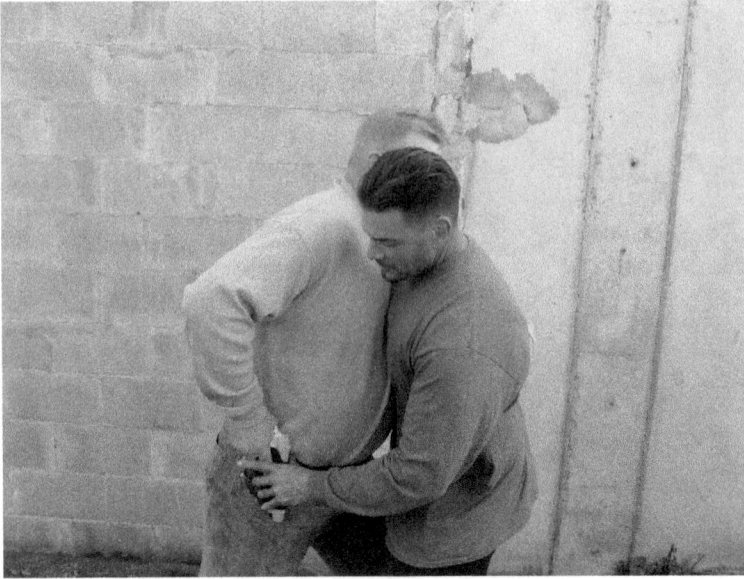

Drive the attacker backward.

Keep the attacker off balance with your momentum and draw your knife.

Thrust the knife into the attacker's back.

Create distance and draw your weapon.

A punch to the throat requires the fist be flattened. This technique requires little skill but needs practice.

As repeatedly mentioned, everything goes wrong under stress and strain. If all else fails and the attacker is pulling you by the holster and denying you an embrace, give him what he wants. Dead run at the savage and throw your support arm around his opposing leg. Pull the leg tight into you as you lower your strong side shoulder. You must keep forcing your handgun into the holster with the strong hand. As you force the attacker back, keep lowering your shoulder, which will create a wedge between you. Your goal is to force him onto his back or cause him to release the handgun. You'll likely wind up on top, and he'll find the holster raid extremely difficult from his back. In the real-life case of the officer who was attacked in the parking lot, it was not possible to close the distance between attacker and defender. The officer's actions were fortunately sufficient for his protection. If the officer had lost his strength before the attacker was exhausted, the situation could have been tragic. A knife in your support hand will force the attacker to remove at least one hand from the gun. Properly preparing the gun belt is an integral part of your gun-retention strategy.

## Practics Muzzle Leveraging

Big people, generally speaking, can pull things away from little people. Leverage changes all that. A little girl can out lift the world's strongest man if sufficient leverage is used. Handgun leverage is intertwined with the mechanics of grip. Whoever holds the grip portion *tends* to have a practical advantage over whoever holds the end of the barrel. Nonetheless, a person with a sufficient strength advantage or the use of a simple leveraging technique can yank the handgun away from the defender regardless of hand placement or superior defender strength. Magnifying the grip-placement advantage by using the defender's entire body to leverage against the attacker is therefore necessary, which will nullify the attacker's use of his entire body, as you'll see in a moment. This technique can allow a small woman to control her handgun against a very large man.

Let's say an attacker grabs the slide of a defender's pistol and pushes the muzzle off to the side. The attacker then takes a step forward to strike the defender or to get between the defender and her gun in order to disarm her. The defender's Practics response is best understood in terms of a clock face. The attacker's location will be considered the center of the clock. The defender will quickly shuffle her body around the clock face as if she were a hand of the clock. Her goal is to get behind the gun, putting it between herself and the attacker. Regardless of where the attacker pushes or pulls the muzzle, once the defender's body is behind the gun, the muzzle will be pointing at the attacker. All that is required at that instant is for the defender to press the trigger.

The defender must avoid a pulling battle over the handgun—a hazard in muzzle leveraging, especially for women. The defender must never stick her butt out and bend her torso forward. It's not necessary. If the attacker wants to pull, go with him. Simply move around the clock face until the muzzle is in line with the attacker. If you lean back and pull, the attacker can charge or release the handgun, causing you to fall backward. Keep your balance, high step, and move quickly. The defender's 120 pounds guiding the handgun grips will out leverage a 300-pound attacker trying to control the weight of the defender and her gun with only his finger and wrist strength. It's just that simple.

She cannot out-muscle her attacker.

He cannot stop her from getting behind her weapon and firing. An exercise in physics.

Her muzzle is forced off target to her left side.

She shuffles her body behind the muzzle and brings it rightward onto her attacker.

## Practics Fallback

A good takedown hurts. Really hurts. The attacker deprives

the defender of the ability to move the leg(s) rearward as the defender is lifted slightly upward and then driven onto his back. On a hard surface a takedown may take your breath, knock you unconscious, or break your bones. Properly done, the takedown is quick and difficult to counter because of the low position of the incoming attacker. Since the attacker is focused on the defender's legs, escape is more difficult than during an upright attack, when a defender might successfully block with his arms. Watch a mixed-martial-arts (MMA) match, and you'll see fighters that fear the strikes of an opponent will often prefer to fight on the ground. The attacker will lower his body beneath the reach of his standing opponent and "shoot in" to grab the legs and execute a takedown. This doesn't always work against a professional fighter, but it will work more times than not in a typical street fight. Fighting a low, quick opponent—whether it's a pit bull or a man—is extremely difficult, and running backwards or sideways is tough to accomplish when your opponent is running forward toward you. If running away or creating a spatial buffer is achievable, the takedown can be prevented or delayed. However, the trained attacker within a confined area has a strong likelihood of success against most untrained defenders. Since proficiency in grappling is probably not in the cards for most defenders, let's accept the probability of a successful takedown.

In Practics we accept the likely success of the takedown and put our time and effort toward our strength: the handgun. Even getting the handgun from the holster in time can be a problem, but if the handgun is drawn and the Gold Standard is met, the takedown defense will be the handgun. When dogs attack police officers, the officers very often wind up firing near their own feet. That happens because of the speed with which the dog can close its attacking distance. A quick, low attack is extremely difficult to counter at close distance. Our response has to recognize our inherent disadvantages as well as our strengths.

What is the Practics answer to the low-leg grab? America's favorite pastime.

Think about a baseball player running toward home plate, fearing the ball is about to be thrown to the catcher. The runner, desiring every inch of space and wanting to force the catcher to reach for him, will always slide home. By going lower than his opponent, the runner creates space and gains time. In Practics we fall back, away from the takedown, also seizing the reach-and-time advantage from the attacker and gaining precious fractions of a second to finish the draw.

Traditional strategies have focused on the defender either blocking the assault or moving beyond the attacker's reach. A competent takedown maneuver renders those old techniques largely ineffective because the approach is too low and difficult to block and the attack is a forward run, making rearward retreat comparatively slow and clumsy. Certainly a skilled fighter will have a greater chance of defeating the takedown through traditional means. But the average defender, not possessing such skill, will find a competent takedown extremely difficult to prevent. None of this is meant to suggest that a defender must use the Fallback defense when a sidestep technique would obviously work, as in the case of an unsteady drunk attacking from a distance requiring more than two seconds to cover. The Practics Fallback is intended when the defender is faced with an inevitable takedown. Even in the case of a high attack, if you know that you are going onto your back, the Fallback allows you some control. If you can do something else—do it. The Fallback is the Practics solution to an inevitable takedown during an incident meriting the use of deadly force.

As noted earlier, the Fallback is also potentially painful. You *are* falling down. Nonetheless, falling down in a controlled manner is infinitely better than being driven onto your back under someone else's weight and force. Keep in mind that the purpose of this technique is to allow the defender time to draw the handgun and the space in which to use it.

Let's examine the elements of the successful Fallback for a right-handed defender:

1. Right leg is moved rearward and to the right one step, putting the defender's body between the holster and the attacker.
2. The body pivots toward the right side, orienting the body at an angle from the attacker. The feet, hips, and shoulders are pointing at about a 45° angle toward the left of the charging attacker.
3. The defender assumes a crouching position as the right hand draws the handgun and the heel of the left hand is forcefully thrust downward at the charging attacker with the purpose of

either grabbing hold of hair, ears, shirt, flesh, or serving to lessen the attacker's charge. The two arms, moving at the same time, will benefit in speed and force through the combined movements of the back and shoulder muscles.

4. The right elbow is lifted parallel to the right shoulder and brought forward, in line with the chest. The right hand and gun are laid high on the left pectoral, pointing the muzzle over the shoulder. This will prevent breaking your elbow on concrete and secure the handgun during impact. Because the body is angled, the handgun will be pointing in the general compass direction of the attacker. If you do not properly index, you run the risk of shooting your support arm or shoulder upon impact with the ground. Even in advanced techniques, fundamental skills are essential. The reason the weapon is secured to the chest is retention. If you hold the gun off to the side, the attacker will have the advantageous momentum to grab it. If you point the handgun too soon, you risk losing it on impact with the attacker.

5. The right foot swings forward past the left foot as the defender's body falls from bottom to top, with the right foot serving as the first portion of the body to strike the ground (the left foot doesn't intentionally leave the ground) and the right hip and buttocks serving as the center point at which the body strikes the ground. The goal is to fall backward not sideways. If the defender falls too far toward the right side, he will strike the right elbow on impact. On soft dirt it won't matter, but on a hard surface it may render your arm inoperable or send your handgun sliding across the floor.

6. Once the hips contact the ground, the defender will pull his knees up to force distance with the attacker. In some cases raising the knees will not be possible due to the attacker having already grabbed the defender's legs above the knees. In either case the attacker's body will prevent the defender's legs from flying upward.

7. The final step is to follow good sub-contact firing procedure: The left hand grabs the attacker, and the right hand thrusts and twists the handgun, which is fired on muzzle impact. Muzzle targeting will depend on the attacker's position. Remember what you're trying to achieve and use proper sub-contact

technique.

The Practics Fallback uses the knees to maintain distance.

## Choking Defenses

Choking can cause unconsciousness and eventually death . . . in time. On the other hand, restricting the blood flow of the carotid arteries can cause unconsciousness within a few seconds, followed by death. The blood-restricting choke is what is referred to in mixed martial arts as a "rear naked choke" and in police circles as a "carotid restraint." Thus an arm across the front of your throat is bad, but compression on the sides of your throat is a whole lot worse. In either case the use of strength as a means of escape is likely to fail. The attacker can choke using both arms, both shoulders, and the upper back, whereas the defender can only pull at the attacker's choke with hand and partial arm strength. Additionally the attacker can use his legs to keep the defender's lower body close and relatively immobile. We've already discussed the futility of eye gouges against a determined opponent. When men are grappling, they tend to "shut" their faces like a fist, bringing the brow and the cheeks close.

Defenders should not expect to stick a finger in an attacker's eye with much effect. Rear chokes protect the attacker's throat and groin too. Watch an MMA match, and you'll see that 99.9% of the time, a properly applied rear naked choke signals the end of the fight. A defender can't do much once the attacker has achieved a proper hold. That is, not much can be done with bare hands.

People do get choked from the front, particularly in domestic violence cases and rapes, where personal rage is the motivator. Frontal chokes are much easier to disrupt because the attacker is exposed. The Practics Choke-Break technique can easily be modified for use against an attacker that is sitting on your chest and choking you, or pushing you against a wall to reinforce a frontal choke.

The worst of the chokes are rear chokes with good side compression that restrict blood to the brain and may render a defender helpless within a few seconds. These attacks are the primary focus of the Practics Rear-Choke-Breaker technique.

**Practics Turtling**—Very often the defender will become aware that a rear-naked-choke attempt is imminent. The defender can greatly diminish the effectiveness of the choke by denying access to the neck. The Practics method is called "turtling." Like a turtle, the defender withdraws his head and hides his neck. This is a two-part movement:

1. The chin is driven into the top of the chest.
2. Shoulders are raised to their full extent, on either side of the neck.

Compression of the neck can cause choking or restriction of the carotid arteries.

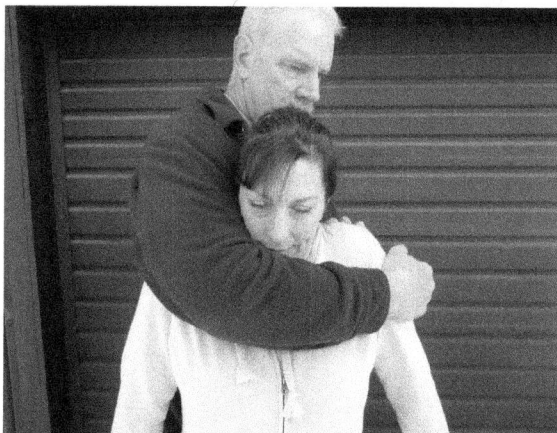

Turtling is simply driving the chin into the chest and elevating the shoulders to protect the neck.

If the above two movements are completed before the choke is attempted, the likelihood of a successful carotid compression is dramatically reduced, and the possibility of an air-restricting choke is virtually eliminated. The defender may get a broken nose and eventually be smothered by the attacker's arm, but even in the worst cases turtling will extend the defender's consciousness long enough to effectively respond.

**Practics Choke-Breaker Techniques**—Let's assume the worst has happened, and the defender has only a few seconds of consciousness in which to break the choke. Of course, our answer is the gun—always the gun. The Practics response is divided into rear- and frontal-attack deviations with similar but sufficiently different elements. One rule is consistent for all variations of the Practics Choke-Breaker techniques: *Never bend the shooting wrist.* If the shooting wrist is kept straight, the likelihood of a self-inflicted gunshot wound is greatly reduced.

*Rear-Naked-Choke Defense (Supine):* The attacker is lying on his back with the defender on top, facing upward. The following movements are done in concert:

- If the legs are free, spread them as far as possible to prevent rolling should the attacker abandon the choke.
- Handgun clears the holster as the shooting-side hip and buttocks are raised.

- Weak hand goes to the throat and grabs the attacker's arm. This will provide some balance for the defender but little else.
- Handgun is thrust (twisting) onto the attacker's thigh or hip area (defender's gun side).
- Shooting arm is as straight as possible. The goal here is to keep the arm and gun pointed away from the defender.
- Firing begins on contact.

She will be unconscious in a few seconds.

The odds are the attacker will release the defender the instant she fires down into his kneecap. The risk to the shooter from the discharge is real. A last resort

Nothing could be simpler than the above movements, but the specific mechanics are strict. The handgun is drawn only to the top of the holster as in the Practics Draw. An attacker may be able to grab a handgun when it is above the defender's waist, simply by dropping the choke arm or choke-support arm from the defender's neck to the torso. Speed and a low draw are critical to reduce the likelihood of a successful gun grab. If the choke continues with one arm and the handgun is held in check for even a few seconds, the defender may lose consciousness or be overcome by the irresistible impulse to fight the choke. A smaller defender fighting a larger attacker must be especially careful to keep the handgun out of the attacker's reach. As we previously discussed, everything in Practics is interrelated. The reader can see how the popular three-point draw would be potentially deadly for a defender suffering a rear naked choke. Clear the holster and thrust the handgun toward the target. Even with a low draw, a much taller attacker may be able to grab the handgun if he becomes aware of the defender's intention. The defender will have the weak hand on one of the attacker's arms, but it is too much to hope that the holster-side arm has been grabbed. In fact, it would be better if the defender would throw his weak arm out to the side for balance, but every human being choked is going to grab at the choking arm. We might as well grab ahold and get some defense out of it. If the attacker has wrapped his legs around the defender, the defender may not be able to raise the hip very high. All that is needed is a couple of inches to provide enough space to place the muzzle. When the handgun is pointing toward the ground and pressing into the attacker's leg, the defender will know the gun isn't pointing at himself. Nonetheless, there is a risk of injury. The more the shooting-side hip can be elevated, the safer it will be for the defender.

*Rear-Naked-Choke Defense (Prone):* The defender is facedown on the ground with the attacker on top. The following movements are done in concert:

- Handgun clears the holster.
- Weak-side hand secures attacker's holster-side arm. It may be the choke arm or the arm that secures the choke but it is the holster-side arm that we want to prevent from dropping onto the defender's gun.
- Legs are spread as far as possible to avoid injury.

- Handgun is thrust into the attacker's thigh, side, or hip area.
- Firing begins on contact.

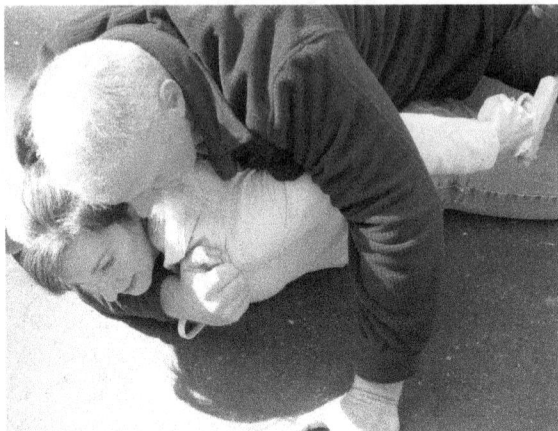

Rear choke defense in the prone.

Greater danger exists with this technique because the gun must be used near waist level and the shooting arm will probably not be fully straight. Securing the attacker's holster-side arm is your only gun-grab defense beside speed. The movement of the handgun toward the attacker is best thought of as an attempt to insert the handgun into the attacker's imaginary holster. In other words, the defender will clear his holster and begin moving the handgun straight back and up toward the attacker. Depending on the attacker's height in relation to the defender, the muzzle may contact the attacker's thigh or the side of the attacker's abdomen. Regardless, the response is the same: angled fire slightly skyward and toward the feet. This technique is much more likely to have a slighter angle-of-fire than the previous one, which means the bullet may more easily pass through a portion of the attacker and keep heading toward the feet of both parties. Hits may not be solid. Twist in and keep firing. By spreading the legs wide, the defender is much more likely to avoid injury from a second-hand projectile. When the legs are spread, the attacker's legs will drop between them. The attacker's legs are not the target—the hip or side of the abdomen is the target. Proper sub-contact technique is essential. The muzzle must be thrust and twisted into the target to avoid a missed shot.

*Rear-Naked-Choke Defense (Standing):* The attacker is standing behind the defender. The following movements are done in concert:

- Handgun is drawn.
- Attacker's holster-side arm is secured.
- Shooting leg moves forward one-half step.
- Torso is twisted toward the shooting side.
- Handgun is thrust into the attacker's thigh or groin.
- Shooting arm is as straight as possible—the wrist must be straight.
- Firing begins on contact.

This technique can be modified if the attacker is backed against a wall. In such an instance, the defender will push backward before quickly taking the half step forward. Forcing the attacker back against a wall will limit his ability to retreat from the handgun. When the attack occurs in open space, the attacker may attempt to sidestep toward the weak side to avoid the gun or may force the defender into a sitting position. The best defense against the possibility of a moving attacker is speed. By executing the half step and twisting toward the strong side (to whatever degree possible), the handgun will tend to point more toward the attacker's crotch than his leg. If the attacker's shooting-side arm is secured, the defender will have good access to the crotch. Keep the shooting arm straight for safety and better insertion.

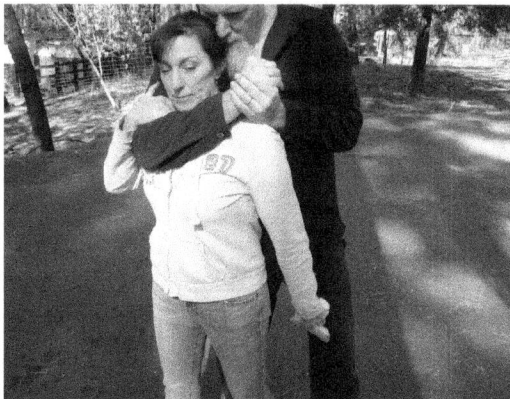

Standing defense from rear choke. Train cautiously to avoid neck injury.

*Rear-Naked-Choke Defense (Sitting):* The attacker kneels behind the sitting defender. The following movements are done in concert:

- Handgun is drawn.
- Attacker's holster-side arm is secured.
- Defender rocks forcefully toward the support side.
- Handgun is thrust into the attacker's crotch or thigh.
- Firing begins on contact.

The inherent danger in this technique is that the attacker has good mobility from the kneeling position with excellent reach. The defender must absolutely control the attacker's shooting/holster-side arm when drawing the handgun. While this is true for all Practics Choke-Breaker techniques, the defender must understand that an attacker in this position is more likely to be aware of the defender's draw than in the previously discussed positions. If the attacker is kneeling on his shooting-side knee, his thigh will be available to the defender. If the attacker is kneeling on the weak-side knee, the defender will need to target the crotch or foot. By forcefully rocking toward the support side, the defender will bring the gun in line with the attacker's crotch, lower leg, or foot, depending on position. In a case where the rocking motion is not possible due to the size or superiority of the attacker, the defender will have to push his arm farther back toward the centerline of the attacker. In either case contact will be made, provided the attacker's arm is secure and the movement is too quick for the attacker to get to his feet. If the attacker releases the choke, then, of course, the choke break is no longer necessary, and the defender can move into the Rollover or Kneel-Up Recovery, as discussed in the Practics Falling-Fire section.

*Frontal-Crush-Choke Defense:* The attacker and the defender are facing one another. The following movements are done in concert:

- Handgun is drawn.
- Attacker's shooting-side arm is secured by grabbing the wrist.
- The handgun is thrust (and always twisted) into the attacker's abdomen.
- Firing begins as soon as the handgun clears the holster.

Whether lying, standing, or kneeling, the movements are the

same. Grab the attacker's wrist with all the strength you can muster in your weak-side hand. At the instant the attacker sees the defender begin the draw, the fight for the handgun will commence. The frontal choke gives the attacker the best view of the handgun. The defender can neither hesitate nor signal his intention prior to the draw. This choke requires space, which means there will be open space between the attacker and the defender. The defender will draw and twist the hand into a punch-fire position as the gun is moved toward the target. Firing begins the instant the gun is clear of the holster and the muzzle has risen to the target, meaning the Frontal-Choke Defense is *en motion firing*. This defense is a race between the defender stopping the threat and the attacker grabbing the gun.

*Frontal-Crush Arm-Break Technique:* When the defender has sufficient strength in relation to the attacker, this technique will remove the attacker's grip and push his arms from between the two parties, ending the choke and freeing the defender. I include this technique with the caveat that it requires the defender to be of somewhat comparable strength to the attacker. My complaint against most "martial arts for the masses" training materials is the constant suggestion that technique can turn all natural law upside down. The above Practics Choke-Break techniques will work for smaller, weaker defenders. This one probably will not if the size difference is dramatic. The following movements are done in the order listed when a frontal, two-handed choke is occurring.

1. Clasp the hands together with the arms extended to the support side.
2. Twist as far as possible to the support side.
3. Violently swing both arms with clasped hands toward the shooting side, striking the attacker's forearms and sweeping them off to the shooting side.
4. While turned toward the shooting side, draw the handgun and turn back toward the attacker.
5. Either sub-contact fire or punch fire as needed.

Violence is the key to this technique. The swinging movement must be fast, forceful, and deliberate. The defender's arms must strike the attacker's forearms, *not* his upper arms. If the attacker is lying on top of the defender, this technique may cause him to fall onto the defender. The standing movement must include a third of a turn toward the shooting side after sweeping the attacker's forearms, which will obscure the draw from the attacker, and the following rollback will provide an opportunity to thrust the handgun in place for sub-contact firing. You will not have secured the attacker's shooting-side arm, making your speed more critical. A standing choke, once broken, will likely cause the attacker to stumble toward the defender, though some space will temporarily exist between the parties. The defender may use this opportunity to gain distance and punch fire.

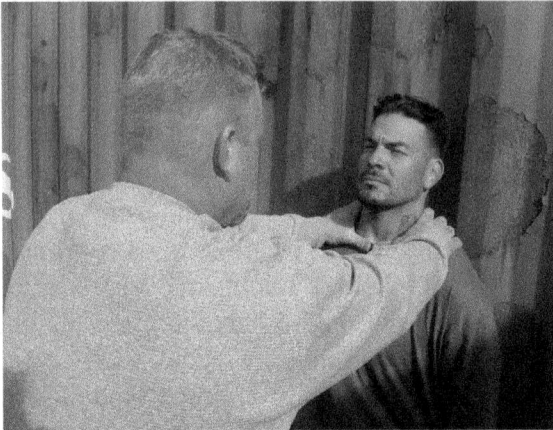

Attackers will often choke smaller defenders.

Lock the hands and use the entire body to swing through the attacker's arms.

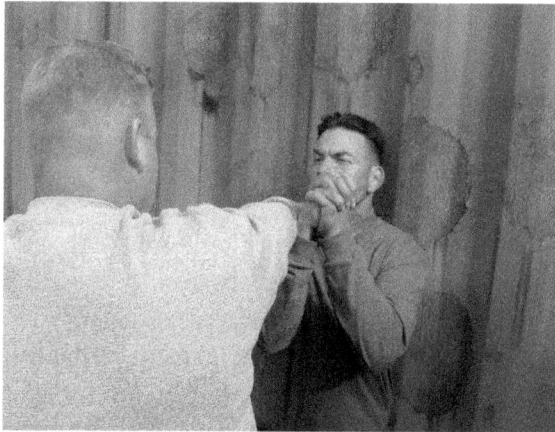

Aim for the far side, not his arms.

You are swinging from your feet to your back with all your strength.

## Contact-Fighting Training

All training in this section is non-firing. Much of what follows requires physical contact between training partner and student in fight simulations. The training goals are to provide the student with an experiential knowledge of position and movement. The fight-simulation exercises are *not* sparring sessions. The training partner need only provide sufficient resistance for the student to properly execute the required movements. Carotid restraints, which restrict blood flow to the brain, will cause unconsciousness and can cause death. Frontal chokes can crush the throat and cause death. Both training partner and student *must* train with restraint. Exercise repetitions at half speed against light resistance will be sufficient to develop a "feel" memory. Further training must be done under the guidance of a competent self-defense instructor.

1. **Practics Holster-Defense Drill**—This exercise requires a storage-safe weapon (no magazine) in the holster. No ammunition or real knife may be present. A training knife can be made out of cardboard, or a rubber knife can be had from the local costume shop. Fill the knife pouch with a piece of material sufficient to hold the training knife tight enough to prevent it from falling out of the pouch or just tape it to the outside of the pouch. The training partner will play the attacker and begin by facing the student and grabbing the holstered handgun with the hand nearest to it. The student will execute a Practics Holster Defense: Secure gun, embrace attacker (eliminate distance), and use knife. After a few repeated back stabs with the fake knife, the training partner will release the gun, and the student will move away from the attacker, ending the drill. The training partner will ensure that the student tightly secures the gun, executes a forceful embrace, keeps moving into the attacker, and uses the knife quickly and without warning. The student's stabs *must* be limited to light taps on the training partner's back. Students may increase the difficulty of this drill by having the training partner grab the holstered gun with two hands or by gradually increasing from half speed to three-quarter speed.

Skill-Installation Requirement: 25 successful consecutive executions

Maintenance Requirement: above requirement weekly for six weeks

2. **Practics Muzzle-Leveraging Drill**—This is more of an event than a practiced movement, which means the drill can provide "feel" but not any reflexive memory. The training partner serves as a bad guy, and a toy gun is used as a training weapon. No firearm or ammunition may be present. The training partner grabs the muzzle of the gun with one hand (his choice), and the student uses proper leveraging technique to line the muzzle up with the attacker's body before saying "Bang! Bang!" This training can be made more difficult by having the training partner use two hands. Both participants are responsible to keep the effort at about half strength. Force may be gradually increased during training but always with common sense as

a guide. The training zone needs to be a safe area with soft ground and no trip hazards. If the action appears to be going beyond the safe area, both parties must stop and move back into the training zone. The goal is to learn a skill, not win a bout. Good movement technique is also a requirement; dragging the feet or stumbling is a disqualification.

Skill-Installation Requirement: 25 successful consecutive executions

Maintenance Requirement: above requirement monthly for three months

3. **Practics Fallback Drill**—Caution is the key to this training. Both training partner and student risk injury if either acts recklessly. A mattress is needed, sufficient to cushion repeated falls. A toy gun will be used as the training weapon. If the toy gun won't stay inside the holster, build it up with duct tape and strips of cardboard. The top strap of the holster must properly secure. A proper draw always requires a full release of all present safety straps and devices, which applies here too. No firearm or ammunition may be present during this training. Once again, the training partner will play the attacker. The drill begins with the student standing one step from the mattress with his back facing the mattress. The training partner will stand two steps in front of the student. As the training partner walks toward the student, the student will begin a proper fallback. Because the parties are not running during this drill, timing is important to maintain relevance. When the training partner takes the first step, the student must move the shooting leg rearward, pivot the body, crouch, and begin the draw. When the training partner is taking a second step and grabbing for the legs, the student is falling. The training partner will follow the student down. The student will try to block with his knees. Both parties must keep the same pace in order for the student to learn the speed required to execute this technique. The drill ends when the student simulates sub-contact firing into the attacker. The training partner is responsible to determine if the student successfully executed the technique, particularly focusing on timing, shooting-arm elbow placement, and delivery of the handgun to the target. The training partner must have read the Practics Fallback section of this text to properly aid the student. Advanced students may wish to *gradually* increase speed. If the training partner is free falling, the pace is much too fast without safety equipment.

Skill-Installation Requirement: 20 proper fallbacks with the training partner only preventing the student's legs from rising. 20 proper fallbacks with the training partner acting as the attacker. Breaks may be taken as needed.

Maintenance Requirement: 10 proper fallbacks with attacker monthly for six months

4. **Practics Choke-Breaker Drills**—Like the previous three drills, these require the training partner to act as a bad guy and both participants to be alert and cautious. *Under no circumstance should any pressure be applied to the choke or carotid restraint.* The attacker will lightly position his arm around the neck without compressing the student's flesh. A toy gun will be used for the training weapon, and no firearm or ammunition may be present. Each of the first five Practics Choke-Breaker techniques will be done. The training zone needs safe, level ground with either soft earth or a gym mat. The training partner will judge whether the student has successfully controlled the attacker's arm, which will require the training partner to attempt gun grabs randomly throughout the training. Both training partner and student must review the training text before executing these drills; the training partner must be sufficiently knowledgeable to spot errors. Drills end with a successful sub-contact firing simulation of multiple rounds.

Skill-Installation Requirement: each of the first five Practics Choke-Breaker techniques · 15 successful executions

Maintenance Requirement: five executions of each technique quarterly for one year

Choking and punching are deadly. You must be able to successfully draw and fire your handgun wherever trouble finds you. Crouch-grimace-and-jerk training won't get it done.

# Chapter Eleven: Architectural Firing

*There is no such thing as darkness; only a failure to see.*

Malcolm Muggeridge

*Weather forecast for tonight: dark.*

George Carlin

Bats, crabs, and defensive hand gunners all work in the dark.

If you carry a handgun professionally for any length of time, you will invariably wind up working in the dark. It doesn't matter how many flashlights you own or whether your handgun has an attached light; you will have to operate without lighting at some point. Most of the time the darkness will be a direct result of an indoor location. That's good for us because Practics provides a reasonable, though extremely limited, remedy for indoor, no-light operations.

Everything is mathematics, or so I have been told. A guy wins a chess match; it's all mathematics. Somebody invents new software —mathematics. Space flight, car safety, and work schedules are all based on math. Architecture is also a case of numbers. If we understand the buildings we encounter and can use them to our advantage, shooting in the dark becomes a simple matter of geometry.

Buildings are built to measurement, square and level. Most rooms are either rectangular or square. Even asymmetrical rooms still tend to have right-angle corners. Imagine a square. Now imagine yourself inside the square and in total darkness. If you can touch a wall, you can find a corner. Find one corner and you will know the angles at which the other three corners are located. You might not know the size of the square, but you'll be able to plot three lines that will reach each of the other three corners regardless of distance. If I gave you a diagram with four dots marking the four corners of a square, could you draw the square? Of course you could. This means that in knowing the corners, you understand the lines of the walls.

Rectangles are mastered by the same theory but with different techniques. The point is we're not lost in the dark. We can, as a mental process, illuminate the walls and corners and know our surroundings. The Practics theory of interior-darkness shooting is simple, and the techniques aren't much more difficult—with a little training.

People tend to hide against walls and in corners. Certainly that isn't always the case, but having searched for more miscreants than I can recall, my experience has been that they are more apt to hide behind curtains than behind couches. In darkness people under duress tend to seek the psychological comfort of a wall. The ability to successfully fire along walls and into corners has value to the blind defender.

The use of Practics Architectural Firing (PAF) has obvious limits. The defender has to know the shape of the room. Firing for a square will cause substantial misses in a rectangular room. A lot of estimating is required for any target other than along the lines of walls or the corners of squares. Conceding all that, I confess that it is reasonable for readers to wonder whether PAF is of any legitimate defense value. The value depends on circumstantial need.

Let's imagine a woman finds herself inside her family's empty concrete-block shop and RV-storage building. When she walks to the back of the shop, the lights go out and a firearm is discharged. The defender knows the building is a square, and she knows the light switch is by the door in the front right corner of the building. She also knows that boxes of Christmas decorations are halfway down the right wall and bicycles are leaning against the front left corner of the building. Between what she knows from experience of the building and what she hears (bicycles rattling), the defender may be able to make a fair determination of attacker location or direction of travel. If she can use the building to direct her fire, the tactical advantage will be hers.

Practics Architectural Firing is of limited value, but within those limits it is irreplaceable. Night-vision equipment is certainly a better choice, provided the defender owns such equipment and happens to have it with her when disaster calls. If the attacker has night-vision goggles and the defender does not, PAF may be the best chance for some level of parity.

The Four Rules of Safety still apply. The defender must know her structure, threat, and immediate proximity of innocents.

## The Return of The Triangle (Sort Of)

Because the legs are spread to provide a bipod against the walls, Practics Linear-Balance firing cannot be used with PAF. The popular triangle is undesirable for the reasons mentioned during our discussion of point shooting (see chapter 5 for review). By keeping the elbows slightly bent (a bit more than natural) and being deliberate with the aim, we can use the old arm triangle with good results. The bent elbows, deliberate setup, and the defender's reliance on the walls for a "true center" feel will minimize the triangle's inherent inaccuracy.

## Mastering the Square

Every square has four corners attached by four straight lines. Find a wall, follow it, and you'll find a corner. Your grandpa's living room and a Hong Kong office space are the same square. You already know every square room in the world. Distance doesn't matter unless the room is so large that the bullet can't reach corner-to-corner. We are all experts on the layout of square rooms.

Shooting the square requires a conversion from theory to practice, which is simply a matter of causing the body to conform to a corner of the room, plumb and level. The defender will use the square corner as a platform for point shooting. Practics has four PAF positions: prone, supine, squatting, and standing. Each position has elevation options to allow the defender to formally train for different aiming paths rather than resort to blind guessing. Estimating can be useful and is often necessary, but even that technique can be developed by formal training.

***Prone***: Kneel in the corner and move outward, lying facedown. Place one foot against each wall with the toes pointed downward and outward. More flexible students may be able to place the feet against the walls with the toes straight outward. The feet must be evenly placed with the body perfectly situated as a centerline between the legs. The arms are brought in front of the head and shoulders, slightly bent with the elbows on the ground. The handgun is in line with the body, forming a straight line from muzzle to the opposite corner of the room. The head is slightly lifted to assist in accurately feeling handgun elevation.

Prone elevation choices: handgun butt on ground (low);

forearms naturally lifted with elbows on ground (mid/27°); and a halfway elevation of the gun with elbows on the ground (high/45°). All three elevations lend themselves to consistency through a natural "feel" based on the sensation of the torso and elbows against the floor.

*Supine:* Very similar to the prone but the defender is lying on his back with his feet evenly positioned against the wall. The legs will have to spread a bit farther to prevent an unnatural twisting of the ankles. The toes will be pointed upward and slightly outward. The arms are brought together in a modified triangle with the elbows slightly bent, which will tend to straighten the aim. The handgun will be held over the centerline of the body. This position enables firing across a room at an upward angle, straight up, and upward at a modest rearward angle. Many industrial buildings have catwalks and second-story lofts requiring greater elevation than the prone position can accommodate.

Supine elevation choices: arms extended over the head at about a 40° angle, with the head tilted slightly up and rearward (high cross-corner); handgun held straight upward in line with eyes (straight up); handgun lowered from the face to the pectoral line (up and back).

*Squatting:* Defender squats with his back to the corner. The hips and shoulders are evenly placed against both walls.

Squatting elevation choices: Arms and handgun are naturally raised at about an 80° angle (high); arms and handgun held straight with a natural elbow bend (mid); arms and handgun held downward at about a 40° angle (low).

*Standing:* Identical to squatting with the exception that the legs are almost fully extended. The defender rests against the corner with hips and shoulders determining true center.

Standing elevation choices: Arms and handgun are naturally raised at about an 80° angle (high); arms and handgun held straight with a natural elbow bend (mid); arms and handgun held downward at about a 40° angle (low).

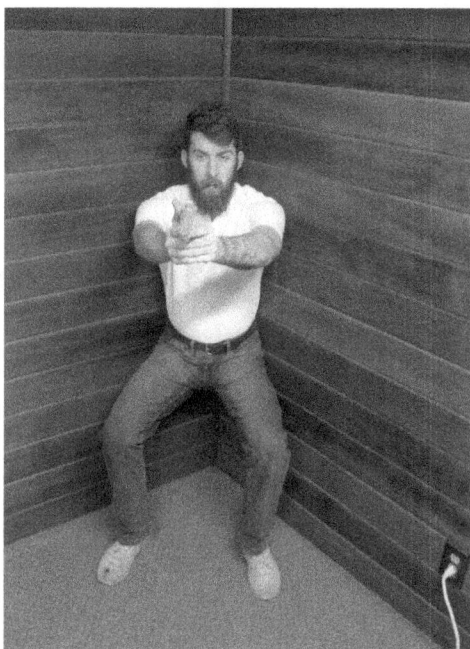

Architectural squatting position

Architectural firing will never be perfect but it may be all you have.

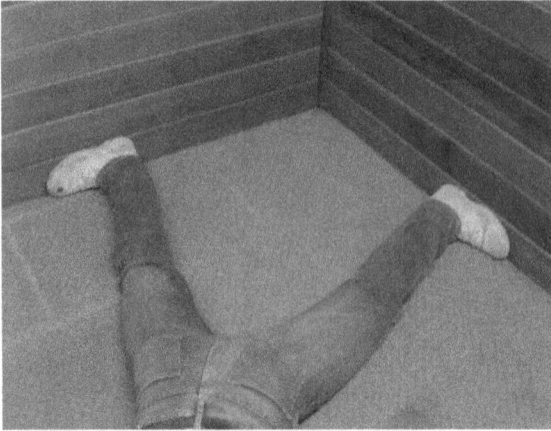

The architectural prone is based on the feet. Try to keep your spine as straight as possible.

## Mastering the Rectangle

The rectangle requires an offset in the shooting position to move the aim inward toward the opposing corner of the rectangle. Offset is easily done by relocating one leg from the square shooting position to closer proximity with the wall. The rectangle shooting positions are as easy to maintain as the square shooting position with some practice. The positions provide the defender with a consistent platform to aim and fire in the dark.

***Prone****:* The defender positions the body evenly and squarely, pressing one foot (as in a square) against one wall and pressing against the other wall with the knee of the opposite leg. The defender will be able to modify the angle of fire by sliding one knee forward or rearward along the base of the wall. When the knee is slid forward, proper body alignment between the opposing foot and knee will accommodate a more squared rectangle. If the knee is slid rearward the angle will accommodate a more exaggerated rectangle. The defender is responsible to train using the appropriate angle for the structure he anticipates defending.

Prone elevation choices: handgun butt on ground (low); forearms naturally lifted with elbow on ground (mid/27°); and a halfway elevation of the gun with the elbows on the ground (high/45°). All three elevations lend themselves to consistency through a natural "feel."

*Supine:* Lying on his back, the defender evenly distributes his balance between one knee and one foot, as in the prone position. Sliding a knee forward or rearward can modify the angle of fire. The knee and foot do not instantly align the body, but rather a conscious effort by the defender will balance or align the torso between the two contact points. Arbitrarily throwing appendages against walls without centering the body is not Practics Architectural Firing.

Supine elevation choices: arms extended over the head at about a 40° angle, with the head tilted slightly up and rearward (high cross-corner); handgun held straight upward in line with eyes (straight up); handgun lowered from the face to the pectoral line (up and back).

*Squatting:* Rectangular squatting begins as the square squatting position. In order to orient the body toward the corner of a rectangle, the foot and thigh on the side the defender wishes to orient toward are placed firmly against the wall—with the body aligned between all wall contact points. An exaggerated rectangle may require the upper arm corresponding to the aforementioned thigh, to also be placed against the wall in order to achieve a greater angle.

Squatting elevation choices: Arms and handgun are naturally raised at about an 80° angle (high); arms and handgun held straight with a natural elbow bend (mid); arms and handgun held downward at about a 40° angle (low). All of the squatting elevation choices can be done even with the greater angle modifications as described above.

*Standing:* Identical to squatting with the exception of the legs being almost fully extended. As described with the squatting position, the defender may choose to use the thigh or upper-arm-and-thigh combination to find the best possible base from which to modify the aim for a particular room.

Standing elevation choices: Arms and handgun are naturally raised at about an 80° angle (high); arms and handgun held straight with a natural elbow bend (mid); arms and handgun held downward at about a 40° angle (low).

## Wall Shooting (Punch Fire)

To fire the length of a wall with the intention of hitting a human-size target, simply place the shooting-side forearm firmly against the wall in a punch-fire position, aligning the firearm and forearm. The grip angle of most modern handguns will be sufficient to send the round straight along the wall. In other words, we use a supported punch fire. What could be easier?

This is how to find a target against a wall in complete darkness.

Wall firing.

## Interior Wall Caution

Firing along the length of a wall is not firing into a wall, at least in theory. Accidents happen and mistakes will occur. For the most part, wall construction will not be of great concern to the interior defender with the exception of three areas: penetration, deflection, and interruptions. We've already discussed penetration as it relates to cover. The interior walls of Balmoral Castle may be cover against anything up to a shoulder-fired rocket; the bedroom walls of your tract home are another matter. Deflection and interruption require a little more thought, particularly with commercial buildings.

Deflection occurs when the bullet strikes something that it cannot penetrate, resulting in angled fire away from the wall. For instance, some metal buildings have tension rods placed across the sheet metal surfaces. A bullet striking a metal tension rod will be deflected.

Interruptions are blockages in the line of fire. An example would be the steel beams used to frame many warehouses. A defender who fires along the surface of the wall will strike the steel uprights on the interior side of the wall. The bullet's forward travel will be immediately stopped, or, worse, the bullet will head back toward the defender. In order to wall fire in such a warehouse, the arm would have to be placed against one of the steel beams rather than the wall.

## Spotting Fire in Darkness

Muzzle flashing can be seen in darkness as a splash of fire. Unfortunately the splash of fire is likely to be behind a mushroom cloud of dark smoke and powder, resulting in the cap of the cloud at least partially concealing the flash from a frontal view. If the gun is pointed at you, the muzzle flash may be hidden from your view. Exceptions in visibility and the light patterns depend on ammunition, barrel length, distance, and the effect of some flash suppressors. For instance, a 2" barreled .357 magnum revolver with hot loads will expel a large amount of unburned powder and smoke, which will form a dark cloud in front of the flash, causing a frontal view to be invisible or no more than a dull ring of light around the edges of the cloud. This light ring will tend to be sufficiently dim so that the defender may think the light was an optical illusion. There are cases where the light ring is clear and relatively bright, but it is still a ring. Military-style flash suppressors on rifles may cause a starburst pattern of light when viewed from the front—the more symmetrical the starburst appears, the more the rifle is pointed directly at you. The takeaway of muzzle-flash spotting in darkness is if you can see a clear fireball or bright flash, the attacker is not aiming directly at you. If you don't see the flash, or doubt whether you've seen the flash but hear the report of a shot fired, or see a perfect starburst or ring of light—get shooting, moving, or covered.

## Practics Architectural-Firing Knowledge and Training

PAF has limited applications. Proper execution depends on the shooter being able to use a natural sense of balance to center his body between two contact points. This phenomenon doesn't work because of poses; it works because of a sense of alignment. Pressure from the bodily contact points will provide sufficient sensory information for the shooter to find true center, but training and knowledge of your buildings are necessary for success. Remember that if you know where the corners are, you can estimate points in-between.

The live-fire drills listed below require some preparation. In order to fire corner to corner, we'll need a couple of corners: one strong enough to support a leaning shooter and the other sufficient for holding a target. If the live-fire portion of this training is beyond your means (some ranges will not permit the use of portable structures), you can use dry fire inside an appropriate room with sufficient safety preparation. The Four Rules of Safety apply even with dry fire. The student must be aware of the backstop and what lies beyond. No ammunition may be present.

The shooting support structure can be made by using plywood and 2·4's to create a corner that has two walls—each of which are at least 4' wide and as tall as the shooter—at a 90° angle and can be weighted or supported from the rear to enable the shooter to rest his body weight against the structure without it moving or tipping over. This is a simple affair for even a mildly competent handyman, but it must be rigid and strong. Unfortunately, unless you're using scrap, the thing is expensive and cumbersome to transport. Nail lightly and you can easily dismantle and reassemble for transporting.

The target structure is another 90° angle with a wood beam or post rising from the corner to a height of at least 5'5". This structure must be stable enough to withstand wind but does not need to have solid walls.

Using four stakes and a tape measure, you can establish a perfectly square "room" on which you may install your two structures. The training room must be truly square, or this training is of no value.

**1. Firing-the-Square Drills (Live Fire)**—Using the above structures, the student will slow fire from all four square positions. Elevation will depend on the height of the target and limits of the range. Shooting may be restricted to low- and mid-level fire. The target will be a full-size silhouette set at a 45° angle in the target corner at typical adult height as if the bad guy were standing inside the corner. Of course, target placement will have to conform to the setup of the range you are using. The student will fire aimed slow-fire rounds from each position, paying particular attention to body alignment and natural balance between contact points. When the student has demonstrated consistently good marksmanship for all positions, the training partner will blindfold the student *after* reloading and holstering has occurred. The blindfold will be removed after each position has been fired or whenever a break in firing is required. The training partner will have complete command of the student and will serve as a safety officer. On the training partner's command the student will slowly draw the weapon and adjust the body position for perfect PAF. On the training partner's next command the student will slow fire a single round. The training partner will inform the student of the accuracy of his fire, and the student will adjust. When the student is consistently accurate, he will fire three rounds on the training partner's command. Three accurate, consecutive rounds count as a successful completion of the drill for each position. Five successful three-round groups are required to qualify for each of the four positions.

Skill-Installation Requirement: five qualifying strings of fire for each position

Maintenance Requirement: above requirement monthly for four months

Ambidextrous training is required for the above drill.

**2. Firing-the-Rectangle Drills (Live Fire)**—These drills duplicate the square-firing drills with these exceptions: A true rectangle must be laid with string and stakes for structure placement and simulated walls made by a couple of rolls of wrapping or butcher paper extended from the target corner outward along the lines of both walls for a distance of 5'. The purpose of these paper walls is to expand the target so the student can see the impact holes, which will advise the student on how to adjust the rectangle firing positions. These positions are malleable, unlike the square firing positions. The ideal setup would be for the student to lay out the training room to duplicate the rectangular room he is likely to defend. Learning positions by feel is committing to muscle memory. Be certain that you are learning something relevant. If the student does not have the ability to duplicate

301

a particular rectangular room, the positional firing experience is still worthwhile, but the student must be cautious to alter the rectangle to different angles during each training session. This will prevent a rigid muscle memory of an irrelevant position. As with the above square requirements, the training partner will have complete command of the student and will serve as a safety officer. On the training partner's commands the student will slowly draw the weapon, adjust the body position for perfect PAF, and slow fire a single round. The training partner will inform the student of the accuracy of his fire, and the student will adjust. When the student is consistently accurate, he will be blindfolded and fire three rounds on the training partner's command. Three accurate, consecutive rounds count as a successful completion of the drill for each position. Five successful three-round groups are required to qualify for each of the four positions.

Skill-Installation Requirement: five qualifying strings of fire for each position

Maintenance Requirement: above requirement monthly for four months

Ambidextrous training is required for the above drill.

**3. Room Survey and Dry Fire**—Safety is the foremost concern in conducting this drill. No ammunition may be present, and the student and training partner will ensure the building is empty and the exterior is clear. The student will conduct dry fire from the corners of rooms he is likely to defend during hours of darkness. The target will be the centerline of the opposing corner of the room. After the student is satisfied that his positions are true, he will dry fire with his eyes closed, concentrating on the feel of the position.

Skill-Installation Requirement: dry fire, sighted and blind, until satisfied

Maintenance Requirement: above dry fire quarterly or when defense locations change

**4. Wall-Firing Drill**—Place the shooting and target structures in a perfect line to reflect a straight wall. The target is a full-size silhouette, at adult height, facing the student from the neighboring corner. Distance doesn't matter, but the training partner needs to be able to spot hits and misses. On command the student will draw his weapon and place his shooting arm in the supported-punch-fire position against the plywood wall of the shooting structure. When the command to fire is given by the training partner, the student will punch fire a single round. The training partner will advise on accuracy. When accuracy is achieved, firing will be done in three-round groups, blindfolded. Five successful three-round groups are required to qualify.

    <u>Skill-Installation Requirement</u>: five qualifying strings of three-round groups

    <u>Maintenance Requirement</u>: three qualifying strings of five-round groups annually

    Both hands must be able to wall fire.

    Now, at least within limits, we can fire in the dark. If only we could fire around corners . . .

# Chapter Twelve: Indirect Firing

*You have to learn the rules of the game. And then you have to play better than anyone else.*

Albert Einstein

In some circumstances an attacker may be able to aim at you, but you may not be able to aim at him. For instance, an attacker lying near a car may be able to fire directly at your feet without you even seeing him. An attacker may thrust a handgun around the corner of an exterior wall and fire wildly in your direction, not leaving you much of a target.

Sending redirected fire in such circumstances may be worthwhile. Indirect firing is unique among shooting skills in that the practice depends on environment. We can only use indirect fire with a striking surface hard enough to cause ricochet and smooth enough to redirect the round with predictable accuracy.

We know some things about the nature of deflected bullets:

- The angle of deflection (post-impact) tends to be less than the angle of the strike (pre-impact).
- Velocity and energy are reduced after the strike, lessening penetration.
- Accuracy and ballistics will be altered by bullet deformation.
- Post-strike accuracy is partially dependent on the striking surface.
- Range is greatly reduced.
- Penetration is also lessened by post-strike bullet deformation.

Perhaps some better mind will put forth a formula for the use of deflected fire. The best I can offer is this: Every bullet, every caliber, every striking surface, and every distance will have a distinct effect on each ricochet. That may sound grim or cause the reader to consider me something of an imbecile for offering indirect firing as a teachable skill, but we can reliably and effectively use ricochets within limits by following some simple guidelines.

- The *actual* striking surface determines ricochet, not the *outline* of the surface.
- Handgun ricochets are effectively limited to close range.
- The Four Rules of Safety remain in effect. Information is required to determine backstop that may not be readily visible. Think first.
- Post-strike angle (bullet exit) will be lower than pre-strike angle (bullet entry). A defender standing at 5:00, shooting at the center of the clock, which represents the center of a wall stretching from 3:00 to 9:00, will *likely* strike around 8:00 or 8:30—not 7:00.

Whether concerned with Practics Indirect Firing or Practics Architectural Firing (previous chapter), a defender must understand the difference between the shooting line of a wall and the surface of that wall. The *shooting line* of the wall is a straight line running along the length of the wall, touching only the high points. For instance, a sheet of corrugated metal has alternating plateaus and valleys built into the surface. The shooting line of that corrugated wall runs across the high points, the plateaus, and does not take into account the valleys within the surface. In other words, if you could lay a giant ruler across the surface of the wall, you would find the shooting line of that wall. If you want to shoot along a corrugated steel wall of a large shipping container or the meandering stone wall of a medieval castle, you will have to keep your fire on or outside the shooting line of the wall. *Surface* means the actual surface that a bullet may strike. The shooting line of a shipping container wall is straight, but the surface is actually a series of 1" to 2" surface distortions. If the round strikes a flat plateau, a normal ricochet may occur. However, if the round strikes one of the walls between a plateau and a valley, the bullet may reverse direction. A rock wall may have thousands of surface points with differing surface angles. Prudence is required.

Bullets will enter wood most of the time, and most of the time they'll shatter glass. Deflection attempts are best reserved for smooth concrete, hard pavement, brick, and steel. Some soft surfaces may deflect handgun bullets in certain conditions. For instance, asphalt has deflected countless rounds when cool and hard but absorbs bullets or lessens their angles of departure when hot and soft. Hollow concrete blocks may deflect handgun bullets if struck at a sufficient angle but will likely shatter when struck with a head-on shot. The point is deflection choices are limited and require the forethought of an intelligent defender.

We will limit our discussion of indirect fire to two specific uses: shooting under cars and shooting around corners. Let's start with cars.

## Bouncing Rounds Under Cars

Anybody can pass rounds directly under a car, of course, but sometimes that is not possible. A defender may not be able to drop and return fire from under a car. Time and safety may not permit it. When standing on an elevated platform, such as a curb or the other side of a parking block, a direct line of fire under a car would not be possible.

The big problem with bouncing rounds under a car is getting your bullet to come out the other side. So far we know that the angle going in will be greater than the angle going out. If we control the location of the striking point, we can ensure a clear path out from underneath the car. Deflected fire under an object is a complicated matter, but we can reduce it to a simple guideline: When the striking point of the bullet is at least to the centerline of the vehicle, the bullet will exit the other side without touching the car. The "centerline" refers to the line of the vehicle (or other elevated object) that divides the vehicle into even halves: closer to the shooter and farther from the shooter. If the defender places his bullet beyond the center of the object he wishes to clear (provided the object surface is one constant height), the bullet will pass through uninterrupted because the angle of departure is less than the angle of entry. All the defender needs to know is the location of the centerline under the car, or other object, in order to pass rounds under the car. To bounce rounds bumper to bumper under a low-sitting Corvette, a defender would have to lie flat on the ground. Standing a few yards from a high-sitting, full-size pickup, a defender will more easily be able to deflect rounds from driver's side to passenger side. Defender height will depend on what angle is required to strike or exceed the centerline. If the centerline is hit, the bullet will exit from under the car at a higher angle than if the bullet strikes beyond the centerline. This allows the defender some opportunity to adjust the exit angle.

Every raised platform has a centerline. Successful indirect fire requires you knowing where the centerline is located.

If you cannot see the centerline, lower your body.

## Shooting Around Corners

There's no great mystery here. The shooting principle that works horizontally with cars works vertically with walls. Again, this will not work with an interior wall but will work in a downtown concrete parking structure.

Here's an example of when and how this technique might be used: A defender is walking through a parking garage. Very few cars are present, with no people and no immediate opportunities for cover. When the defender walks past a parked van, an attacker fires at him from between the front of the van and the concrete wall of the garage. The attacker has decent coverage, with the van's right front wheel, engine, and windshield, from which he continues to fire at the defender. Unable to effectively fire directly at the attacker, the defender decides to use indirect fire. The defender must choose an aiming point on the concrete wall, between himself and the attacker. The aiming point is selected based on the distance between the two parties. Closer shots require an aiming point within the defender's half of the striking area (concrete wall, for instance). When the parties are farther away, an aiming point on the attacker's half of the striking area may be selected to allow for a lesser bullet-entry angle and a gentler angle of bullet departure. The defender may not strike the attacker with the first shot, but the attacker will be immediately aware of his own vulnerability as the front of the van is struck.

Indirect fire is weaker, is less accurate, and has less penetration and bullet expansion than direct fire. Additionally, indirect fire is extremely difficult to develop as a skill due to the difficulty of live-fire training opportunities. In short, bouncing bullets is never a first choice. Having a handgun for self-defense is recognition that you do not get to make all the choices in your life. Indirect fire is used when it has to be used. In the above example the defender would fire under movement, creating distance and moving toward cover or a firing advantage. We always want to upgrade our defense. Practics is a series of interconnected and complementary skills—we never stop.

The target is sufficiently visible for direct fire. If he retreats back a step, indirect fire may be necessary

# Indirect-Fire Training

Indirect-fire training requires steel plates or concrete surfaces, both of which are beyond the means of most students. I want you to be aware of the opportunity indirect fire affords you, although I was reluctant to include it in the text. Knowing the principles of indirect fire will give you some ability to use it, should the need ever arise.

The safety concerns mentioned throughout this chapter are the most important elements of this skill. You can shoot yourself if firing without sufficient angle of deflection. Many of you may have learned this by firing at steel plates with too light a round from too close a distance. Fortunately, with eye protection and ranges greater than 15 yards *most* ricocheting bullets do little harm when they are 180° reversals. Indirect fire, however, can kill. If the student intends to train for this skill beyond what is recommended here, it is the student's responsibility to seek a professional instructor with knowledge in this area and a range specifically set up for indirect fire drills. This is not Handgun 101 stuff.

**Practics Round-Skipping Drill (Live Fire)**—The best and safest way to do this drill is to get a 4'·4' square of steel from your local metal shop. If you get a piece of diamond plate, be sure to use the smooth side. Concrete works but will be cosmetically damaged. Good solid concrete will only scar when the angle is soft, but resurfaced or crumbling concrete may chip or crack. Take a large piece of cardboard or plywood and non-deflective stands from which you may suspend the four corners of the cardboard. Milk crates or blocks of softwood are good choices. The center of the cardboard obstruction must be positioned directly over the steel, forming a simple elevated platform to simulate the bottom of a car. Folding other pieces of cardboard and standing them on the downrange side of the concrete (3' h · 2' w) will make deflection targets. The targets may be weighted for stabilization but only with non-deflective materials (sandbags are good).

The drill begins with the student drawing his handgun and selecting a striking point at or beyond the centerline of the cardboard obstruction. Student will attempt to strike the cardboard deflection targets with indirect fire. The training goal is to be able to select proper aiming points to clear the cardboard obstruction and hit the intended deflection target. This drill should be fired until the shooter can reliably hit any target within about 15' of the obstruction. Remember that the angle of rise requires distance, so you won't be able to hit

310

chest-high targets a few feet from the deflection point. Do NOT use an automobile for this training due to the risk of severe damage. Remember, this technique does not guarantee precise fire—train accordingly.

This primitive device is good enough to begin training for bouncing rounds under cars.

Skill-Installation Requirement: above drill until consistent accuracy is achieved

Maintenance Requirement: above drill annually

Don't forget to execute the above drill with the weak hand.

311

# Chapter Thirteen: Long Range

*The shortest distance between two points is a straight line.*

Archimedes

Every defense huckster from Maine to Malibu has been living off the snake-oil pitch that because most fights are at close range, nobody needs to be taught how to hit their mark. We've already sufficiently discussed that absurdity. Close range doesn't mean a stationary silhouette with a full frontal view. More than that, although the average distance of gunfights being only a few feet is true, that average comes from chest-to-chest encounters *and* wide-open spaces. We certainly should emphasize training in response to statistical averages, but we can't ignore the entire range of conflicts from which those averages are derived.

Here is the revenge of the marksmen. It's well and fine to know how to fire at 6', but what will you do if a rifle shooter fires at you from 200 yards? You can't cry "foul" and refuse to participate.

About 60 years ago, trick shooter Ed McGivern and firearms innovator Elmer Keith began exploring the possibility of police using the .357 Magnum on man-size targets out to 600 yards (with proper sights). While McGivern could make those shots, it was a bit much to expect of rank-and-file peace officers. Nonetheless, the man was shooting a revolver on human-size targets at 600 yards.

I mention this to the reader because we have come to think of handguns as 25-yard weapons. A good mid-caliber handgun in competent hands can give decent defense against a mediocre rifle shooter. The handgun is no match for a rifle, all things being equal, but all things are not equal, and the trained defender can give an untrained rifle attacker a whole lot of trouble.

Near the beginning of this book I assured the reader that this was not a marksmanship book. I also said that my assumption in writing this book was that only marksmen would be reading it. If you are not a consistently accurate shot capable of self-correction, then you must seek professional training. This chapter is of no value to a shooter without good fundamental marksmanship skills.

Following are three problems with long-range shooting (beyond 100 yards) with a service handgun:

1. Range estimation
2. Bullet drop (trajectory)
3. Wind

Solutions to the above problems are relatively simple but require experimentation and documentation by the student. I will tell you how to acquire the information you need for long-distance firing, and it will be your job to conduct the tests, record the results, and sufficiently memorize the information so it may be recalled under duress.

## Service-Handgun Limitations

The defender with a service handgun firing at long distances will eventually see the accuracy of his fire break apart as bullet velocity deteriorates. At some point the defender is firing artillery rounds into an area rather than shooting bullets at a target. When that occurs depends largely on caliber, ammunition, and barrel length. Service sights are not made for long-range shooting. The marksman knows how to use the sights to their mechanical limits and the restrictions of his own vision, but at some point the sights become no more than guideposts. People bother to carry rifles for this reason.

What does this mean to the defender? I'm afraid it means that the best we can do is about the best we can do. Crude but informed adjustments for wind and elevation will get your rounds into the ballpark at a few hundred yards and let the other fellow know you're awake, but the long-distance use of the handgun is only a stopgap measure. Get covered, get out of the area, get help, or get a rifle. In the meantime squeeze the best out of your handgun and ammunition.

## Target Problems

Even a jumbo training target may not be sufficient to capture hits. In such a case targets will have to be placed side by side. Patience and determination are required to capture the needed long-range data.

## Range Estimation

Your ammunition begins a slow, inevitable submission to

gravity the instant the round leaves the barrel. Quick compensation for bullet drop requires knowledge particular to each handgun-ammunition combination. The defender must be able to accurately estimate target distance and then compensate for that distance by adjusting point of aim.

Practics range estimation has two elements. The first requires the defender to measure his front sight blade against an average-size man at 100, 150, 200, 250, and 300 yards. We'll consider how to do that safely in the training section of this chapter. The second element requires the defender to write down his front-sight observations for later study and memorization.

The poor-man's range estimator is easy to use. Because human beings tend to be relatively the same size (tall men and short men are separated by less than two feet) and the size of your front sight never changes, measuring between them can give you a fairly accurate range estimate, at least enough for our purposes. If you know in advance that at 200 yards a man will appear to be the height of *your* front sight blade, and you subsequently sight on a man that appears to be the height of your front sight blade, you know that he is about 200 yards away. It is that simple. Now that you know your range, you must know where to aim to compensate for bullet drop *at that particular distance.*

## Compensating for Bullet Drop

Compensating for bullet drop is easy once you know how far your bullet will drop at a particular distance, which you'll learn during training. A defender must know bullet drop for his handgun-ammunition combination for 100 yards to 300 yards at 50-yard increments. If you know that your bullet will drop 60" at 100 yards and your target is estimated to be at a distance of 100 yards, you need to fire 60" above the head of your target, about one-third higher than the attacker appears in your sights. That's all it takes—unless there's wind . . .

## Compensating for Wind

In the same way that the defender needs a method for measuring target height for bullet drop, a measuring standard for windage is also necessary. Again we use the front sight blade to measure the width of a man at known distances: 100 yards to 300 yards at 50-yard increments. The other half of the equation is the wind itself; we must quantify wind force and convert it into front-sight-blade widths in order to be able to execute windage adjustments.

Measuring the effect of wind requires an immediate visual test by the shooter and the knowledge that wind force will move the bullet at specific distances. The visual test is to take a few blades of grass, grains of sand, pocket lint, or other lightweight matter and let them drop from the height from which you intend to shoot. If you carry a handkerchief that won't signal your adversary, you can dangle it in the wind for measurement. Measurement for any of these methods is to *note the angle of drop against a straight vertical line*. If the sand, handkerchief, or other matter drops straight to the ground, there is no wind requiring compensation. Our meteorology will be limited to a standard of "good enough for service handguns" with quarter-value winds (22–23°), half-value winds (45°), three-quarter value winds (67–68°), or full-value winds (90°).

Direction is everything in wind. A full-value wind blowing directly at the shooter or from directly behind the shooter is the same as no wind at all. If a full-value wind crosses the shooter at a 45° angle (in other words, the shooter is not facing the wind nor has his back to the wind but is turned partially into or away from it), it is actually a half-value wind. Only when crossing the shooter perpendicularly to the line of fire is the wind considered to be at its full force value. Account for the direction of wind in relation to your orientation.

In the training section the student will find how to measure and record windage.

## Long-Distance Shooting

Defensive shooting at extreme distances is marksmanship. There's no way around that. Every adjustment must be exact.

The front sight tip must be crystal clear. *Eye relief must not be altered if at all possible.* Eye relief is the distance between the dominant eye and the rear sight. This positioning provides a perspective of the sights that will change if the eye relief is changed. The reader should remember from earlier in the book that prone firing tends to group shots at a different point than standing fire due to the alteration in eye relief. If the defender shoots differently at 600 yards than at six yards, his shooting experience and knowledge is unusable for informing his long-distance shooting. It is natural that when forced into long-distance shooting the defender will attempt to use a supportive handgun rest. In such a case the defender must try to position the head, arms, and weapon for normal eye relief. If you want to master a different eye relief to add long-range prone or rest positions to your skills—then train for it.

Long range tends to mean more available time. The threat is farther, and the fire is usually slower. The defender's first priority must be his own protection. Cover first; shoot later.

Most shooters will not see a lot of difference between ammunition in close-range firing. That is not true at 200 yards. Part of a good long-range firing strategy is consistency in ammunition. If you change ammunition, retrain for it.

Light plays havoc with long-range sighting. In bright light, lighter colors "bleed" onto darker colors, causing the lighter target areas to appear larger and the darker target areas to appear smaller. Darkness has the opposite effect. Light colors reflect light; dark colors absorb light. For instance, in a bright summer sun, a white shirt will appear longer and black trousers will appear shorter than they are. The fix is to lower your weapon and focus below the target while keeping sight alignment and then raise the weapon to achieve a fresh sight picture. Don't keep staring at a wavering or shimmering image in bright light.

I do not recommend the use of artificial devices such as makeshift slings when firing at great distances. The best tool of the defender for long-range fire is marksmanship, which demands knowledge based on consistency of experience. In the end, it's all front sight tip.

## Long-Range-Firing Preparation and Training

Firing accurately at long distances requires the defender to have specific knowledge concerning his gun and ammunition performance prior to firing a shot. The following requires some work by the reader and the training partner.

Safety Requirements: To avoid sighting on a human being, cut a full-size cardboard silhouette of a real man's head and body and secure it to a stake. The top of the head should be about 5'8" tall when the stake is placed in the earth. The following research should be done on a dry, windless day for best results.

1. **Elevation-Measurement Research**—The student will measure and record man-size targets at 100 yards and in 50-yard

increments to 300 yards. Use the silhouette to sight each measured distance. The defender sights his handgun on the target and notes the man's size in relation to the front sight blade. For example, if the man-target appears to be half the size of the front sight blade at 250 yards, the defender will annotate it as 250 YARDS = 0.5. The benefit of that knowledge occurs when the defender is forced into a long-range defense and sees a man appear half the size of the front sight tip. The defender will know his target is approximately 250 yards away and adjust elevation accordingly. People do not often conveniently stand and face someone firing at them. We can calculate a sitting or kneeling man at half the height of a standing man, and we can calculate a prone man as one quarter the height of a standing man.

2. **Ammunition-Performance Research**—The defender must know how far his bullet drops at each of the recorded distances. The easiest way to gain such knowledge is to go to a rifle range and fire at a large paper target (at least 10' · 10'). Place a brightly colored aiming point at the very top of the target (a red circle 12" to 24"). Aim at the red disk and fire deliberate slow-fire shots. The training partner will spot, using a scope or binoculars, and record the hits on a mini-target as they occur. This will allow the student to inform the training partner which shots to dismiss due to shooter error. After firing five good slow-fire shots, the student need only measure and determine an average distance from the red disk to the accepted bullet holes on the target to know the bullet drop for that specific distance. All that remains is to record the results, such as 250 YARDS = 8' DROP. If the defender measures a man at 0.5 front sight blades at 250 yards, 8' will be about three-quarters of the front sight blade. The defender will hold his sight alignment three quarters of the front sight blade's height over the head of the target. It's that easy.

3. **Wind-Measurement Research**—This research can be done at the same time as the elevation research. Where elevation is measured against the height of a man, windage is measured against the width of a man. For our purposes a man is about 18"–20" wide. If a man appears to be about a third of the width of the front sight blade at 250 yards, the result will be recorded as 250 YARDS = 0.3.

4. **Wind-Performance Research**—This research requires a little cooperation from nature. The student goes to a rifle range and uses his giant target, with the difference being that the red disk is moved to the upwind side of the target to allow as much target space

as possible for bullet drift. After taking a wind reading to determine the value of the wind, the shooter fires good slow-fire shots at the red disk. The training partner again spots and records the shots on a mini-target, omitting the student's declared errors. After firing five good shots, the student measures and gets an average for bullet drift for a particular wind value at a specific distance. The results are recorded as 250 YARDS (HALF-VALUE) = 5'. The student must be dedicated enough to attend the range during each of the different wind values to record results. I know that estimations can be made, but I also know that there is no substitute for firsthand knowledge that includes the imperceptible quirks of individual shooters. Ballistic reports and wind-calculation charts are not enough.

The above four factors, when recorded in your long-range data book, will tell you where to hold for each incremental distance and wind value. The example used in the above text would be recorded to tell the defender the following:

- 250 yards = Man is half the height of the front sight blade.
- 250 yards = 8' bullet drop
- 8' bullet drop at 250 yards = three-quarters of a front sight blade
- 250 yards = Man is a third of the width of the front sight blade.
- Drop test = half-value wind
- Half-value wind at 250 yards = 5' of windage adjustment
- 5' at 250 yards = one front-sight-blade width of adjustment

The defender in the above example would hold three-quarters of a front sight blade above the target and one blade's width to the upwind side of the target. Please bear in mind the above example is for illustrative purposes only, having no bearing in reality. Actual drop and windage will go from feet to several yards, depending on distance and caliber. The student must record actual results using his defense handgun and ammunition.

Long-range shooting requires discipline and the acceptance that at some point ballistics break apart and accuracy is reduced to general direction of fire. The training for long-distance firing is to do it as often as you are able. If you have no means to fire at long distances, devote yourself to perfect close-range fire. The elements of a good shot are the same at any distance. The difference is only in where you put the front sight tip.

Skill-Installation Requirement (Live Fire): standing slow fire at 25, 50, 75, and 100 yards using a large black cross drawn on the blank side of a large target. Qualification is 10 shots at each distance, beginning at 25 yards, with hits no farther from the crucible than 3" @ 25 yards, 6" @ 50 yards, 10" @ 75 yards, and 18" @ 100 yards.

Maintenance Requirement: standing slow fire at 100 yards, 50 rounds, semi-annually

Long-range training must also be conducted with the weak hand. You don't want to be disarmed due to one broken hand.

If the reader has difficulty with the above training, please seek competent local instruction. Marksmanship is well within your grasp.

# PRACTICS 104: Strategy and Tactics

# Chapter Fourteen: Planning the Defense

*However beautiful the strategy, you should occasionally
look at the results.*

Winston Churchill

## The Seven Practices "Everys"

1. Every round will misfire.
2. Every shot will miss.
3. Every firearm will break.
4. Every magazine will fail to feed.
5. Every holster will prevent a good draw.
6. Every knife will fail to open.
7. Every plan will prove inadequate.

The solution to the Seven "Everys" is training and quality equipment properly maintained. Planning has no value if based solely on unrealistic expectations of fair weather and good sailing. A proper plan anticipates disaster and failure. Practicality trumps idealism in strategy. Removing bad guys from the basement would be nice, but I will not drag myself down the basement steps to be shot in my skivvies and gun belt. No thank you. They can help themselves to a box of Christmas decorations. The preservation of life is our ultimate goal. Everything else is a distraction.

## Priorities

This may seem simple, but enough recorded tragedy proves priorities are often not sufficiently considered by home defenders. Make yourself a list of whatever you may want to save during a home emergency. Your list might look like this:

1. Wife and kids
2. Restored 1971 Chevrolet Chevelle
3. Grandfather's war medals
4. 105" HD television

Now go back through your list and drop any item for which you are not willing to sacrifice everything else. Your new list should look like this:

Wife and kids

The defender needs to plan a defense around that ultimate priority and then honor it. Getting killed clanging around in your garage with a shotgun does nothing toward preserving the lives of your family. A good plan weighs risk against the possibility of success. Cops weigh risk all the time. That's why they park half a block from a reported disturbance and wait outside for cover units to arrive. The military does the same thing. You don't kill your own people over replaceable things. Nobody wants to be robbed, and an armed man that is in the right doesn't want to hide with his family while savages defile his home. We all can empathize with the righteous indignation of the homeowner. But the defender must remember two things: Success *is* achieving your defense priority, and being the defender is always better than being the attacker. Whenever you can get into a protected defensive position, you have exponentially increased your odds of success. Leave pride and ego behind you.

Home-invasion crimes are different than in years past. Before, attackers could sever the telephone line and effectively cut off a single home. Today, attackers know that if you're awake, you will probably grab your cell phone and call for help. They have to move fast, which is bad for them and good for you. Never be rushed beyond safety.

Help is the local sheriff's office or next-door neighbor. Know the real response times of whomever you're counting on for assistance. If you're 15 minutes or more from a law enforcement response, you may wish to consider a cooperative agreement between competent, law-abiding neighbors.

You can't defend what you don't control. That means you need to gather those you are responsible to protect. You will need a defensible area or an escape route. Access to real-time communications and whatever extra weapons you may possess are also required. Above all, know what you have to do and how you are going to do it, and don't let adrenaline or emotion change your plan.

## Planning for Disaster

The first priority is life. A sole defender may be responsible for only himself, or he may have a dozen people to defend. Protecting life requires control of the people under your care. More plainly put, the defender must gather those he will defend. He needs a rallying point. Office space and bedrooms have different limitations. The house may be smaller and therefore quicker to move through, but the office space may provide alternative paths of travel. In either case the defender must be able to move through the space, gather his people, and lead them to a secure or at least defensible position. Since we know everything fails, the defender will need a primary and a secondary collection or evacuation route.

Finally, there must be a planned conclusion for success. Whether the defender shelters in place, calls for aid, and defends his charges until the good guys arrive or whether he leads his people to safety, he must have a planned conclusion beyond picking up a gun and heading for the kids' bedroom.

## Collection Vs. Evacuation

*Collection* means local protection. *Evacuation* means liberation. A ground-floor office in the back of a commercial building may lend itself to evacuation through an exterior door facing a heavily treed area. Three second-story bedrooms in a 3,200 sq. ft. house will probably require a collection and stationary defense of the family. Of course, getting people to safety is always better than involving them in a gunfight. Know what your end game is, collection or evacuation.

## Moving the Group

Whether the kids are moved into the master bedroom or the parents are moved into a child's bedroom depends on circumstances. Defending a child's room may be safer and quicker if moving the children requires another exposed movement past the top of an open staircase. The intelligent defender will include environment in his planning. During the cover-and-concealment portion, we discussed how to plan evacuation routes based on cover and concealment options adjacent to an occupied building. Consider likely paths of fire when planning movements. The general rule is to move whom you must as far as you must and not one step farther. People are more vulnerable during movement than when covered, so avoid convoluted paths and get where you need to be safely and quickly.

Routes may be seasonal. If you plan to move down a hill,

consider whether that plan will be reasonable when the hill is covered in snow and ice. If Mom is one-month pregnant today, the plan must work for a woman in her third trimester. You need at least a primary and an alternate route whenever possible.

Planning is actionable thought, not desire. Don't make big plans to carry three children across a golf course while holding your handgun in your teeth. Teach kids to hold hands when moving. Little ones have limits on what they can be expected to do when terrified in the middle of the night. The same is true, to some extent, for untrained adults. The defender will be doing well if untrained and frightened adults can be made to move without a lot of discussion. Aim for the kids being quiet, holding hands, and obeying very simple orders quickly.

Getting the cooperation of surprised adults is easier with a simple summary statement that includes the reassurance of a solution prior to a specific request for action: "Bob, burglars are downstairs. The cops are coming. Please get your wife and move quietly into the master bedroom." Compliance seems to be easier when you begin by using the other person's name. The defender's objective is to give the other person enough information for them to act with a sense of being both informed and in agreement. People are funny. Very often they will not move until they can emotionally accept their circumstances, even if imminent danger is apparent. Bob's first impulse, when woken in the middle of the night, will be to resist reality: "Are you sure it isn't a raccoon?" After that Bob will become possessive and protective: "I'm not moving my wife anywhere." Finally, old Bob will want to be involved in decision-making: "Shouldn't we just lock the doors?" Once Bob is on board, he'll want to save face by asking "intelligent" questions: "What did the police say?" The defender who thinks before speaking will save himself a lot of time while attempting to gain the compliance of startled adults.

## Sheltering in Place

If collection is your reasoned choice, you'll need to make preparations for a secure space. Remember the Sphere of Responsibility and the countless possible avenues for incoming fire? Inside your home, the sphere points are lumped into four walls, a ceiling, and a floor. A second-story home (or any home, for that matter) is not likely to have forced entry from the roof. But shots can be fired through walls, floors, and ceilings. A piece of heavy metal from your local welding shop can provide a safe place for family to sit when sheltering upstairs. A piece large enough to protect an adult and a couple of small kids will fit under most dressers. In the event of an invasion, move the dresser and park the family on the metal. A second-story exterior wall is unlikely to be a target, and a chest of drawers, on wheels, with a reinforced back will serve as a decent barricade, provided the defender doesn't use that position for returning fire.

Fire draws fire. Keep a little distance from your family and use the same diligence in protecting yourself. Planning is about logistics: guns, phones, people, and routes. Know what you want to accomplish, and planning becomes easy.

## Building the Plan

All plans have goals; otherwise, we have no impetus to accomplish anything. The goal is simple: Protect innocent life. That's the goal for every defender, every time. Objectives are those things that must be achieved in order to meet your goal and are ordered by priority.

A. **Set your priorities in order of importance.** Priorities are choices that become your plan's objectives. You may have to abandon some priorities due to circumstances beyond your control. Know your priorities, and you can plan your objectives.

Following is an example of a prioritized protection list:

1. You
2. Co-workers sharing your office
3. Warehouse worker downstairs
4. Customers and sales staff in adjacent building

Each of the above priorities will require planning consideration. Collecting co-workers and the warehouse guy in the same trip may not be reasonable. Time is everything. If you need several minutes to lead co-workers to safety, the warehouse worker may have to be abandoned. On the other hand, if you can get them to a doorway opening onto a busy sidewalk within two minutes, your other priorities may be entirely achievable. Don't plan for impossible objectives and be reasonable in recognizing when objectives are no longer possible.

B. **Convert your objectives into footsteps by mapping routes and preparing any shelter-in-place positions.** This is the time for logistical considerations. The sooner help is requested, the quicker help will arrive. How will you call for help? Your Practics belt phone won't be in your office. Plan on cell phones failing and landlines being disrupted. If your plan includes use of an automobile, it had better include a set of keys as well. An unprotected car can easily be disabled. Every point in your plan needs an alternative:

1. Call police on the office phone to give them instant address information through the 911 system.
   *Alternate*: Call 911 on a cell phone if office phone system is disrupted.
   *Second alternate*: Alert police by Internet if the cell-phone call fails. (Preload police Web address into your device.)
2. Grab the medical bag from under the coffeemaker stand.
   *Alternate*: Empty the company first-aid box.
3. Gather all six co-workers in the office.
   *Alternate*: Move to restrooms to collect stragglers.
4. Lead the group to the stairwell (never the elevator).
   *Alternate*: Exit to the rooftop from a copy-room window and low jump onto the grass hill.
5. Direct the group to flee toward the main thoroughfare under cover of the brick wall.
   *Alternate*: Send the group through the drainpipe into the wooded area toward the mall.
6, Enter the warehouse by the stairwell door and collect the warehouse worker.
   *Alternate*: Enter the warehouse from the window by the grassy hill and collect the warehouseman.
7. Send the warehouse worker along the edge of the building toward the drainpipe.
   *Alternate*: Send the warehouse worker into the parking lot.

8. Enter the adjacent building by the employees' door.
   Alternate: Enter the building by the men's room window.
9. Direct all occupants to flee through the loading dock into the wooded area toward the mall.
   *Alternate*: Direct occupants to flee through the main doors into the parking area.
   *Second alternate*: Shelter in place all occupants in the basement; defend the stairwell.
10. Re-contact police by cell phone.
    *Alternate*: Call 911 from the basement landline.

Keep the plan simple. You have to be able to remember it, and complex plans tend to be easily disrupted. Notice the above plan provides for a medical bag but does not specify a time or place to administer first aid. Obviously, there is no way to know if anyone will require medical aid and no way to plan for it. The plan does not preclude additional necessary actions, nor does it get bogged down guessing at them. Simplicity is key.

Knowledge-Installation Requirement: Make a plan for your defense responsibilities.

Maintenance Requirement: Update the plan with changes in people, location, and environment (i.e., wooded area gets clear cut, drain pipe has bars welded across opening).

# Chapter Fifteen: Navigating the Route

*Distrust and caution are the parents of security.*

Benjamin Franklin

Self-defense with a gun comes down to three things: shooting a gun, not getting shot, and moving. We have already discussed shooting and cover. While we have looked at methods of walking and crawling, moving through a challenged area to execute a defense plan requires some additional thought.

## Sole-Defender Movement

I have been on too many robbery or burglary clearances with cops that insist on Hollywood poses instead of intelligent, purposeful tactics. Many times I have seen men expose themselves to the danger of a gun grab by using SWAT or special operations movement techniques that do not properly serve the sole defender. The sole defender must move slower and keep Sphere of Responsibility awareness.

In your home the most dangerous movement will be passing from room to room. That's easy enough to understand; bad guys wait against doorways. Let's begin by considering how to retain weapon control.

**Handgun Proximity**—When moving through confined spaces, keep your muzzle pointed forward but close to your torso by bringing your elbows rearward. Let your forearms contact your torso. If an attacker grabs your muzzle when it is close to your chest, the attacker will either have to be in front of the muzzle or immediately to the side. A close chest clutch of the weapon enables you to take one step in the direction of the attack, while turning toward the attacker, and have your muzzle pointing at your opponent's chest. Remember Practics Muzzle Leveraging. You are now in a position to fire or to step back and raise the weapon into a punch-fire or linear-fire position. When a defender moves with extended and locked arms (even when

SWAT-dipping the muzzle through doorways), he is exposing his weapon to a gun grab. A hand on the muzzle of your weapon can easily be countered, but when both parties share similar leverage, the defender is at extreme risk.

**Practics Horse Heading**—A tactical team has a rearward-looking member; a lone defender does not. You must look to the rear every three seconds when you don't know where the bad guy or guys are located. If you can move, they can move. One method of keeping an eye on what is behind you is Practics Horse Heading. A horse can see to his rear with a very slight turn of his head. A human can achieve a similar view but requires a greater angle of head turn. Peripheral vision covers side to side in humans. If the head is turned to the right at a 45° angle, the defender will be able to see from 10 o'clock to four o'clock. If the focus is kept straight ahead, the defender will have peripheral vision focus *from both eyes at the same time.* If the focus goes to either side, the defender will not notice movement within the peripheral vision of the opposite eye. Proper horse heading requires the head to turn to both sides. When the head is turned 45° to the right, step at an oblique angle toward the right by crossing the left foot over the right, which will turn the shoulder carriage and give a direct rearward peripheral view even if the focus is kept at the original 45° angle. A step to the left will do the same for the left eye (look left, step left). These steps and peeks allow a defender to see behind while still looking ahead. Remember that the goal is to keep the vision in line with the direction of the head but to periodically angle the head for a greater field of peripheral vision. Don't twist your head to the rear making yourself blind to a frontal attack.

Horseheading is a matter of splitting the difference between forward movement and rearward awareness.

**Closed Doors**—This is a tough obstacle for one defender. If you must enter a closed door, you need to consider some things. A bad guy knows you have to turn the knob or kick down the door. No matter what you choose to do, you will likely signal your location before you discover his.

Having kicked open my share of doors, I do not recommend kicking open a door when other alternatives exist. While I am rather large, I have encountered doors that I couldn't budge. The problem is, after the failed kick attempt, you're left standing in front of the door. Granted, most interior doors shouldn't be a problem. Let's assume you have a big foot and flimsy doors. Success brings its own misery because after the door is kicked open, it will often swing back toward you—which never happens in a movie. How many times do you want to have to open the same door? You might as well hire a marching band to go in with you. Bear in mind that not every door you need to open will swing inward; some doors must be pulled open.

A better method is to use a quick movement to turn the knob along with a gentle push (or pull) and a light retreat. Broom or mop handles will push a door and give the defender a little more distance. Due to the Americans with Disabilities Act (ADA) regulations, more and more buildings are equipped with door levers instead of doorknobs. That's good for defenders, who can pull handles from a slight distance using a belt or cord. An open doorway, by any means, is ready for Slicing-the-Pie.

**Stairs**—Generally, going up the stairs is safer than going down them. I suppose that only matters when you're setting up your home and no reasonable alternative to using your staircase exists, but it's worth bearing in mind. Your feet can be seen coming down a partially closed stairwell that is open on the lower level before your eyes can see the bad guy and your hands can react. It's easy to suggest going down head first, but that is not realistic. The shooter needs to be on his feet before reaching the bottom of the stairs. Otherwise you'll get shot in the back as you slither into view, or you'll have to flip onto your back and fire upward once you reach a certain level in your descent. You can use the headfirst position to take a peek and then creep down in a crouch, but it is a tough slog any way you do it and requires practice.

A reasonable method is to get your butt down behind your knees (sitting on the steps) and put your arms and handgun between your knees. This position may bring your vision and weapon low enough to use whatever opening you have to see the room below. Crab walk your way down the steps until you have enough visibility to stand.

Treat short stairwells like an open door. Longer stairwells require a tactical guess. You are better off being against the same wall as the bad guy. If he's hiding on the right side at the top of the stairs, you want to approach close to the right edge of the stairway. Force the attacker to come farther away from the corner of the wall to shoot. As I said, this is a tactical guess, and there can be more than one attacker.

It is better not to slide yourself against the wall on your way up the stairs. Sliding makes noise and may reveal your position. Having said that, if you must get up those stairs and you are wobbly (understandable), put your nearest shoulder blade against the wall. You must not look down as you climb the stairs. Remember to high step, raising your feet a little higher than you normally would. Keep weight on the rear foot until the lead foot is fully seated, which will prevent stumbling on junior's roller skate and lessens the nervous temptation to look down.

As you get near the top of the stairs, you may Slice the Pie as if breaching a doorway.

**Doorways and Other Contained Openings**—The common rule is "get out of the fatal funnel." That's a good rule, but, as always, use common sense. Don't stand in a framed, backlit doorway, but don't give up a dark doorway to jump into a well-lit commercial kitchen.

When entering a room, move to the right or left immediately. By "immediately" I don't mean without looking where you're going. Generally speaking you have two options for entering through a doorway. The first is to quickly cross the doorway to the other side (right to left, left to right.) Crisscrossing is not the most desirable method due to increased exposure but may be an architectural necessity.

The preferred method is to buttonhook. Buttonhooking is passing through a doorway using only your half of the opening and winding up on the other side of the doorway against the same wall. Few adults can actually only use half an interior doorway, I get that, but you can see the benefit to minimizing your target silhouette during room entry. The way this works is you finish Slicing the Pie and determine to the best of your ability that the other side of the doorway is safe. Stand close to the wall on one side of the opening. For this example we'll say you're on the right side. Move through the doorway quickly and "hook" to the right side. Finish with your back against the wall and scan with your weapon.

**Speed**—A word about scanning and moving with your weapon. You can't go any faster than you can see, recognize, and react. If you walk or scan beyond your ability to recognize danger and address it, your speed can kill you. Training often pushes students to move too quickly. Don't waste time but make sure your hands and feet don't outrun your eyes and brain. Speed is good only when speed is needed. He's the criminal, he's in a hurry, let him rush. Use the time you need to clear obstacles. Don't let the other guy set your pace.

**Elevation**—*High* is generally better than *low*. The second-story sitting room that overlooks the first-floor living area is a desirable location if the bad guy is below. You want the high ground in most cases. Why? To begin with, you command a better field of vision. You can see behind him, but he can't see behind you. Also it's physically harder to fight up. You know that if you've ever moved furniture upstairs—it comes down a lot quicker.

Higher will not always be better than lower though. In most indoor situations neither party has much view. The lower floor has easy access and egress. Upper-floor movement is harder to keep quiet. The second floor is vulnerable to smoke and fire. One area in which indoor height really helps is defending against room entry, like crouching on top of a tall chest of drawers against the entry wall. Few people will bother to look up when entering a room. Rooms have walls, floor, and ceiling. Be certain to see each of them and use interior height when defending wherever it makes sense. When searching, think of a room not as a three-dimensional space, but as six flat planes. Look straight, left, up, right, down, and behind, and you will have visually covered a room.

In the outdoors the high ground becomes a clearer choice, with some exceptions. A man in a tree or tower may do well until he is discovered. Then he has nowhere to go. All questions concerning location should include what comes next. If you're likely to be trapped under fire, the risk of moving may be worthwhile.

**Tracks**—Liquid leaves tracks when walked through. If you just got out of the shower, try to prevent dripping. Wipe your feet on the couch if it comes to that. Some surfaces become like glass when wet. Don't expose yourself to the bad guys but try to avoid walking through liquids. On the other hand, you can use liquids (milk, water, soda, and so on) as a tracking trap for your bad guy. It won't prevent his movements, but it will lessen the benefit he receives from them. If you're alone and invaders are in your house, you can multiply your effectiveness with common house paint. Pop the lid and cover the floor with it. Paint is tough to wipe off shoes, leaving well-marked prints for a decent distance. (I know it ruins carpets and so forth, but this is a self-defense book, not a marriage guide.)

**Lighting**—Anyone entering your house should never have a natural sight advantage over you. Keep hallways lit. Put the fear on the other guy. If he has to stand in a lit hallway to peek into a dark room, he won't like it. Lights can be turned off, but hallway night-lights require some exposure on the part of whoever wants to bend down and turn them off or kick them out of the sockets. Light matters. Some years ago a young girl was abducted in a horrible case that gained nationwide attention. The poor child was later found murdered.

The criminal told police that he only selected her house because the street light in front of the house wasn't working. Make criminals do their business without cover of darkness. Some will press on under lighting, but they won't know for sure if they're being watched. Prepare your area of responsibility for your defense. Don't make it a fair fight.

## Limiting and Tracking Access

Alarm *system*s cost money, but alarms cost nothing. The following trick is a little hokey, but it works. Windows that you believe are likely to be used as a source of entry can be alarmed with soda cans. Go to the dollar store and buy a couple of bucks' worth of kids' marbles. Pour a few marbles in some soda cans. Tie the cans about 10" apart with string. Place the cans on the inside window ledge or on a table under the window. Let the string drop down to be less conspicuous. A curtain between the cans and the window is preferable, preventing them from being seen altogether from the outside. If anyone tries to come through the window, they would have to grab all the cans at once. Usually, if the arrangement is casual, the crook will assume the cans are empty and quiet. If they don't see them, all cans will get knocked over at once and make a racket. Of course, you can use knickknacks, glassware, and so on. The point is to make the bad guy reveal himself. This would chase away many sneak-entry rapists, who won't risk premature discovery.

When living in urban apartments or working overseas, I found it helpful to know if someone had entered my dwelling while I was away. This is easy to do and can be used to learn where an intruder has gone, provided it was set up in advance. All you need are some small wood splinters (like you might pick off firewood); tiny, neutral-colored slivers of thick paper; or thin slivers of cardboard. Even bits of grass or leaves work well. The objects used should be less than 1/4" and bent into an "L" shape, or at least not flat. Spread them out on the surface of the floor, three or four pieces to every square foot. If noticed, it will look like normal debris tracked in from outdoors. When anyone steps on the pieces, they will crush flat, leaving a record of entry. The more you can use, the more exact information you can learn. Generally, unless you dump 50 pounds of wood chips on your living room carpet, the bad guy will never notice. You'll need light to see the results, though, and you'll have to vacuum afterward. An alternative tracking method is to vacuum a carpet all the way to the door from which you are exiting. Toss the vacuum a few feet and note its position. Any intruders will leave footprints on your carpet and won't be able to cover their tracks with the vacuum cleaner, or at least you'll notice the carpet was disturbed or the vacuum was moved. This is a helpful method if you suspect your building's handyman is a bit too curious.

A sole defender must control space more actively than a team member would. When the defender passes through a cleared room, placing a chair in front of a doorway will either prevent entry or alert the defender to an intruder's movements. Dumping the contents of a garbage can on a stair landing denies an attacker stealthy movement. The defender should not become distracted with setting elaborate traps, but simply rearranging items in a room can increase defender control.

A trick used years ago by some Marine embassy guards was to keep a container of old motor oil salted with metal bearings. If the embassy was overrun, they could pour the oil and bearings down the marble steps, making access to the second floor practically impossible. Use the tools you have to accomplish what you otherwise couldn't.

## Supplies

Small medical bags with a few bandages and tourniquets should be staged throughout your area of responsibility. Keep these bags small, light, and simple. The purpose of the supplies is to stop or slow bleeding until professional medical help is available. In most cases these incidents will end within minutes. Keep med-bags in your work desk, car, bedroom, basement, garage, wherever your evacuation or collection route may take you.

Extra weapons and phones may be concealed along your route. The reality is that a defender may not be able to reach his gun belt at the instant he becomes aware of trouble. Additional weapons must be well hidden. Test hiding spots with a trusted friend. A good knife or baseball bat is very effective in tight, close quarters. Cheap prepaid phones are worth their weight in gold to a defender. Get as many as you can keep charged and staged throughout your area of responsibility.

## Route-Movement Training and Preparation

Everything in this book has relevance during movement along an evacuation or collection route. Anything is possible. The defender's movements, use of cover, shooting tactics, and use of deadly force are all pertinent during route movement.

1. **Practics Horse-Head Drill**—This unarmed drill will help the student develop the skill of looking in both a forward and rearward direction at the same time. The student will walk through a home or office building with the training partner trailing behind by about 15'. The training partner must ensure the student is viewing rearward no less frequently than every three seconds. The student will horse head by taking an oblique step (crossing legs) to either side with the head following the oblique angle. Eye focus is straight in line with the head. In other words, the foot steps at about a 45° angle, and the head and eyes go to the same angle and direction. Practics Horse Heading depends on *peripheral* vision to enable both forward and rearward sight at the same time. The training partner must stay behind the student to force the student into proper technique. The student's objective is to see the training partner with every execution. As soon as one oblique step is taken, an oblique step to the opposite side must be immediately completed. The two steps combined count as one "look to the rear." This simple skill is only difficult because it takes effort to not turn the eyes to the rear. Lock your eyes in the same direction your nose is pointing but use peripheral vision for viewing straight to the front and rear when horse-heading.

Skill-Installation Requirement: Walk 50 yards executing proper Horse-Head technique.

Maintenance Requirement: above training requirement annually

2. **Buttonhook Drill**—All this unarmed drill requires is a toy gun, gun belt, and doorway with sufficient space to allow training movement. The student must wear the gun belt because the belt is extra bulk that may limit how closely the student can hug the doorframe. Beginning with the student standing with his back against the wall immediately adjacent to the doorway and the toy gun in a high-ready/close torso hold, the student will pivot toward the doorway with a lowered body position and place the foot that is farthest from his side of the doorway in the center of the doorway opening. If you

are entering the doorway from the right side, your doorway entry foot will be your left foot. Once the foot is set, the student pushes through the doorway by tucking the doorframe-side shoulder downward. For instance, if you're moving off the left foot, tuck the right shoulder down in order to clear the doorframe. Allow the back of the shoulder to slide along the doorjamb. The goal is to force yourself exclusively into one quarter of the doorway opening. That's the goal. It's not realistic, but we aim for it in order to achieve the smallest possible target area when clearing a doorway. The head must be forced upward, craning the neck. You must look ahead when clearing a doorway; too many SWAT guys stare at their feet because they depend on the first guy in the line. You are the first guy in your line—look at what's waiting for you. Likewise, it will be natural for your handgun to dip when your torso is bent forward. Clear the doorway with the muzzle pointing forward, in line with your vision. Once the corner has been turned, so to speak, place the other foot inside the room about a foot from the wall. Step onto the ball of that foot and pivot yourself into a back-against-the-wall position. Shorter students may have to take a couple extra short steps to clear a doorway. Raise your toy gun and scan the room. The training partner will stand inside the room to be entered and center himself on the doorway. It is the training partner's primary job to determine if the student is minimizing exposure to the greatest extent possible. The training standard is using one lower quarter of the doorway opening. The training partner will determine the realistic limits of the standard on the student. The second concern of the training partner is to ensure the doorway is cleared with no portion of the body or equipment intruding into the opening at the conclusion of the movement.

Skill-Installation Requirement: 20 successful buttonhooks from each side of the doorway

Maintenance Requirement: Repeat the above quarterly for two years.

Repeat the above training with the weak hand. Don't let your position outside a doorway deny you the best possible entry; be able to use either hand.

3. **Crisscross Drill**—This technique is often necessary when a doorway is set into a corner, preventing a buttonhook. Execution begins similarly to the buttonhook; the difference begins with the choice of lead foot. If you are entering a doorway from the right side,

your lead foot will be your right foot. The lead foot is placed in the center of the opening. Step through the doorway and place the trailing foot about 12" from the wall as far inside the room as possible. When the lead foot is brought into the room, the student's back will be against the wall, and scanning will begin. Eyes and muzzle are up, just as with buttonhooking. The student must not allow the muzzle to point at his feet. The training partner will watch to ensure the student is as low as possible without slowing the movement. Eyes and muzzle are forward. The goal is to use no more than half the opening. Of great concern is the speed with which the doorway is cleared. Good form doesn't matter if the student is in the doorway one fraction of a second longer than necessary. Hustle.

Skill-Installation Requirement: 20 successful buttonhooks from each side of the doorway

Maintenance Requirement: Repeat the above quarterly for two years.

Students must train to crisscross with the weak hand, too.

## 4. Route Preparation

Preparation Requirement: Examine your route for possible defender obstacles, such as self-locking doors, creaking floors, slippery rugs, vicious dogs, and so on.

## 5. Staging Requirement

Staging Requirement: Prepare some medical bags by placing a few large bandages and a tourniquet inside each small bag and store them along your routes. Place phones where needed and extra weapons in secure, hidden locations.

Everything in Practics is intended to bring innocent people to a position of safety. A good, well-chosen, well-prepared route or collection point is as important as good shooting. Remember what the legal defender is trying to achieve.

# Chapter Sixteen: Mindset

*We cannot solve our problems with the same thinking we used when we created them.*

Albert Einstein

*Let our advance worrying become advance thinking and planning.*

Winston Churchill

I will make a confession: I hate writing about mindset, shooter psychology, or "thinking to win." The significance of emotion on precision shooting or in the handling of threatening situations cannot be overstated, but in my experience too many shooters are babbling about some New Age mind scheme when they ought to be training for reliable, effective, reflexive action under duress. Nonetheless, the subject of mindset merits our attention, understanding, and mastery because it is fundamental to self-defense. I could have included this chapter earlier in the book, but proper mindset begins with a few informed decisions, and I believe that the reader is better served to first consider the gravity and broad scope of the responsibility for armed defense before making those decisions.

People behave in stressful situations as they are trained to behave. For instance, a teenager who has had no guidance in life and has had nothing required of him, will often, when faced with an emergency, stand and blink through the crisis. He was trained to do nothing, and nothing he will do. Several years ago, when four CHP officers were killed in a shoot-out near Newhall, California, one fallen officer was found with brass in his trouser pocket. Apparently, under fire he resorted to his range experience and dumped his expended revolver brass into his hand and then into his pocket. Think about that. An intelligent, knowledgeable man in fear for his life took a precious second to prevent littering the ground. CHP didn't formally teach that error. It was born from range shooters not wanting to have to pick up brass after qualifying. The training is in the actual *doing*, not the accepted written procedures. If you have to think before reacting, you're not trained to react; you're effectively trained to hesitate. The patrolman *knew* better, of course, but like all of us he could not help doing what he was trained to do, especially under shocking duress. Proper training is the means by which we overcome the confusion and doubt wrought by stress.

Many people will candidly state that under no circumstance would they ever shoot another human being. Hand salute. I mean it. Self-awareness is critical to marrying the proper training to the individual. A man who cannot bring himself to punch another man in the face should not waste time learning to throw punches when he could instead learn how to grapple. If you can't or won't fight, train to run or use non-lethal means to the best possible advantage. The use of deadly force has a moral component. A defender must truly believe, in good conscience, that he has the right to use deadly force to protect himself or others from death, serious injury, or great bodily harm. This is not a courage test, because the people legally using deadly force are doing it in fear for life. Right? A moral decision must be made, and that decision (whether or not to use legal deadly force) is the basis of defender mindset. If you can't answer that question now, I urge you to give it serious consideration before taking up firearms. Find some alternative if your conscience prohibits the use of deadly force. Something is always better than nothing.

Let's assume that the reader has decided that under the legal and moral guidelines of the Practics Gold Standard, he will use deadly force. It remains that the defender must be mentally prepared, and here is where the topic tends to fall into kill-or-be-killed, camouflage-pants-wearing silliness. You can't be fully prepared all the time. Many books by many knowledgeable people contradict what I'm about to tell you, but I'll leave it to the reader to reason through all of it. A recent gun-magazine article recommended holding reading material low enough to allow a defender to scan the area over the top of the reading material. The author was both knowledgeable and sincere, but in real life better advice would be to do your reading at appropriate times and places. Do you really have to read at midnight while sitting at a lonely bus stop? *Most practical preparedness is in the general choices made by the defender.* For instance, a well-trained, off-duty cop is not prepared for an attack when he leaves his family room to walk toward his bathroom. Who would be? On the other hand, he can verify his home has not been entered while he and his family were away during the day, and he can secure the home after their return. But only in books is he in Condition Rambo after two plates of lasagna and two hours of inane television. Officers that have been in high-stress situations, such as an initial encounter with armed robbers, are relieved from the duties of scene security as soon as possible to prevent mental/emotional fatigue overriding training and sound practice. Being "ready" is exhausting. So let's be realistic about preparedness and mindset.

As mentioned, the first and most essential element to mindset is the moral decision that the defender must make long before action is required. Continuing with defensive firearms is foolish if the defender has not fully accepted the moral premise of the right to self-defense. That decision, once made, allows the possibility for an instinctive response. Absent a firm decision to defend life using force, even the best technically trained defender will only be practically trained to hesitate. Each person must decide beforehand.

For the remainder of this book, I'm going to assume that the reader has already claimed a moral right to use the Practics Gold Standard of deadly force. Mindset consists of two elements: mental and emotional, addressed separately below.

## Mental

Mental preparedness is like an open gate at a stockyard: a little fear, a little stress, and the whole herd will start running through. Once the thought process has been laid *and maintained*, the reactionary pathway will be there under duress. If I have determined that no matter what happens I am going to warn old Mrs. Jones in apartment #C32, that settled desire combined with fear of the moment will help to get me pounding on Mrs. Jones's door during a building fire. The process for converting an idea to a settled decision for action consists of three things:

- **Decide.** The decision is made after an internal process wherein the defender affirms that any expected risk is acceptable in light of the intended action (the benefit of fighting back is determined to outweigh the risk of being punched). It cannot be a case of "I'll try to let Mrs. Jones know if I can remember." To make the decision, the issue of risk must be embraced and settled: "I won't leave the building without getting to Mrs. Jones unless I'd be burned to death or die of suffocation."

344

Think about a paramedic, who is exposed to deadly blood-borne pathogens throughout a career of riding in ambulances. The paramedic makes the decision to handle bloody people before ever being required to encounter an injured person. Emergency medical personnel don't respond to an accident scene and then have a debate over the risks of HIV exposure. Before taking their first ambulance ride, paramedics have already decided to minimize risk through equipment and procedures and then to accept that reduced and specific risk. We all go through a similar process as it relates to driving on a public roadway. Will I take the risk in order to accomplish the goal? That's the question the defender must answer before he needs to draw a gun; run across an exposed field of fire; or charge a larger, more powerful intruder. Weigh the risk against the intended action and decide.

- **Keep it alive.** Naturally, mental preparedness must involve the training of thought. Neglected ideas are moved to the back of the mind. We all experience that phenomenon when last year's passionate but discarded plan comes back to us in the happenstance of misplaced memory. Preparing requires preservation of the idea. Every time a jumbo police officer gets into a midsize patrol car, he needs to think how he can pull himself out the passenger door in the event of an emergency by placing his left hand on the dash, spreading his knees to miss the steering wheel, pushing off the driver's seat with his left foot, and grabbing the passenger door with his right hand. That takes two or three seconds' mental maintenance every day. If Sally in Human Resources intends to flee out the window in the event an armed, disgruntled employee comes into her office, Sally needs to think about unlatching and lifting the window, passing through the opening, and freefalling down to the company-designated smoking area. Otherwise Sally is just going to sit in her chair for a few critical seconds until a fresh idea comes to her.

- **Train.** The thought gets things going, but action has to be effective. In the above example of a jumbo cop, he has to actually be able to squeeze out from under the steering wheel; otherwise, the mental planning is pointless. Whatever we desire to do in a crisis, we must train ourselves to do prior to the crisis. No surprise, defensive shooters go to the range to prepare. But in a crisis you do not "go to the range." The actual *reaction* must be trained. Target shooting develops a skill; repeatedly rolling out of bed and grabbing your handgun ingrains a reaction. Defenders need both.

## Emotional

Now we have the thought-to-action process down, but what about the other major influence on our ability to turn desire into action? Emotion plagues our action through fear and insecurity. Doubt creates hesitation. Training for an instinctual reaction can defeat destructive emotional influences, but during lulls in the crisis when decision-making is required, training alone is not enough to control emotion. We must use reason, and the defender must construct a bulwark of reason by adopting and maintaining the following precepts.

- **The defender has a responsibility to win this struggle.** God grants humans the right to defend their lives. Humanity has traditionally recognized the right and necessity of self-defense. It is the responsibility of the individual soul to morally preserve his life and the lives of the defenseless under his care, or civilization will die under the historical onslaught of natural and man-made violence. It is the defender's duty to win. The attacker alone decides through his actions what will be a deadly force situation. The defender merely seeks to preserve life through appropriate reactions.

- **Feelings are not indicative of fact.** Many people have waited for news, expecting it to be bad, and then were pleasantly surprised when good news arrived instead. In life we have many erroneous beliefs based on our insecurities. The defender must realize that his insecurities are not based on who he is but on whom he is afraid of being. If I don't care about a feeling, it cannot have any impact on my readiness to act. The ability of insecurities to cause hesitation is greatly reduced when training has fully answered the question "Am I ready?"

- **The defender knows what he is doing.** If we engage in specific physical actions, specific physical results will occur. Nothing in the natural order of this world can change that.

346

Training results, not fleeting emotional insecurities, demonstrate the reality of a defender's capability. If you have already successfully done a task a thousand times in training, it is reasonable to believe you can do the exact same task again under duress. Maybe not as well, but good enough.

- **A best defense requires action.** Bad decisions may be dangerous, but not making a decision is worse. When chased by a dog, a rabbit will make a series of running turns. Occasionally a rabbit makes a wrong turn, but the survivability of rabbits would dramatically decrease if rabbits stood still to consider the failure of municipal leash laws. Act now; worry later.

Mindset is thoughtful preparation, not psychological tricks. If you are a person who believes human emotion can influence the mechanical operation of firearms, ballistic performance, or environment, no one will be able to teach you how to function under duress. On the other hand, if you are able to accept the fact that your "feelings" do not control reality, you have the means to navigate through stress and limit the crippling effects of fear. Think—reason—act.

## Situational Awareness

The application of good mindset enables the preventive state of situational awareness. Understanding your immediate situation allows you to avoid danger or react to danger in an effective and efficient manner. Earlier I mentioned the need for realism when considering mindset—it goes double for situational awareness.

On occasion I've gone to dinner with friends and heard one of them announce an unusual seating preference: "I can't sit with my back to the door." This Dirty Harry sort of declaration is particularly amusing when the speaker is unarmed. I never know what to make of it. The assumption is that an armed robber could come through the front door of the restaurant. That's certainly possible, but it's also possible that a nut in the men's room is getting ready for a shooting spree or that a disgruntled ex-employee is coming from the kitchen, as many restaurants tend to leave the outside kitchen door open for cooling. As a uniformed police officer, I avoided eating in restaurants that I thought unsafe or was unable to view my surroundings—the uniform and gun being a potential target. Consequently, most of my evening meals were eaten inside a patrol car in the middle of a deserted parking lot. Of course, we can be vigilant while doing mundane activities, but there's a limit to what can realistically be done.

When cops need to take witness statements at large disturbances, they wait until enough officers are on scene and everyone who needs to be handcuffed has been handcuffed. They wait to conduct necessary, but not immediately critical, tasks rather than risk dividing their attention to write on a clipboard while agitated people are moving around them. Potentially dangerous situations require decision-making much more than they require technical skills.

The cornerstone of situational awareness is the defender's honest self-assessment. A relatively safer method for reading a newspaper in a public place exists, sure, but a decision to not read in any place that requires security vigilance would be the better choice. Seeing trouble before trouble sees you has a legitimate advantage, but the advantage depends on two things: having a planned and effective response and knowing your capabilities. For instance, planning to use your gun in a crowded restaurant—that involves possibly firing from a table in the back of the restaurant to the cashier's counter 10 yards away—assumes that you can consistently shoot quick 2" groups at that distance during training. Otherwise, under duress you'll kill innocent people. Knowing (and admitting) your capabilities is a significant part of situational awareness. In the case of a restaurant shooting, the defender may do better to grab his wife by the wrist and flee through the kitchen door. Having a plan doesn't mean declaring some kind of tough-guy stance. It actually means having a realistic and achievable plan. If you walk down a ghetto street at night, you must deliberately watch for danger approaching from the rear. In the movement section of this book we discussed looking to the rear while walking. That is a good skill for a dark, dangerous street, but here's a better idea: Don't walk down a ghetto street at night. It's not my intention to be flippant or funny. Some people are forced to walk through bad neighborhoods at night, but most aren't, and I have found a surprising number of victims over the years that got in trouble because they believed themselves more capable than they were. Earlier in the book I mentioned an FBI study concerning cop killers. Many of the victimized officers believed themselves to be good at "reading" people. They weren't.

PRACTICS - HANDGUN DEFENSE SYSTEM

Too many armed defenders are no more than gun nuts, people who enjoy firearms as a hobby but have no will or desire to learn fundamental shooting skills. If that's you, it is incumbent upon you to recognize it and change or to consider your handgun suitable only for defense from a stationary attacker who stands seven yards in front of you and allows you time to do your crouch-grimace-jerk technique. Whatever we can do in training is likely to be more than we can do under threat of serious injury. How well are you really trained?

Knowing our situation—being aware of our circumstances—consists of the following:

- **Self-awareness.** Know who you are, not just in terms of abilities and skills but emotionally as well. If you are prone to pessimism, recognize and accept it as your current state. I am not qualified to give advice concerning mental and emotional health, and most of us won't make about-face personality changes during our lifetimes. That's not the point. Wherever a defender is in terms of how he processes information must be self-recognized and anticipated. The pessimist needs to possess enough self-awareness for his reason to dispute his ingrained emotional patterns of behavior. In other words, when the pessimist has a minor setback, rather than defeating himself through hopelessness, he must recognize his tendency toward expecting misery and force his thinking back to the facts. Rather than "my magazine malfunctioned; I'm going to die," it can be "load a fresh magazine and live." Self-awareness requires vigilance over a lifetime. People change throughout their lives, perhaps not dramatically, but change nonetheless. A parent who has recently lost a child will certainly undergo a period of personal change. What we knew of ourselves 10 years ago may not be true today. We must measure and match our abilities to our circumstances as would a disinterested observer, devoid of pride or insecurity. Each defender must recognize his particular sensitivities and self-doubts. Predators manipulate human insecurities. People have died because they were afraid of offending criminals. A woman in a Subaru may roll her window down in a bad part of town to disprove a taunt of racism. An educated and successful man may be induced to show someone his watch just to prove he doesn't look down on poor people. Know who you are.

- **Weigh everything.** You have to be stubborn and relentlessly logical in your pursuit of security. Allowing your feelings to overrun your common sense is a recipe for disaster. Cops subordinate emotion to reason every day. Police officers will wait outside a house until another officer arrives while a woman screams from inside the home. Neighbors will gather and berate the officer for not acting. The cop has a strong, natural temptation to immediately charge the front door, but he knows from experience and training that an incapacitated or dead police officer helps no one. Weigh everything. Risk and reward are balanced through reason, not emotion and not through old patterns of ineffective or dangerous behaviors. Must any driver read yet another pointless text message while hurtling down a busy highway at rush hour? People kill themselves through an inability to set proper priorities based on their actual life experiences. Just because your phone rings doesn't mean you have to answer it, and just because someone holds an elevator door open for you doesn't mean you have to step inside. If you can't find a safe place to park downtown, don't go. Think about it. It's doubtful any sane person would agree to go to a theater in a bad part of town if the proposition offered were "This movie is really great; you'll love it. It's worth getting raped, robbed, and having a few teeth knocked out." In self-defense, like in all aspects of life, we must weigh possible benefits against potential risks. How much of a chance are you willing to take for some incidental pleasure or convenience? Weigh the risks and benefits and act accordingly.
- **Determine the likely approaches of danger.** In every place that a human being can be found are approach paths for potential danger. Approaches of danger are simply the lines of travel in which danger (human, dog, bullet, and so forth) can reach the defender. If your back is against a brick wall, danger probably won't be coming from behind. In the press of a stadium crowd, potential approaches of danger may be literally touching you on all sides. Realistic expectations must rule the day. While working in your garden, a meteor may drop on your head, but let's limit our standard of concern to

common human experience. We can be aware of danger in three zones: close, mid, and open. The zones are concentric circles with the defender in the middle. The sizes of the circles depend on the surroundings. In a movie theater with the defender seated, *open* may be the lobby and the world beyond the emergency exits. *Close* might be the surrounding block of seats, and *mid* would be everything in between. Each zone has its own general response: *Open* requires escape, *mid* requires improvement such as acquiring a weapon or a better position, and *close* requires defense. Other than just being some pretentious nonsense you read in this book, the three zones have a practical purpose. The defender should strive toward the open zone at all times, recognizing, of course, that wherever you go will become your new close zone. The danger zones are about constantly improving your physical security circumstances where appropriate, which means we strive for open zones but never actually arrive. The zones are a process of movement, not a stationary goal. The zones are intended to inform the choices the defender makes during movement and are only static when danger makes them so. If you ran into your mid zone, but gunfire prevents further movement, you'll have to make a mid-zone response and improve your security situation in place. Don't walk 100 yards under a dark, occupied overpass to get to your car when you can spend an extra 15 minutes and walk three blocks on well-lit suburban streets to arrive at your car. If a woman is at a gas station and a fight breaks out between groups of men, she need not walk through the fight when she can go to the restaurant next door and have a cup of coffee until the cavalry arrives or the combatants flee. We are all constantly moving from one zone to another, and the zones change continually and instantly based on where we go, which is exactly the point: Have a sense of where you are and where danger may be and improve your situation when it makes sense to do so. The food court at the local shopping mall may have open-zone threats such as a large window to the north and a second-story walkway running parallel to the food court on the south side. If you're standing in front of Suzy's Truly Authentic Italian Pizza, your mid zone may extend to Bobby's Real Chinese and the hallway leading to the public restrooms. Your close zone may be the line you're standing in and the people moving around behind you in the seating area. Should you forfeit the opportunity to enjoy Sally's Authentic Pizza and flee to Bobby's Chinese to work toward a better zone? Of course not, but you should look out the window once, at the mall walkway a couple of times, listen for screams or shouts out of place in the food court, and select a table by a nice, quiet woman who is eating bad pizza and reading my book on her e-reader. Know where you are and from where danger is most likely to come.

- **Discover escape, evasion, or defense alternatives.** When in a crowded conference room on the fourth floor of a hotel, take 10 seconds to locate the exit signs. If you work in an office building, you ought to know if you have access to the basement. Find out from the building-maintenance guy if the emergency exit doors are really alarmed. A woman who is uncomfortable getting on the elevator with the office pervert ought to know whether the stairwell doors are self-locking on all but the ground floor. She may prefer to wait for an elevator with her friends who work on a lower floor. Know where you exist in this universe and how to navigate its lesser-known passageways.

If you can do the above while moving through life, you will have a usable and reasonably effective level of situational awareness. You won't be James Bond, but you won't be Barney Fife either.

## Mindset Training

Train for situational awareness by being aware of your immediate circumstances. The following unarmed drill will help you organize your defensive thinking.

**Situational Awareness Drill**—During the course of a five-day period, go to three public places and situate yourself within the movement or activity of the people present. Imagine that a particular threat causes you to move through the zones. Your imaginary threat can simply be a general concern over a possible assault or be a very specific scenario, but you must define it prior to beginning. Locate the most likely approaches of possible danger, assess your position, and consider your own capabilities. Determine the boundaries of your close, mid, and open zones. Relocate yourself toward the open zone but recognize that each new location becomes your new close zone. Continue pursuing an open zone until you completely remove yourself from the public place that you selected for the drill. Observe the following while conducting this drill:

- Choose paths of movement based on security needs, not convenience. The drill is of no value if you walk through the danger from which you are trying to escape. As an example, you mustn't use an elevator during a natural disaster that may cause a loss of power. Fleeing a sniper may rule out using exposed walkways. Move with the objective of immediately and constantly reducing your level of danger.

- Once you leave your close zone, you will be entering another (and hopefully better) close zone. Constantly reevaluate your circumstances. Your original goal of moving to the open zone will remain unchanged, but your actual open zone will change as you progress. At first the open zone may be the boulevard beside the shopping center. As you reach the sidewalk, the open zone may be the open field on the far side of the boulevard, and so it should continue until you decide that you are absolutely and positively safe. Constantly reevaluate where you're headed; otherwise you're just practicing walking from point A to point B.

You are responsible to reasonably know who is behind you. The Sphere of Responsibility requires your awareness. Know what and who is near you. Look up, down, to the sides and to the rear. You can't just stare at your feet and hope for the best.

Skill-Maintenance Requirement: One day a week, for a two-month period, place a rubber band around your wrist or use some other physical reminder. Whenever your attention is drawn to the rubber band, determine your zones and available escape routes. Accept your immediate circumstances as a mid zone and pretend you are prevented from further movement. Immediately determine how you may improve your security situation with cover, weapons, and other advantages.

# Chapter Seventeen: The Pyramid Test

*Testing leads to failure, and failure leads to understanding.*

Burt Rutan

Some years ago I attended a social gathering—more or less—at an old Yugoslavian vineyard. Among the guests were members of the Russian airborne infantry. The wine being free, camaraderie and goodwill abounded, and I told the Russians that during my early years in the U.S. Marine Corps I was taught the absurdity that Soviet soldiers were larger and stronger than we were, and, therefore, we were trained to "fight up," thrusting the bayonet high and punching above our own heads. The Russians told me they had been taught that the Americans were bigger, stronger, and taller than them. Had we ever gone to war, I am certain we would have disgracefully abused each other's hats. The point is it was considered advantageous by the two nations capable of space travel and intercontinental nuclear war to always train for the disadvantage.

I suppose this chapter will be equally frustrating for all students. Our purpose here is a test, and like all tests it is neither perfect for measuring the subject skill set nor sufficient for determining a student's actual readiness for real-world application. But this test is a pretty good starting point for all Practics students who have completed the skills-installation training found throughout this book. Some will struggle to ever successfully meet the test standards, and others will have to continually increase testing difficulty to encourage further improvement. Either way, the goal is continuous improvement, not just passing. No one knows what may be required of him or her during an emergency. Proficiency never surpasses need. We want to do our best today, but better tomorrow.

We know that most shootings will occur at close range and be resolved within a few rounds and a few seconds. Everything in this book was influenced by the sad statistics concerning the injuries and deaths of too many peace officers and their law-abiding employers during typical American gunfights. If you have successfully completed the training in this book, you have skills that, if maintained and developed, may dramatically improve your chances of survival. The Pyramid Test allows you to combine some of your Practics skills under the stress of a severe time limit.

The Pyramid Test is simple enough: The student draws the sidearm while issuing a command and fires at a simulated and unsteady primary defensive target during evasive movement. It's all over in a few seconds. Despite the simplicity of the test, some tactical thought is required.

## Arc of Retreat

In any unarmed-defense training, it seems to be a struggle for students to retain which of their hands is supposed to grab which of the bad guy's something-or-other. It's always the same. When you add a lack of training maintenance, stress, and fear, the whole thing becomes a recipe for getting punched in the face. On the other hand, boxing students find it difficult to learn to punch while moving but seem to easily grasp the rudiments of "slipping a punch." When an opponent throws a punch at the defender's head, the defender goes below and to the outside of the punch. I don't know why punch slipping is easy to learn and wrist grabbing is hard, but I suppose moving to the outside of a punch is more intuitive than calculating right-to-left and left-to-right.

In any case, defenders *should* strive to move to the outside when facing an attacker, whether he is armed or not. Earlier in this book, I mentioned that over gripping the handgun is the most common error amongst the shooting population. Over gripping causes shots to go low and to the inside. Approximately 80% of the world's population is right handed, which means that during face-to-face confrontations most bad guys will be shooting to your right. Since most gun attacks are at close range, we can assume that missed shots will tend to be between the defender's lower abdomen and thighs, striking the ground a few feet behind and to the right of the defender. Of course, there are left-handed attacks, and so our goal is to react to the "punch" and move to the outside when that is possible. It is easier and more natural for a shooter to adjust fire inward than it is to swing the arm outward, at least from an accuracy perspective. Therefore, the defender will prefer to force the attacker to adjust fire toward the outside. Some locations will not allow you to move to the outside of an attacker's shooting arm. Should you stand in place? Absolutely not. The attacker will adjust fire, get lucky, or move closer—you can't stand still. The natural, reflexive movement is to go backward, but that doesn't work well in an unarmed assault (remember the takedown) and does nothing at all when the attacker has a gun because the bullet travels in a straight line until it loses altitude and strikes the ground. Defenders can't stand still, and they can't move to the rear in a straight line.

The Practics response is to move away from the attacker in a rearward arc. An oblique retreat is better than just moving straight back, but if the attacker pivots onto the defender's oblique line of travel, the defender is, despite intentions, moving straight back. An arcing movement cannot be "locked on" through a single attacker body-position change and requires the attacker to track the defender's retreat in order to successfully fire. To clarify, a straight-line retreat allows several attacker shots to be fired in the same direction without adjustment, but an arcing-movement retreat forces the attacker to do more than point once and repeatedly jerk the trigger. The arc of retreat is among the most difficult elements of the test, and most students will find that after the initial first step away from the target, they tend to retreat in a straight line. We don't want to go slower for the sake of form, but the arcing movement is important enough to demand the dedication to master it. Once the habit has been acquired, it will easily be maintained.

## Commands

Early on in this book we discussed taking control of an attacker through verbal commands. Verbal commands are helpful because they may be sufficient to gain compliance, avert the need to use further force, and provide a concrete example of the defender's good will. By telling the attacker to stop the attack, the defender is demonstrating a preference to avoid the use of force. This has become a standard for police and, unfortunately, a virtual requirement. Shouting commands is not always possible, due to urgency. If the defender needs to act to save life, he must never delay that action for the sake of a command. Aiming while shouting commands is difficult and has proven a recipe for missed shots (that's why Practics requires defenders to shout at their front sights rather than at the attacker). Even when done properly, talking diverts focus and delays reaction time.

The close-range Practics answer to commands is to shout a short universal command while drawing. "Stop" means stop, whether an attack is armed, unarmed, a beating, or an abduction. Shouting "Stop!" is a good-faith attempt to prevent a greater use of force. Aimed-distance encounters allow for the more specific commands, such as "Raise your hands." Close or quick encounters are satisfied by "Stop!" Use the stop command during your training. Think about it and make it reactionary. The desired mindset is to shout the command during the defensive reaction, meaning the mouth speaks while the mental focus is on the defender's required physical response. Don't speak and wait; shout as you go. If the attacker complies with the command, you will see that and hold your defense, but you must assume that the command will be ignored. Consider that no human being able to put on his own shoes needs to actually be told not to commit a violent felony in order to know that the criminal action is unwanted by the victim. That doesn't matter, however, because ultimately the command is given for the sake of the defender. If the attacker accepts the command, great. But the value of the command is for the conscience and legal well-being of the lawful defender. Whenever you point a gun, time permitting, shout "Stop!"

## Danger Line

The line of danger is the initial straight path that exists between attacker and defender. The attacker's weapon doesn't matter, because all attacks are easier when the target is straight to the front. Every defender begins from a point within the Danger Line. The first goal is to move left or right in order to get out of the line of danger. As previously discussed, moving straight to the rear does nothing, because the defender can't outrun a bullet or a quick forward attack. Of course, the attacker will respond to the defender's movement out of the Danger Line, and that's why the Practics student continues moving away in an arcing retreat, but the initial move out of the line of attack forces the attacker to adjust. Adjustment requires time, and time is life to the defender. Even if you are not physically capable of a walking or running retreat, strive to slide one step out of the Danger Line, and, as previously discussed, the attacker's outside is the preferable direction of movement.

## Preparing for the Pyramid Test

This test requires the presence and control of an alert safety officer to ensure the firing stays downrange and the area remains clear throughout the test. It is essential that the testing-area ground be flat, dry, level, and free from obstructions for a 30' radius from the target. Use chalk or paint points to mark a 22' semicircle centering on the target. This area is the hot zone, which the student must exit during the test. The target is a piece of cardboard cut to fold into a pyramid about 8" h x 8" w x 8" d. A piece of clothesline is run through the pyramid from the center of the bottom through the top of the pyramid. The free end of the rope should be about 20" long and suspended by a crossbeam attached to an upright wooden pole. In the case of severe winds, the pyramid may be weighted with any soft object, such as an apple, small bag of sand, pine cones, and so on. A stopwatch is required, and a whistle is helpful for cease-fire commands.

The Pyramid.

A good measure of many of your Practics skills.

## Conducting the Pyramid Test

Loaded and fully holstered, the student will stand 4' from and centered on the pyramid target, which simulates the PDT. Hands will be held in front of the belt buckle prior to the start signal. When the safety officer is satisfied that conditions are safe and the student is ready, he will issue a start command that identifies which direction the student must arc toward, such as "right hand." By identifying the hand in which the attacker is holding a gun, the safety officer is requiring the student to translate the threat into a direction of retreat. This is easy to do after the first couple of runs, but it does assist in getting the student to think about attacker gun hands. Simultaneously with issuing the start command, the safety officer will begin the timer. At six seconds the safety officer will give a cease-fire signal and ensure a proper, safe holstering is conducted. The safety officer will also note whether qualification standards were met during the test, paying particular attention to the arc of retreat (a straight-line retreat is a failure).

## Qualification Standards

1. Minimum of four hits to the PDT with at least a 70% hit-to-miss ratio (Four out of six is acceptable.)
2. Move beyond an 18' radius from the target/attacker (three times the average distance of most gunfights). Movement must be constant. Stopping to fire is a disqualification.
3. Arc of movement: Less than a half second to break the Danger Line and begin the arc of retreat
4. All done from the holster in less than six seconds
5. One clear verbal command must be given prior to firing—"Stop!"

Some defenders do not possess the physical ability to move 18' in a hurry. Those defenders will still benefit from the Pyramid Test by breaking the Danger Line and then striving for a higher hit ratio. If you're on a cane or in a wheelchair, do what you can. Even a retreat limited to leaning toward the outside has value because as little as half of an inch may be sufficient to prevent injury. Bullets are small.

You may use any of the movement and firing techniques in this book, provided you obey the qualification standards. Pick the Practics skills that suit your abilities and competence levels. Running Fire requires one-handed Punch Firing and the ability to run. If your accuracy requires you to slow down, try a fast Groucho Walk with two-handed fire. Know your abilities and which skills best meet *your* needs. Work at it. If you are able to *consistently* meet the Pyramid Standard, then add shots, increase the hit-ratio requirement, or reduce the maximum allowable time.

## Additional Assistance

If you are unable to achieve any hits on the pyramid while moving, substitute the above pyramid with one that is twice as large (16"·16"·16"). The larger pyramid is NOT the test but only a training aid to assist you in preparing for the test. However, the substitution of the pyramids should come only after you have revisited all training in this book. The goal of the Pyramid Test is not to pass a test, but to give you some sort of real measure of your actual defensive skills. Don't focus on beating the test. Focus on improving your skills. If the test results tell you that more training is needed—get to work.

## Defender Objectives

- Create distance to increase safety.
- Strike the primary defensive target to efficiently stop the threat.
- Minimize missed shots to avoid unintentional injury to the public and prevent delay in stopping the threat.
- Move in an arcing retreat from the threat to deny the attacker the benefit of a consistent angle of fire.
- Complete the action within a few seconds to reduce the likelihood of sustaining injury.

The successful attainment of the Pyramid Test Standard guarantees nothing, but the exercise is a simple and revealing measure of a defender's skill versus what we know about the last 100 years of criminal deadly force attacks. Common sense tells us that since trained peace officers have only been accurate with 40% of their rounds at spitting distances, any test reflecting those same conditions would necessarily be difficult to pass. Further, passing this test without the threat of actually losing one's life must be considerably different than the real-life incidents upon which the test is based. The answer is in perfection. Defenders must train to stretch their competency and continually raise their own training standards for the sole purpose of making training perfection "good enough" in real life. If you can hit the pyramid, you can hit something twice as large. If you can fire an accurate five rounds while moving in less than six seconds, you can beat the statistical average of three rounds with one hit at 6'.

Before taking the test, it is best for the student to have read the entire book at least twice and completed all possible installation training. If you have done that, it is likely apparent to you that reading and doing are two very different things. You have probably also formed strong preferences for some Practics techniques over others. That's the point at which you are ready to begin Pyramid Testing, using *your* Practics skills to accomplish the test.

I am absolutely certain that at this point in the book it is unnecessary for me to remind the reader that the Pyramid Test requires the student also be tested using the weak hand. So I won't even mention that. Nor will I say that each hand will have to be successfully utilized in each arc direction, requiring a minimum of four runs through the test. As the reader fully understands that practical preparedness assumes disaster, I will not torture the subject by saying that two additional runs are necessary (six runs total) to test the weak-hand draw in both arc directions. In short, wild horses could not drag an ambidextrous word out of me.

If or when the Pyramid Standard is consistently attainable for you, it is your responsibility to make the test more difficult. You are training to beat hideous odds. There's no room for comfort or self-satisfaction. Use the Pyramid Test to prompt improvement. Be satisfied with nothing less than continued measureable improvement.

# Chapter Eighteen: Conclusion

*The education of a man is never completed until he dies.*

Robert E. Lee

A firearm is a tool for the civilized. Predatory animals survive through fear, live by force, and devote themselves to the rewards of violence. All prey live reactively to the presence of the predator. A civilized person chooses to live in liberty, free from fear. The firearm diminishes the advantages of physical strength and destroys the rewards of violence. When a murderer climbs through a window at night, he comes prepared. Most have spent time in a prison system that physically strengthens and makes cruel. The home intruder often enters with the willingness and ability to do evil from a lifetime of preparation. The defender is not so prepared, having lived by means other than the victimization of others. Yet the defender has an advantage—discipline. Anyone can be armed, but to be successfully armed is a skill earned through study and regimented experience. The ability and willingness to legally use a firearm for defense is a heavy check against lawlessness and the destruction of civilized culture. A firearm is a responsibility that imposes itself on the owner. Museums keep guns; only diligent citizens master and maintain arms.

As the reader now knows, Practics demands a considerable commitment to disciplined training and self-evaluation. Human nature desires knowledge and skill. Wanting it all now and without much effort is even more human. Reality dictates that perishable skills require a commitment as serious as the objective of those who seek to acquire those skills. Golf can be practiced at the leisure of the golfer. Bad golfers rarely wind up in the hospital as a result of insufficient training. More to the point, bad golfers don't accidentally kill their family members, lose their estate in civil court, or endure criminal prosecution. If you only want to have a gun to show your friends and occasionally take to the range, you don't need Practics, but you do need safety, operation, and marksmanship training. However, if you intend to provide you and yours with a legal armed defense, you're going to need a training program for the duration of that responsibility. Either you are ready and competent when the need arises, or you are not.

Our world has always been a dangerous place, and it's not getting any better. The generalization that criminals have the upper hand in how the law reacts to the private use of force for self-defense may not be fair, but the home defender being increasingly scrutinized and caricatured is undeniable. Knowing how to shoot is no more sufficient for the private defender than it is for the working peace officer. The traditional moral and legal burdens of self-defense are now joined by an ever-shifting social scrutiny that threatens to distort statutory law. The emotional and often uninformed opinion of the masses is beginning to influence police and prosecutors. In short, you had better know what you're doing before you pick up a weapon. Knowledge, continued training, and an honest regard for your fellow man require as much forethought as learning how to shoot.

I hope the material in this book will help in keeping your piece of the world a bit safer and just a little more civilized. After all, a peaceful life is the goal—firearms are only a means.

# About the Author

Albert League is a former U.S. Marine Corps marksmanship and close-combat pistol instructor. In addition to overseeing firearm training programs, his law enforcement work included assignments in SWAT, patrol, counter-sniper team, coroner investigations, and command of an international police taskforce station. Formerly a Washington D.C.-based security contractor and consultant, League is the author of *The Perfect Pistol Shot* and the founder of the Practics firearm system.

www.ingramcontent.com/pod-product-compliance
Lightning Source LLC
LaVergne TN
LVHW051619080426
835511LV00016B/2080